3

LEARNING services

01209 722146

Duchy College Rosewarne
Learning Centre

This resource is to be returned on or before the last date stamped below. To renew items please contact the Centre

Three Week Loan

P

Professional Practice for Landscape Architects

Second edition

Nicola Garmory, Rachel Tennant and Clare Winsch

AMSTERDAM • BOSTON • HEIDELBERG • LONDON • NEW YORK • OXFORD
PARIS • SAN DIEGO • SAN FRANCISCO • SINGAPORE • SYDNEY • TOKYO
Architectural Press is an imprint of Elsevier

ELSEVIER

Architectural Press

Architectural Press is an imprint of Elsevier
Linacre House, Jordan Hill, Oxford OX2 8DP
30 Corporate Drive, Suite 400, Burlington, MA 01803, USA

First edition 2002
Second edition 2007

British Library Cataloguing in Publication Data
Garmory, Nicola
  Professional practice for landscape architects. – 2nd ed.
  1. Landscape architecture – Great Britain   2. Planning – Law and legislation –
  Great Britain   3. Landscape architecture – Practice – Great Britain
  I. Title   II. Tennant, Rachel   III. Winsch, Clare
  712.3'0941

Library of Congress Cataloguing in Publication Data
A catalogue record for this book is available from the Library of Congress

ISBN-13: 978-0-7506-6902-3
ISBN-10: 0-7506-6902-0

For information on all Architectural Press publications
visit our web site at http://books.elsevier.com

Typeset by Charon Tec Ltd (A Macmillan Company), Chennai, India
www.charontec.com

Printed and bound in Great Britain
07 08 09 10   10 9 8 7 6 5 4 3 2 1

Contents

Introduction		**ix**
1	**Landscape practice**	**1**
	Professionalism and Ethics	1
	The Landscape Institute	1
	The Landscape Institute's Code of Professional Conduct and Practice	3
	The Landscape Architect's Responsibilities and Obligations	7
	Forms of Organization	9
	Companies	16
	Sole Principal	20
	Other Forms of Association/Collaboration	21
	Establishing a Private Practice	22
	Methods of Appointment of a Landscape Consultant	26
	Approach and Offer of Work – Factors to be Considered by the Landscape Architect	31
	Acceptance and Confirmation of Appointment	31
	The Landscape Institute's *The Landscape Consultant's Appointment*	33
	Calculating and Charging Professional Fees	36
	Payment of Fees	41
	Fee Tendering	42
	Appointing Sub-Consultants	44
	Quality Assurance	45
	Copyright	47
2	**Liability and the law**	**49**
	The Importance of the Law	49
	The Legal Systems of the United Kingdom	49

The Law of Contract   51
Law of Tort ('delict' in Scotland)   59
Liability   65
Health and Safety Legislation   73
Limitations Act 1980   82
Insurances   82

3   **Planning legislation**   **86**
Introduction to the Planning Framework   86
The Hierarchy of Planning Policy and
    Development Plans   87
Development Plans   91
Responsibility for Development Plans   98
Development Control   101
Special Development Areas   107
Heritage Planning and Special Forms of Control   110
Penalties for Non Compliance with an Order   112
Planning Consent Procedure   120
Environmental Impact Assessment   141
Landscape Assessment   146
Strategic Environmental Impact Assessment (SEA)   148
Building Acts and Regulations   149

4   **Environmental legislation**   **152**
Introduction   152
Planning Law   153
Management of Scarce Resources   155
Protection of Areas for Amenity, Landscape Quality
    and Natural Habitat   174
Convention on International Trade in Endangered
    Species (CITES)   187
Specific Sites and Species   206
Access to the Countryside   208
Pollution Control   219
Organization of Countryside and Conservation
    Authorities   227

5   **Tendering**   **231**
Work Stages   231
Work Stage F: Production Information   231
Work Stage G: Bills of Quantities   234
Schedules of Rates   238

The Quantity Surveyor   238
Work Stage H: Tender Action   239
Competitive Tendering   240
Non-competitive Tendering   242
Advantages and Disadvantages of Alternative
    Types of Tendering   243
Procedure for Single-Stage Selective Tendering   245
Post-tender Period   251

6 Contract and contract administration   **252**
Types of Contract   252
Standard Forms of Contract   253
Forms of Contract   253
Subcontracts   257
Roles of People Engaged in Landscape Contracts   258
The Pre-Start/Pre-Contract Meeting   264
Progress Meetings   267
Definitions   268

7 The JCLI Agreements   **276**
The JCLI Agreement for Landscape Works   276
The JCLI Agreement for Landscape Maintenance
    Works   284

Index   **287**

Introduction

The second edition of this book provides essential updated and enhanced guidance for all levels of landscape architects from students to seasoned practitioners and is a point of reference for everyday professional landscape life. It covers the fundamental principles of successful professional landscape practice.

Topics covered include practice formation and professional ethics; an outline of liability and the law; planning and environmental law; contract administration and procedure.

There is no companion website for the second edition but web addresses are included in the text to enable readers to follow up references themselves. This is particularly relevant for issues that change frequently such as environmental and planning legislation.

Nicola Garmory, Rachel Tennant, Clare Winsch.

Acknowledgement

In memory of John Coultas.

1 Landscape practice

Professionalism and Ethics

A professional person is one who offers competence and integrity of service based upon a skilled intellectual technique and an agreed code of conduct.
Report of the Monopolies Commission on the
Supply of Professional Service, 1970

A professional person enables a client to do something, which they are unable to carry out themselves and a client will employ a professional on the basis of their:

> **• QUALIFICATIONS •**
> Through which they are a member of a profession.

> **• SKILLS •**
> Including their knowledge and experience.

> **• TRUST/ETHICS •**
> A professional will look after the client's interests unlike in a commercial relationship.

The Landscape Institute

A profession has a professional institute or body that protects the status of its membership and governs its members. The Landscape Institute controls who enters the profession, via the Objects of the Institute, by safeguarding the first basis of professionalism, which is your qualification.

The Objects of the Landscape Institute, as set out in the Royal Charter of the Landscape Institute Paragraph 5(1), are 'to protect, conserve and enhance the natural and built environment for the benefit of the public':

- By promoting the arts and sciences of landscape architecture and its several applications.
- To foster and encourage the dissemination of knowledge relating to landscape architecture and the promotion of research and education therein.
- To establish, uphold and advance the standards of education, qualification, competence and conduct of those who practice landscape architecture as a profession.
- To determine standards and criteria for education training and experience.

The Landscape Institute was granted Royal Charter status in July 1997. The title of 'landscape architect' is the professional title now protected by Charter in the UK. This has the following principal effects:

- Only members and fellows are able to use the protected title of 'chartered landscape architect' and use the letters MLI or FLI.
- Only registered practices can describe their practices as 'chartered landscape architects'.
- Graduates are 'associates' and cannot use the letters MLI.
- The Government has a statutory duty to consult with The Landscape Institute.

To become a Chartered Landscape Architect the Landscape Institute has introduced the "Pathway to Chartership" which replaces the Professional Practice Examination in Autumn 2006. The new system focuses on the accumulation of the knowledge and understanding required to practice as a landscape architect with a chosen mentor which culminates in an oral exam. (Refer to LI website www.landscapeinstitute. org.uk for further details).

Landscape architects are obliged to act in accordance with the requirements of The Landscape Institute Charter of Incorporation which defines the professional title of 'landscape architecture', see Paragraph 5(2).

Landscape Institute's Charter of Incorporation: Paragraph 5(2)

- The application of intellectual and analytical skills to the assessment and evaluation of the landscape and its character and the resolution of existing and potential conflicts through the organization of landscape elements, spaces and activities based on sound principles of ecology, horticulture, design, planning, construction and management.

- The planning and design of all types of outdoor and enclosed spaces.
- The determination of policies and planning for existing and future landscapes.
- The appraisal and harmonious integration of development and the built environment into landscapes.
- The conservation, modification and continuing management of the landscapes of town and countryside and sustaining their characteristic features and habitats.
- The promotion of greater knowledge and understanding of materials and technology to enhance the appreciation of and resolution of practical landscape issues and problems.
- The promotion of a better understanding of the principles of and purposes of natural, biological and physical systems affecting or relating to the landscape.

The Landscape Institute's Code of Professional Conduct and Practice

The codes of professional conduct of a professional body are devised to protect the interests of the clients of the profession and to maintain the status of the profession in the eyes of society.

The Landscape Institute controls the standard of work and professional ethics via the Code of Professional Conduct and Practice. Members are governed by and are obliged to conduct themselves in accordance with this Code. The Institute's Professional Performance and Conduct Committee can enforce a breach of the Code of Conduct.

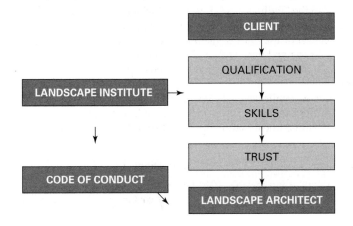

The Landscape Institute updated the Code of Conduct in the summer of 2000. The new code is based on that issued by the Architects Registration Board in 1997 with the aim of achieving a consistent approach to all professional codes. The Code consists of four sections including a forward, introductory clauses which cover the scope and limit of the Code, the 12 Standards with sub clauses, and general guidance on interpretation of the Code, legal proceedings, employees and further advice. (Refer to LI website for the full document) The Code is seen as:

> *Central to the professional life of a Landscape Architect and a source of ethical guidance and common sense indicator of good practice.*

The code is due to be updated in 2007 (refer to www.landscapeinstitute. org.uk for updates).

THE STANDARDS OF THE CODE

Reproduced by kind permission of The Landscape Institute.

Standard 1: Landscape architects should at all times act with integrity and avoid any action or situations which are inconsistent with their professional obligations.

- LAs should not make/support/collaborate in any statement which is *misleading, unfair or discreditable to the profession.*
- An LAs private life can not give rise to disciplinary proceedings except in the case of personal insolvency as this may lead to professional insolvency.
- LAs must *withdraw from or obtain agreement* regarding the terms of their engagement if a *conflict of professional or personal interest* occurs with the client or relevant parties.

Standard 2: Landscape architects should only undertake professional work for which they are able to provide proper professional and technical competence, and resources.

- This duty refers only to work for which a contract has been entered and not for speculative or competition work.
- LAs are *responsible for the competence and adequate supervision* of employees or other people acting under their instruction.
- A sole practitioner must have arrangements in place for the conduct of the business in the event of their death, incapacity or absence from work.

Standard 3: Landscape architects should only promote their professional services in a truthful and responsible manner and such promotion shall not be an attempt to subvert professional work from another chartered landscape architect.

- LAs can advertise services and special expertise, provided it is *neither untruthful, misleading nor claiming to be better* than other professional members.
- Adverts must conform to the British Code of Advertising Practice and ITC and Radio Code of Advertising Standards.
- The business style of a practice should not be misleading or confused with another practice or service.
- LAs shall not attempt to gain a contract for services provided by another member.

Standard 4: Chartered landscape architects shall carry out their professional work with care and conscientiously and with proper regard to relevant technical and professional standards.

- When providing advice or acting between parties, LAs shall *provide impartial and independent professional judgement* to the best of their ability and understanding.
- LAs shall perform with *due skill, care and diligence* within an agreed timescale and costs with the client, where practical. The LA shall advise the client if any issue will affect the cost or progress of the work.
- LAs shall *observe the client's confidentiality* and shall not disclose confidential information without prior consent.

Standard 5: In agreeing to carry out professional work and in the execution of that work landscape architects shall have regard to the interest of those who may be reasonably expected to use or enjoy the product of their work.

- LAs have responsibilities to the character and quality of the environment. They should manage change for the benefit of current and future generations, enhance the diversity of the natural environment and enrich the human environment in a sustainable manner.
- LAs must have due regard to the Objects of the Institute set out in the Charter.

Standard 6: Landscape architects should maintain their professional competence in areas relevant to their professional work and shall provide such educational and training support to less experienced members or students of the profession over which they have a professional or employment responsibility. *(Refer to Landscape Institute Document – The CPD File 2004.)*

Standard 7: Landscape architects should ensure that their personal and professional finances are managed prudently and shall preserve the security of monies entrusted to their care in the course of practice or business.

- Bankruptcy, liquidation, accommodation of creditors and failure to pay judgement debts are all acts by an LA which could be examined concerning wilful disregard of responsibilities or lack of integrity.
- LAs should hold client monies in a separate interest bearing bank account entitled 'client account'. Money can only be withdrawn to make payment on behalf of the client or on the client's written instructions. All interest is due to the client. (NB The Architects Committee fined an architect in 2002 for serious professional misconduct for failing to set up a separate client account for the project grant finances. Another was struck off the register) for unprofessional conduct for failing to manage his financial affairs.
- LAs shall deal with creditors and debtors in conformity with best practice and in accordance with legislation regarding timely payment of accounts.

Standard 8: Landscape architects shall not undertake professional work without adequate and appropriate Professional Indemnity Insurance.

- Cover must extend to work undertaken outwith the LA's main professional practice/employment and to work undertaken by employees.
- Employed LAs must ensure that PII cover is provided by their employer.

Standard 9: Landscape architects shall organize and manage their professional work responsibly and with integrity and with regard to the interests of their clients.

- LAs shall not undertake professional work unless the terms of the contract have been recorded in writing as to scope, allocation and limitation of responsibilities, fee/method of calculation, provisions for termination, provisions for dispute resolution.
- LAs should not accept or continue work where there is a business, personal or financial conflict of interest with the client.
- Where clients, whose interest may be in conflict, require the services of the same LA the professional work shall be managed in a manner that avoids the interests of one client adversely affecting another.
- Clients' property (plans, papers, etc.) to which they are legally entitled shall be returned directly upon demand.
- LAs shall have appropriate and effective internal procedures, including monitoring and review procedures, and ensure qualified and supervised staff to enable it to function efficiently.
- LAs shall not take on a partner/director who is unsuitable (disqualified or suspended LI members or other professionals).

Standard 10: A Landscape architect is expected actively and positively to promote the standards set out in these Standards of Conduct and Practice.

- LAs should order their own professional lives according to the Standards of the Code and ensure observance by other LAs. Any activities that do not accord with the Code should be reported to the Director General. *(Refer to Code for likely activities and required action.)*

Standard 11: A landscape architect is expected actively and positively to promote and further the aims and objectives of the Landscape Institute, as set down in its Charter, and to contribute to the work and activities of the Institute.

Standard 12: Complaints concerning professional work of landscape architects or their Practice or business should be dealt with promptly and appropriately. *(Refer to Code for action required relating to complaints.)*

NB The Landscape Institute has updated their disciplinary procedures – refer to LI website.

General Guidance within the Code of Conduct – Employees

An employer must have due regard to the fact that the conduct of an LA, who is an employee, will be governed by the Code in addition to any duties as an employee. If the two sets of obligations conflict the LA should follow the Code or in the last resort resign their employment. In the case of an employed LA, the more senior the position held the greater the responsibility to ensure conformity by the employer with the Standards of the Code.

THE CODE OF PROFESSIONAL PRACTICE IN A NUTSHELL

The professional standards expected of landscape architects in the areas of:
- Technical Competence (Standard 2, 4 and 6)
- Propriety, Competition and Promotion (Standard 1, 3, 4, 9 and 10)
- Finance/Insurance/Complaints (Standard 7, 8 and 12)
- Obligations to the Environment (Standard 5 and 11)

The Landscape Architect's Responsibilities and Obligations

The Landscape Institute's Charter of Incorporation and Code of Professional Conduct and Practice set out the parameters of landscape architects' professional obligations and their responsibilities.

A landscape architect has a responsibility to the environment, society at large, the client, the landscape profession, their own organization/colleagues, and also to other professionals and contracting organizations. These responsibilities are expressed through the undertaking or provision of:

• PROFESSIONAL SKILLS •
Undertaking all aspects of work in accordance with the normal standards of the profession.

• ADVICE/INFORMATION •
Providing accurate advice and information to the client, the design team and the contractor within the required time frame.

• LEGAL KNOWLEDGE •
Up-to-date knowledge of statutory laws and other legal controls.

• OFFICE AND PROJECT MANAGEMENT •
Providing the right conditions and procedures for the effective running of the office and projects.

• CONTINUING PROFESSIONAL DEVELOPMENT •
Ensuring professional competence is maintained in areas relevant to professional work.

• QUALITY CONTROL •
Ensuring that the work is carried out for both design and construction to the highest standard and in accordance with the design brief and contract documents.

A landscape architect has a responsibility to the client as:

A Skilled Professional Person

- 'The landscape architect will use reasonable skill, care and diligence in fulfilling their services to the client in accordance with the **normal** standards of the profession'. *(Landscape Consultant's Appointment: Clause 3.2 Duty of Care. Refer also to Standard 4.2 of the Code of Professional Conduct and Practice 'LAs shall perform with due skill, care and diligence.')*

- Landscape architects are obliged to conduct themselves in accordance with The Code of Professional Conduct, which governs the standard of professional conduct and self-discipline required of Members of the Landscape Institute.

↓

A Responsible Agent

- The landscape architect is the client's representative and will act on behalf of the client on matters set out in the terms of their appointment. In this capacity, the landscape architect must act in the client's interest and must always remember that the acts done by the LA on behalf of the client will be deemed to be the acts of the client.

↓

A Quasi-Arbitrator/Arbiter

- The landscape architect will be impartial in administering the terms of a contract between client and contractor. Under the JCLI conditions of contract, the landscape architect as contract administrator is named as Agent, which allows for a quasi-judicial function in resolving issues on a fair and reasonable basis. *(Refer also to Standard 4.1 of the Code of Professional Conduct and Practice 'When providing advice or acting between parties, LAs shall provide impartial and independent professional judgement to the best of their ability and understanding.')*

Forms of Organization

• PUBLIC SECTOR •

• PRIVATE SECTOR •

The Public Sector

Landscape architects can practice in the public sector in a variety of ways but local authorities continue to be the main source of employment. The main forms of public sector organization are:

• CENTRAL GOVERNMENT •
Department for Environment, Food and Rural Affairs (DEFRA), Department for Transport (DFT), National Assembly for Wales (NAW), Scottish Executive, Northern Ireland Department

> **• CENTRAL GOVERNMENT AGENCIES •**
> Forestry Authority, Countryside Agencies,
> Government Enterprise Companies and
> Regional Government Offices

> **• LOCAL GOVERNMENT/AUTHORITY •**
> Councils

Local Authority Structure

The Local Government Act confers on all local authorities power to arrange for any of its functions to be discharged by a committee, subcommittee or an officer. All local authorities conduct their affairs by a committee system. Committees consisting of elected councillors are entrusted with specified functions of the council, e.g. planning committee, finance committee.

The client in the public sector is the council committee, e.g. planning, housing, leisure and recreation. As with private clients, these public ones decide priorities and allocate funds. Their approval is necessary before work begins. A committee representative, usually the chairman, also signs tenders once they have been received back from tenderers.

Decisions are recommended to the council or to the relevant committee usually by the corresponding department's director. If approved it is then the duty of the appropriate officer (e.g. landscape architect) of the council to implement the decision, satisfy the committee's requirements and report back to them if required to do so (e.g. by Standing Order).

Compulsory Competitive Tendering (CCT) and Best Value

The 1980 Local Government Planning and Land Act introduced the idea that direct labour sections involved in construction and maintenance of local authority buildings had to tender for this work in competition with private construction companies. Similar legislation came into force in 1992 to cover maintenance of council land, sport and recreational facilities, and professional and 'white collar' services including housing management, financial services and design.

The Government in 1997 heralded 'best value' as an alternative to CCT. Best Value is even more challenging than CCT because 100% of council services and everyone in the council – all council employees and Elected Members – are directly involved. Moreover, although tendering is no longer compulsory, councils still have to consider competition and 'alternative forms of service delivery'. This may include Voluntary Competitive Tendering (VCT), Private Finance Initiative (PFI), Public Private Partnerships (PPP) Trusts and other forms of partnership.

Under the Local Government Act 1999, best value rules also apply to the authorities for national parks, police, fire, waste disposal, metropolitan county passenger transport and the London Development Agency.

The Private Sector

The main forms of practice or organization in the private sector are:

> • **PARTNERSHIPS** •
> (Unlimited and Limited Liability)

> • **COMPANIES** •

> • **SOLE TRADERS/PRACTITIONERS** •

Partnerships (Unlimited Liability)

This is the most common form of association because it is a form of contract, i.e. it is legally binding and it has the benefits of mutual support and combined resources. There is also a default duty of good faith between partners which creates a 'partnership ethos' which does not exist in companies or Limited Liability Partnerships. A partnership is not a separate legal entity from its partners (except in Scotland), therefore when a third party enters a legal agreement with a partnership, they do so with the partners themselves.

A partnership is less formal than a company, with freedom of action and privacy of its affairs. However, it is subject to unlimited liability with personal assets at risk; it has limited powers to borrow money and the taxation position is more complex than in a company.

The principal elements in understanding partnerships are:

> • **Recognition of partnerships**
> • **Partnership agreements**
> • **Management and types of partners**
> • **Finance/accounts**
> • **Size of partnerships**
> • **Liabilities**
> • **Dissolution of partnerships.**

Recognition of a Partnership

The essentials for recognition of a partnership are contained in the Partnership Act 1890 which states that a partnership is a '*Relationship which subsists between a collection of persons carrying on a business in common with a view to profit.*'

Sharing of facilities or shared ownership of property does not necessarily mean two people practise in common, but sharing of net profits is evidence of the existence of a partnership.

Partnership Agreements – Rights of Partners

Obligations are borne by the partners as individuals and hence it is very important that their rights and duties are set out in a written partnership agreement. In the absence of this the provisions set out in the Partnership Act 1890 will apply:

- Property brought into the firm or bought with the firm's funds is partnership property.
- Profits, capital and losses will be shared equally.
- Every partner is entitled to take part in the management of the business and to inspect the accounts.
- There are no rights for remuneration for acting in the partnership business.
- No new partners may be introduced, no fundamental changes can occur to the nature of the partnership and no partner may be expelled unless majority consent is gained.
- Every partner is entitled to dissolve the partnership at any time by giving notice to the other partners.
- A partnership must indemnify each partner in respect of liabilities.

Management/Types of Partner

Management is by the partners. The law makes no distinction between junior and senior partners except in decisions on profit making, which will be deemed as equal unless stated otherwise in the partnership agreement.

The term 'salaried partner' should be avoided as persons described as partners should have full share and responsibility in the decision-making and the professional conduct and liabilities of the practice. The title 'associate' is not referred to in the Partnership Act and it has no meaning in law. The title is often used to retain important members of staff while preventing them having any real responsibility in the management of the practice or share of the profits.

Finance/Accounts

Partnerships are liable to income tax on their profits whether they are drawn out or left in the practice. The partnership's profits are shared equally, or as stated in the partnership agreement and no audit is required of the business accounts.

Size

There are some restrictions on the size of partnerships, however for architects and similar professions this restriction was removed by the Partnerships (Unrestricted Size) No 4 Regulations 1970 provided that no less than three quarters of the partners are registered architects.

Liabilities

In addition to all their normal individual liabilities, each partner has added responsibilities as a member of a partnership. The nature of the liability for the contract debts and torts (including professional negligence) is defined by sections 9 & 10 of the Partnership Act and is summed up as follows:

- Every partner is an agent of the firm.
- If a partnership is sued a partner can be proceeded against 'jointly and severally', i.e. singly/together.
- Partners are jointly liable for a partnership's contract debt, in the absence of agreement to the contrary. (Each partner is bound to contribute to the debts in proportion to his share of the profits. This may be to the whole extent of his property.)
- Partners are jointly and severally liable for the partnership's torts (including negligence) and this cannot be avoided by agreement.
- Partners are jointly and severally liable for the partnership's contract debts if they have expressly agreed to be so liable.
- The estate of a deceased partner is also severally liable for the partnership's contracts, subject to the prior payment of their private debts.
- Partners are not liable for the criminals actions of other partners unless they contributed to them or had knowledge of them.
- A new partner entering a firm does not normally become liable for debts, obligations or wrongs incurred or committed before his entry. However, if a partner retires or dies he or his estate will still be liable for debts or obligations incurred before his retirement.
- A partner will continue to be treated as a member of the firm and attract associated liability until there is notice of change in the constitution of the partnership.

There is also a default duty of good faith. If the conduct of one partner appears to conspire against another it could be construed as a breach of that duty of good faith which may give rise to remedies for that breach including damages or dissolution and winding up of the affairs of the partnership (Blisset v. Daniel 1853).

Dissolution of a Partnership

Partnerships can be dissolved or ended in a variety of ways:

- If no time is fixed for the duration of a partnership it is termed a partnership at will, and may be dissolved at the insistence of any partner, i.e. by giving notice.
- At the end of a fixed term or a single commission, if it has been so set up.
- By dissolution by the court on the grounds of insanity, incapacity, misconduct of a partner or of the hopeless state of the business.
- On the death or bankruptcy of any partner unless the agreement makes provision for its continuity.

The Government has sought recommendations on the changes in partnership law put forward by the law commission in 2004. Two key areas for review were the continuity of partnerships irrespective of changes in the membership and including simplification of the process of solvent dissolution.

Limited Liability Partnerships (LLPs)

The essential feature of an LLP is that it allows collective limited liability and the mutual, co-operative characteristics of a partnership with its associated organizational flexibility and tax status. This is possible because it is a corporate body – an entity with a legal existence independent of its individual members.

The principal elements in understanding Limited Liability Partnerships are:

- **Formation**
- **Legal status and management**
- **Management and types of partners**
- **Finance/accounts**
- **Size of LLPs**
- **Liabilities**
- **Dissolution.**

Formation

Under the Limited Liability Partnership Act 2000, a Limited Liability Partnership (LLP) can be formed by registration and obtaining an authenticated certificate of incorporation from the Registrar of Companies House. The Act extends to England, Wales and Scotland. Some provisions of the Act regarding tax, National Insurance contributions and commencement extend to Northern Ireland.

Legal Status and Management

An LLP is a legal person in its own right. It is a body corporate, formed on incorporation. It has unlimited capacity and is able to undertake the full range of business activities which a partnership could undertake.

LLPs are governed by their members. For an LLP to be incorporated, two or more persons associated for carrying on a lawful business with a view to profit must be named in the incorporation document. These are classified as designated members and are not employed by the LLP, which is a separate legal entity.

Members are not obliged to have a formal written agreement but as with partnerships it is advantageous to do so to regulate the affairs of the business and avoid disputes. In the absence of a written agreement, regulatory default provisions under section 15 C of the Act apply that cover the rights and duties of the members:

> • Entitlement of members to share equally in the capital and profits of the business.
> • Every member may take part in the management of the LLP.

These provisions can be expressly excluded within written agreements.

Finance/Accounts
The profits and property of the business of an LLP will be taxed as if the business were carried out by partners in a partnership rather than by an incorporated body. This ensures that the commercial decision between using an LLP or a partnership is a tax neutral one. Accounts are filed at Companies House.

Size
There are no restrictions on the size of an LLP.

Liabilities and Powers
Liabilities of members of LLPs are very different from partners in an unlimited partnership.

> • Every member of an LLP is the agent of the partnership. The LLP is bound by what a member has agreed unless he acted outwith the scope of his authority.
> • The LLP's existence as a separate corporate entity with unlimited capacity means it has the ability to enter into contracts, hold property, sue and be sued as with a company.
> • A member is not liable for the torts or obligations incurred by the LLP, other than in tort for their own negligence. Therefore it is only possible to sue the LLP in contract and not the member. However the member can be sued under the law of tort.
> • A member is liable for the debts of the LLP in the event of it being wound up to the amount which he has contributed to the LLP as capital.

Dissolution of an LLP
LLPs can be dissolved or ended in a variety of ways:

> • By agreement between the members.
> • By being struck off the register (e.g. for no certificate of incorporation).
> • By winding up/insolvency.

The Limited Liability Partnership Act 2000 gives powers to apply the provisions of company and insolvency law, which safeguard the interests of those dealing with LLPs.

Companies

The principal elements in understanding companies are:

- **Formation**
- **Management**
- **Types of company**
- **Finance/accounts**
- **Size**
- **Liabilities**
- **Dissolution.**

Formation of Companies
A company can be formed in three ways:

- By Royal Charter.
- By Special Act of Parliament.
- Registration under the Companies Act 1985 and as amended in 1989.

Registration under the Companies Act is the most common. The Registrar of Companies will issue a Certificate of Incorporation and give the company a registered number. Without a certificate a company does not exist in law and cannot do business.

Management
A company is controlled by the Companies Act 1985/1989, which covers its formation and operation. It is owned by its members or shareholders and is governed by its directors or managing director with the supervision of its shareholders.

A company is a distinct and separate entity in law from its members and directors. It can own property, sue and be sued, and enter into contract in its own right. The company continues whoever leaves or joins; it is not affected by the death, bankruptcy or retirement of a shareholder or of a director or other employee.

Types of Company
Two types of company exist: limited liability or unlimited liability companies.

Limited Liability or Unlimited Liability Companies
- Limited liability companies are where the shareholders' liability to contribute to the company's assets are limited to the amount unpaid on

their shares. Shareholders may also have different interests, e.g. 40% and 20%, therefore their liability and profits will be different. Companies can also be limited by guarantee where shareholders are liable as guarantors for an amount set out in the memorandum in the event of a company being wound up.

- Unlimited liability companies are subject to the same rules as a limited company except that shareholders are personally liable for all the company's debts and obligations only on the winding up of the company. This liability is unlimited, although it may be limited by agreement on entering into transactions and creditors. The accounts need not be filed at Companies House (unless the company is controlled by a limited company) nor does the ownership of shares have to be notified. The state of affairs of the company is therefore not available for public scrutiny.

Companies, whether limited or unlimited, may be either public or private.

Public and Private Companies

- A public company is the only sort of company that is permitted to offer its shares to the public by trading on the Stock Exchange and only companies with a certain nominal share capital and at least five years' track record may be a Public Limited company (PLC) with full Stock Exchange listing. Two tiers exist below that for smaller or newer companies: the Third market and the Unlisted Securities Market.
- Reasons for flotation on the Stock Exchange, apart from the raising of finance, include the provision of evidence of the standing of the practice, improved efficiency from the necessary disciplined management and the ability to acquire other businesses to widen capabilities. A number of large multidisciplinary environmental practices are now PLC.
- Private companies do not offer their shares to the public. In general a smaller practice will incorporate a private company and the individuals who would otherwise be partners will be the directors and also the shareholders.

Accounts/Finance

Profits are distributed among shareholders in accordance with the rights attached to their shares, which relate to the class of shares owned. Preferential shareholders will receive profits in the form of dividends first before ordinary shareholders and if there are insufficient funds ordinary shareholders may receive no dividends. Directors and employees are paid salaries out of the profits of the company, which are tax deducted. Accounts must be audited and filed at Companies House.

Size

The number of shareholders that a company may have is unlimited.

Liabilities of Shareholders

Companies are distinct and separate entities in law. On this basis the liability of shareholders differs from partners in a partnership.

- Shareholders are not liable personally for the torts or obligations incurred by the company or by other shareholders (other than in tort for their own negligence).
- Shareholders are only liable for the debts of the company to the amount unpaid on their shares if the company is limited.
- Shareholders are fully liable for torts and obligations if the company is unlimited **only** on the winding up of the company; otherwise it rests with the company itself.
- If a company is dissolved by winding up, both members and past members (within the past 12 months) will be liable to contribute towards the assets of a company so it can meet its liabilities.

Liabilities of Directors

Directors are normally given the power to manage the company under the ultimate supervision of shareholders and therefore their liabilities are more limited than those of shareholders.

- Directors are not servants/agents of the company but they are liable for their own torts.
- Directors are only allowed remuneration specified in the articles/memorandum.
- A director owes the company a duty of loyalty and faith and must exercise reasonable care in the conduct of business.
- Directors must prepare annual accounts and report on the company's finances/dividend. Companies are audited annually and the audit, report and accounts must be filed with the Register of Companies for public inspection.
- Directors must hold an annual general meeting.

Dissolution of a Company

Companies can be dissolved in the following ways:

- Winding up under the Insolvency Act 1986 which is either voluntary or compulsory. Once wound up no judgement may be forced against it.
- By being struck off the Register under the Companies Act 1985, which will occur when the company is no longer carrying on business or fails to present the annual accounts. Companies may seek this form of dissolution to save the cost of a formal liquidation.

Partnership and Companies – Key Differences

Partnerships (Unlimited Liability)	Companies
1. No separate legal personality (except in Scotland).	1. Has separate legal personality from its shareholders.
2. Partners have unlimited liability.	2. Shareholders are liable only to the amount unpaid on their shares but may be liable on personal guarantees for some liabilities, e.g. borrowing.
3. Interest of a partnership that may be difficult to transfer.	3. Interest of a shareholder is his shares which are usually easy to transfer unless subject to limitations in articles.
4. It may be difficult for a young architect to join a partnership as he/she will have to amass capital to buy a share in the partnership or take over a retiring partner's interest.	4. It will be easier to join the company as it will not necessarily involve buying in.
5. The only promotion is to become a partner, so career prospects may be limited.	5. There are more possible kinds of promotions.
6. Management through meeting of partners.	6. Management through Board of Directors, supervised by shareholders, who meet annually.
7. Partners will share profits edequally unless there is an agreement to the contrary.	7. Company profits are divid- according to rights attached to the shares.
8. Can be formed informally by just starting up business with another person.	8. Must be registered to come into existence. It costs money to register a company (£200+) and it will require time unless an 'off the peg' company is purchased.
9. No restrictions on the powers of partnership.	9. A company only has the powers in the objects clause of its memorandum. Other powers will be *ultra vires* and void.

(Continued)

Partnerships (Unlimited Liability)	Companies
10. Each partner can bind the partnership.	10. No shareholder can bind the company.
11. There is no place where partnership details may be inspected by members of the public.	11. Matters filed with the Registrar of Companies are open to public inspection. Such matters include the memorandum, articles, details of directors, secretary and registered office.
12. Partnerships need not publicise their accounts.	12. Companies must file their accounts with the Registrar of Companies.
13. No audit is required of accounts.	13. Annual audit required.
14. A partnership does not require much paperwork or administration.	14. A company requires more paperwork and administration.
15. A partnership cannot borrow money to the same extent it can only receive loans.	15. A company can more easily raise money (if allowed by its Memorandum), e.g. by debentures and fixed and floating charges.
16. Death or departure of a partner causes dissolution of the partnership.	16. Transfer of shares will not end the company's existence.
17. There are many ways to dissolve a partnership. It can be dissolved instantly by agreement.	17. A company is dissolved only by liquidation in accordance with the Companies Act 1985/89 and the Insolvency Act 1986.

Sole Principal

Sole practitioners have considerable freedom in the running of their business:

- No formal documentation required for setting up/constitution.
- No legal requirements regarding form of accounts, annual returns (except for Inland Revenue) or statutory books.
- No restrictions on financial drawings.

Against this are set:

- All business and personal assets are at risk.
- There is no legal continuity on death.

Other Forms of Association/Collaboration

Other forms of practice exist and in addition, regardless of whether they are practising as partnerships or companies, practices may join forces in various forms of collaboration.

- CO-OPERATIVES -

- TRUSTS -

- GROUP PRACTICES -

- CONSORTIA -

Co-operatives

A co-operative is a method of working rather than a form of practice. It is based on a commitment to the principles of co-operative working and collective decision-making. Liability, capital and valuations of the business and members' capital should be clearly defined. A co-operative can be registered either as a company under the Companies Act or as a society with the Register of Friendly Societies under the Industrial and Provident Societies Act 1965–75. It can be carried out through a promoting body such as the Co-operative Union Industrial Common Ownership Movement (ICOM rules).

Trusts

The key principles of trusts are that they:

- Are non profit making organizations.
- Have a board of Trustees (normally with other business interests).
- Depend on sponsorship, i.e. charity, central government or local funding.
- Are not taxed.
- Have employees.
- Must disclose accounts as per limited company to Register of Companies for inspection by the public.

There are many organizations that employ landscape architects that operate as trusts such as The Groundwork Trust and The Central Scotland Forest Trust.

Group Practices

Individual private firms of one profession, under various forms of agreement, may be grouped for their mutual benefit and to give better service, i.e. greater availability of skills and resources, while each retains their own identity and a measure of independence, for example:

Association of Individual Firms

- Beyond agreeing to a division of overheads and expenses they retain the profits of the individual firms and their normal responsibility to their respective clients.

Co-ordinated Groups

- For large jobs work can be undertaken by two or more firms with one of them appointed to co-ordinate the activities of the others. The co-ordinating firm is solely liable to the client, but the individual firms are still liable to the co-ordinating firm for acts committed in their area of activity.

Consortia

In law, consortia are little different from group practices. The term normally implies the association of firms and different professional skills acting as one for carrying out either a specific termed appointment or on a regular basis for a variety of projects jointly, yet retaining their separate identity and each with their own responsibility to the client.

Establishing a Private Practice

The principal elements to be considered when establishing a private practice are:

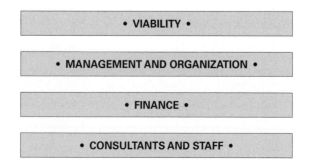

- VIABILITY -

- MANAGEMENT AND ORGANIZATION -

- FINANCE -

- CONSULTANTS AND STAFF -

> • MATERIALS AND RESOURCES •

> • BUSINESS DEVELOPMENT •

> • PERSONAL ISSUES •

Viability

The viability of a practice requires to be established and this can be achieved through:

- Market sector research and targeting.
- Competitor research.
- Professional or government advisory services. (The Landscape Institute offers advice and information on setting up in private practice.)
- Preparation of a Business Plan.

Management and Organization

A number of principles need to be established and organization systems set up:

Decide the Form of Practice

- Partnership.
- Company.
- Sole trader or other.

Comply with Statutes and Regulations

- Companies Act 1989: register company name and arrange for auditing of accounts.
- Partnership Act 1890: set up partnership agreement.
- Competition Act 1998 (prohibits anti competitive agreements and abuse of a dominant position in the market): penalties enforced by OFT (10% of turnover).
- HM Revenue and Customs: VAT registration (if turnover in excess of a specified sum approx. £60 000.00), PAYE and tax.
- Contributions Agency: registration for National Insurance Contributions.
- Rates: register with local authority for assessment of rates.
- Staff employment: Equal Pay Act 1970, Race Relations Act 1976, National Minimum Wage Act 1998, Disability Discrimination Act 1995, Employment

Rights Act 1996 (Rev '98), Employment Relations Act 1999 and Employment Act 2002, and current European Community Work Directive and corresponding UK Acts of Parliament and associated Regulations (Maternity/Paternity Leave, Flexible Working, Part-Time Working, Employment Equality).
- Health and Safety: Offices, Shops and Railway Premises Act 1963, Health and Safety at Work Act 1974, Health and Safety Information for Employees 1989, The Fire Precautions (workplace) Regs 1997, and The Management of Health & Safety at Work Regs 1999.
- Disability Discrimination Act 1995 (Access for all not just disabled).
- Register with the Landscape Institute in order to practice and to obtain benefits such as advertising.

Take out Appropriate Insurances

- Professional indemnity insurance (a requirement of the Landscape Institute).
- Building and contents insurance.
- Motor insurance.
- Employers' liability insurance against personal accidents to staff or diseases incurred as a result of the business. (Employer's Liability (Compulsory Insurance) Act 1969)).
- Occupier's liability insurance against personal accidents to visitors. (Occupier's Liability Acts 1957 and 1984).
- Other insurances: private medical insurance, pensions, life assurance, crossover insurance.

Set up Office Quality Management Systems

- Quality Manual.
- Quality Policy.
- Auditing systems.

Finance

Options for raising finance and setting up financial control systems within the office should be considered and initiated:

Raising money

- Personal savings.
- Bank loan (business plan required).

Establish a Bankbook System

- Records incoming money (fees and expenses) and outgoing money (salaries, overheads and direct expenses).
- Balances the end of the month account with the bank statement.
- Used by the accountant to prepare the annual accounts.

Cash Flow Forecast for Long-Term Financial Planning

- Monthly forecast of fee income.
- Monthly summary of expenditure.
- Forecast of annual fee income and expenditure.
- Profit and loss ratio.

Annual Statement of Accounts and Balance Sheet

Produced (normally by the practice accountant) for:
- Annual accounts audit.
- Tax purposes.
- Annual practice forecasting.

Consultant and Staff Appointment

Consultants

Consultants are external professionals that are essential for the management of the practice. They will include a bank manager, solicitor and accountant.

Internal Staff

The appointment of internal staff will depend on the size of the practice and will usually consist of administrative and professional (junior and senior) staff. Employment of staff is now strictly regulated under The Employment Act 2002 and the main terms of a contract between employer and employee are governed by the Employment Relations Act 1996. Staff recruitment requires the practice to:

- Prepare a person and job description.
- Advertise (internally/externally) or through word of mouth.
- Interview.
- Appoint and set up a contract of employment (within 2 months).
- Arrange for development training or CPD.
- Arrange for training in office systems, quality assurance, health and safety, etc.

Materials and Resources

The following list of materials and resources is not exhaustive but will be
dependent on the size of the practice.

- Office space.
- Office transport.
- Office furniture.
- Computers, telephones, fax, email, etc.
- General office materials and stationery.

Business Development

Establish practice goals and set out a long-term business development
strategy. Ensure its review and update to prevent stagnation of business;
this may require employing an external consultant. A business development strategy should cover:

- Business goals.
- Finance.
- Marketing.
- Staff.

Personal Issues

The following need to be taken into consideration:

- Effects on personal life, i.e. time commitments.
- Relationship with colleagues (directors/partners) – ensure similar goals.
- Restrictions placed by former employers.

Methods of Appointment of a Landscape Consultant

The Landscape Institute has produced a series of publications dealing
with appointing a chartered landscape architect which are now grouped
together as a complete guidance set:

- *Appointing a Chartered Landscape Architect: Guidelines for Best Value*
- *The Landscape Consultant's Appointment*
- *Appointing a Landscape Consultant: Guidance for Clients on Fees*
- *Guide to Procedure for Competitive Tendering*
- *Landscape Competitions: Guidance for Promoters*

All these documents are under review by The Landscape Institute with a view to replacing them by early 2008 (Refer to www.landscapeinstitute. org.uk).

Guidelines for Best Value provides advice on good selection and appointment procedures appropriate for the type of commission, which can also comply with 'best value' frameworks as set out by the Government.

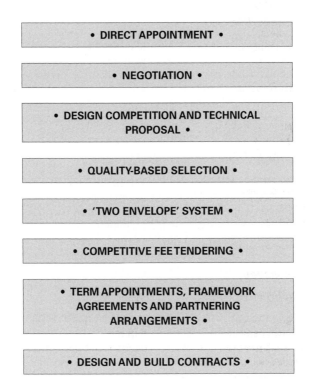

• DIRECT APPOINTMENT •

• NEGOTIATION •

• DESIGN COMPETITION AND TECHNICAL PROPOSAL •

• QUALITY-BASED SELECTION •

• 'TWO ENVELOPE' SYSTEM •

• COMPETITIVE FEE TENDERING •

• TERM APPOINTMENTS, FRAMEWORK AGREEMENTS AND PARTNERING ARRANGEMENTS •

• DESIGN AND BUILD CONTRACTS •

Alternative methods of selecting a chartered landscape architect described in the Landscape Institute document include:

Direct Appointment

Landscape architects can discuss a potential appointment with a prospective client without obligation. Examples of previous work and/or the individuality of design approaches by practices can be ascertained by a client in order to consider the practice suitability. Many clients build an established working relationship with one or more practices to their mutual benefit to create a 'win-win' situation for both parties. Public sector clients have to abide by procedural rules that govern tendering and appointment, which restrict their ability to appoint consultants directly.

Negotiation

On large or extended commissions clients can negotiate with one or more practice to obtain the most favourable fee agreement appropriate to the commission. Discussion between client and landscape architect on the particular requirements on the project enables the consultants to tailor the brief and fee basis to mutual advantage.

Quality-Based Selection

A chartered landscape architect is selected on the basis of the relevant qualities and experience required for the project. The project and services are then defined jointly, drawing on the consultant's expertise, and finally the fees for the agreed services are concluded by negotiation with reference to the LIs publication *Appointing a Landscape Consultant: Guidance for Clients on Fees* and also the CIC's *A Guide to Quality-Based Selection of Consultants: A Key to Design Quality*.

Design Competition and Technical Proposal

Design competitions are a way of discovering the range of design options available on major projects. To enable a consultant to be selected on the basis of a design competition or technical proposal the client has to ensure adequate information is available to competitors including the basis of remuneration. The criteria and methods used to assess and select from the competition entries must be determined in advance by the client, e.g. on the basis of the design or on the fee proposal.

'Two Envelope' System

The 'two envelope' system is a method used to evaluate the quality of proposals and the fee tenders at the same time.

Each shortlisted consultant submits a design or technical proposal with a separate sealed fee tender; the client opens all proposals and after evaluation ranks them in preferred order, endorsing the fee tender envelopes with this ranking. The fee tender envelope of the first choice tenderer is then opened and the commission is awarded unless the fee is unacceptable. Only if the fee is unacceptable is the second choice tenderer's fee envelope opened.

When the commission is awarded, all remaining fee envelopes are returned unopened to the unsuccessful tenderers.

Competitive Fee Tendering

When fee competition is used to select a consultant, the client prepares a short list of fully acceptable consultants, either by:

- **Pre-Tender Qualification**
- **Known Practices**
- **The Nomination Procedure**

The number of consultants on the shortlist is determined by the project size and will usually range from three to six. In order to invite bids the client prepares a full brief and full project definition. A suitable basis for this process is set out in the Landscape Institute's *Guide to Procedure for Competitive Tendering*, which is divided into five sections with appendices. The Institute emphasises that unless the process of tendering selects the best consultant for the project with least effort from all parties, it will not give the best value for money.

Guide to Procedure for Competitive Tendering

Part 1: General Introduction

This document advises Landscape Consultants and their clients in the commissioning of landscape consultancy by tender. It seeks to ensure that the procedure followed is fair and equitable to all parties, and allows the client to make a valid judgement between tenders received. It provides advice on drawing up a shortlist of suitable practices and guidance on the items to be covered when preparing a tender information and brief to be used when approaching a number of landscape consultancies for competitive fee quotes.

Part 2: Pretender Selection of Landscape Consultants

Provides advice to the client on drawing up a shortlist of suitable practices. Each practice invited to submit a competitive fee tender should be fully and equally acceptable to the client on all their criteria in order that fee price should be the sole criteria for selection.

Part 3: Tender Information and Brief

Provides a guide to the brief to be used by clients when approaching a number of Landscape Consultancies for competitive fee quotes. The tender information and brief is considered under the following headings:
- Description of the proposed project.
- Background information.
- Client's requirements: the project (covers feasibility studies, design and contract administration and landscape management projects separately).
- Client's requirements: consultants services.

Part 4: Tender Procedure

Provides guidance on standard procedure, timescale and assessment of tenders and notification of results.

Part 5: Form of Tender

Appendices
- Schedule of Services and Fees.
- Memorandum of Agreement.

Term Appointments, Framework Agreements and Partnering Arrangements

These arrangements offer benefits including reduced administration, improved efficiency and economy, established communication, flexibility and consistency of service. Government and industry initiatives encourage the use of these longer-term arrangements as an alternative to single project tendering, particularly where a series of smaller and or similar projects is anticipated.

Design and Build Contracts

These encourage co-operation between designers and contractors and allow the skills of both to be integrated into the design and implementation. The document stresses that such contracts will only achieve a good quality landscape outcome if the relevant component is clearly defined in the brief and forms part of the assessment of tenders.

The Landscape Institute's document *Appointing a Chartered Landscape Architect: Guidelines for Best Value* sets out selection procedures for landscape architects that cover:

- The nature of the project and understanding the requirements of the project.
- The professional services, skills and resources required to undertake the project.
- Landscape architects possessing the services, skills and resources and quality required.
- The selection process.
- The criteria for selection (quality or price) and scoring systems.
- Stages in the selection process.
- Developing the brief.

The Landscape Institute recommends a 3-stage selection process for major or complex projects or, if required, to be advertised according to project size/value thresholds under The Public Contracts Regulations 2006 (e.g. in the *Official Journal of the European Union – OJEU*).

- Stage One – Compilation of the Select List.
- Stage Two – Preparation and Evaluation of the Tender Submissions.
- Stage Three – Final Selection by Interview.

Feedback should be provided to all unsuccessful tenderers dependent on the selection criteria.

Approach and Offer of Work – Factors to be Considered by the Landscape Architect

When first approached by a client to undertake work the landscape architect should consider certain factors before accepting/undertaking a commission whether it be by direct approach or through a tender:

> ### • COMPETENCE •
> Whether the landscape architect has relevant experience and is competent to deal with the type of work required. (Standard 2 of the Code of Professional Conduct and Practice: *'Landscape architects should only undertake professional work for which they are able to provide proper professional and technical competence, and resources.'*)

> ### • COMMITMENTS •
> Whether present commitments will permit the landscape architect to devote adequate time and staff to the work. (Standard 2 of the Code as above.)

> ### • FINANCE •
> Whether the office can carry the job financially. (Standard 7: *'Landscape architects should ensure that their personal and professional finances are managed prudently…. Bankruptcy, liquidation, accommodation of creditors and failure to pay judgement debts are all acts by an LA which could be examined concerning wilful disregard of responsibilities or lack of integrity'*).

> ### • THE CLIENT •
> The known standing and integrity of the client.

Acceptance and Confirmation of Appointment

Acceptance and confirmation of appointment can be made in the following ways:

> ### • VERBAL AGREEMENT •

> ### • UNDER SEAL •

• EXCHANGE OF LETTERS •
• MEMORANDUM OF AGREEMENT •

Under Seal

This is a formal document drawn up by lawyers detailing the requirements of the client as the first party and the manner in which the professional will undertake and discharge his duties as second party. It is signed, witnessed, sealed and embossed. It is used mainly by large organizations for contracts involving large sums of money, e.g. government contracts. The most important consequence, and often the reason the parties choose this method of contracting, is that the limitation period for making a claim is twelve years instead of the usual six (refer to Chapter 2).

Exchange of Letters/Memorandum of Agreement

This is a written formal offer to the client setting out the terms of appointment and other relevant information and asking for confirmation to proceed. Misunderstandings may arise from exchange of letters. The Landscape Institute recommends using its Standard Memorandum of Agreement and Schedule of Services and Fees as contained within *The Landscape Consultant's Appointment* as well as issuing the client with a copy of the document itself. The memorandum ensures that the agreement covers the terms of the commission, the scope of the services, the allocation of responsibilities and any limitation of liability, the payment of fees including the rates and method of calculations, and the provision for termination.

Standard 9 of The Landscape Institute's Code of Professional Conduct and Practice states that '*Landscape architects shall not undertake professional work unless the terms of the contract have been recorded in writing as to:*

- *Scope of services.*
- *Allocation and limitation of responsibilities.*
- *Fee/method of calculation.*
- *Provisions for termination.*
- *Provisions for dispute resolution.*

Other relevant information:
- Project description and location.
- Additional or unusual services.
- Conditions of appointment.
- Other consultants/professionals appointments.

A letter or memorandum of agreement should be sent by registered post or recorded delivery as, should litigation arise, it may be necessary to produce evidence of the client's receipt.

Implications of an agreement between the landscape architect and the client

Once there has been an agreed acceptance and confirmation it signifies the commencement of a contractual relationship. This is reinforced by an assurance of special professional competence and by the Code of Professional Conduct of the Institute. If this relationship breaks down and the contract is breached because there is a failure of either party to perform in accordance with their agreement then the law will give remedy and redress can be sought through the courts. This could include *(refer also to Chapter 2)*:

- Professional negligence by the LA (error and omission).
- Tortuous negligence (breach of duty of reasonable care).
- Breach of contract (e.g. unpaid fees).

The Landscape Institute's *The Landscape Consultant's Appointment*

Background

The Landscape Consultant's Appointment was first issued in 1988 by the Landscape Institute. Its predecessor, *The Conditions of Engagement and Professional Charges*, was withdrawn by the Office of Fair Trading in 1984 under the Restrictive Trade Practices Act 1976 because of the detailed formulae it contained for calculating fees.

The aim of the new document is to ensure that the landscape consultant and the client achieve a clear understanding of the services required by the client and that the conditions concerning the provision of these services are clearly defined.

The document was revised in May 1998 as a result of the Housing Grants, Construction and Regeneration Act 1996, which came into force in April 1998. The Act covers architectural, design and surveying work in relation to construction operations. The Act makes provision for adjudication in the case of disputes and stage payments. The right of suspension and 'pay when paid' clauses is no longer permitted save on the grounds of insolvency by the payer. All contracts signed after the Act came into force are subject to these provisions. If the contract itself does not say how this is to be done then the provisions set out in the 'Scheme for Construction Contracts 1998' will apply automatically. The Landscape Consultant's Appointment has now incorporated adjudication and payment within its revised version.

The document comprises:

> **• THE MEMORANDUM OF AGREEMENT •**

> **• APPENDIX 1 •**
> **LANDSCAPE CONSULTANTS APPOINTMENT**
> Part 1: The Landscape Consultants Services
> Part 2: Other Services
> Part 3: Conditions of Appointment

> **• APPENDIX 2 •**
> **SCHEDULE OF SERVICES AND FEES**

The Memorandum of Agreement

The Landscape Institute advises its members to use the Memorandum of Agreement and the Schedule of Services and Fees to prepare formal agreements with clients to prevent uncertainties occurring for either party as the commission progresses. It is the formal agreement between the client and the consultants and covers:

> - Names of the parties.
> - The conditions of appointment.
> - Schedule of services and fees.
> - Project description and location.
> - Payment provisions.
> - Signatures and witnesses.

Memorandum of Agreement – Points to Note

- A duty is placed on the landscape consultant to provide invoices to the client in instalments/dates as specified in the schedule. The date of receipt (2 days after posting) of the invoice is the date the fees are due by the client.
- A duty is placed on the client to acknowledge receipt of the invoice, no later than 5 days after receipt, to the landscape consultant and specify the amount to be paid and the basis of calculation.
- The final date for payment after sum is due is written in to the agreement as 17 days (or other as specified).
- Notice for withholding payment has to be given within 7 days before the final date for payment.

- NB The Late Payments of Commercial Debts (Interest) Act 1998 came into force on November 1998. It covers commercial contracts for the supply of goods or services where the supplier is a 'small business' and the purchaser is a 'large business' or UK Public Authority. The rate of interest has been set at 8% above base rate.

Landscape Consultant's Appointment: Appendix 1

Part 1: Landscape Consultant's Services

This describes the preliminary and standard services which a landscape consultant would undertake after accepting a commission and covers design, construction and management, Stages A–L Inception to Completion. These services are then subdivided into work stages but not all will apply to each commission.

Part 1: Landscape Consultant's Services – Points to Note

- **Preliminary services:** Inception and feasibility to be classified as preliminary which enables this initial work, when a client may be considering options for the brief or methods of implementation, to be charged on a time basis. Once the actual project is defined, a brief established, and basic services commenced, fees can be related to a capital sum on a percentage basis.
- **Basic services:** Work Stage C – CDM: designers duties are covered.

Part 2: Other Services

Part 2 describes the services which are provided outside the design, construction and management process and augment the preliminary and standard services such as public inquiries, environmental impact assessments, landscape planning, landscape appraisal and evaluation and also other consultants' services.

Part 3: Conditions of Appointment

This describes the conditions which normally apply when a landscape consultant is appointed and includes the landscape consultant's duty of care, project control, appointment of other consultants, liabilities, termination, adjudication, and requirements under CDM regulations.

Conditions of Appointment – Points to Note

- **Cl 3.2: The landscape consultant's duty is defined:**
  'The landscape consultant will use reasonable skill, care and diligence in accordance with the normal standards of the profession.'

- **Cl 3.4: The landscape consultant's authority is defined:**
  'The landscape consultant will act on behalf of the client in the matters set out or implied in the landscape consultant's appointment. . .'
- **Cl 3.12: The sub-consultant's liability is set out:**
  'Where a consultant is appointed under 3.10 the landscape consultant shall not be held liable for the consultants work. . .'
- **Cl 3.15: The contractor's responsibility is defined:**
  'The client will employ a contractor under a separate agreement to undertake construction or other works not undertaken by the landscape consultant. The client will hold the contractor and not the landscape consultant responsible for the contractor's operational methods and for the proper execution of the works.'
- **Cl 3.20: Copyright** (also covered under Cl. 2.29 and 2.2.10)
- **The clients obligation is also defined in the Introduction:**
  'They must provide adequate information on the project, site and budget and fully understand and approve the landscape consultants proposals. . .'

Schedule of Services and Fees: Appendix 2

Names the parties and the project; refers to the memorandum of agreement; covers the services and specialist conditions which apply and details the method of charging fees, stage payments, expenses and disbursements.

Schedule of Services and Fees – Points to Note

- Lump sum payments are defined as a single figure.
- Time charge fees allow a detailed breakdown of hourly rates.
- Interim payments allowed for time charge and percentage fees.
- Expenses and disbursements are clearly defined.

Calculating and Charging Professional Fees

The Landscape Institute's Engaging a Landscape Consultant: Guidance for Clients on Fees

In August 1996 the Landscape Institute Practice Committee produced a fee guidance supplement with the aim of promoting the principle of quality, balanced with price, in providing the best value for money. It was revised in 2003 when fee guidance for planning supervisors was added as an appendix. The booklet is divided into three sections and has attached tables, a fee graph and examples. The document supersedes the *Conditions of Engagement and Professional Charges 1984* withdrawn by The

Office of Fair Trading and supplements the information and guidance contained within the following Landscape Institute documents: *The Landscape Consultants Appointment, A Guide to Procedure for Comprehensive Tendering* and *Appointing a Chartered Landscape Architect: Guidelines for Best Value.*

This document is now under review again by The Office of Fair Trading (Refer to The Landscape Institute for updates on this situation).

Methods of Charging Fees and Expenses

Part 3 of the document sets out the common methods of charging fees in:

> - **PERCENTAGE** •
> - **TIME CHARGE** •
> - **LUMP SUM** •
> - **RETAINER** •

Other methods exist and include Ceiling Figure, Unit Price Fees, Incentive Fees and Betterment Fees but the principal methods are described in detail below.

Percentage Fees

These are fees expressed as a percentage of the total construction cost of the landscape contract or subcontract. Before fees can be calculated both client and landscape architect must establish the services to be provided, the approximate construction budget and the nature of the work, e.g. hard or soft landscape or combined, main or subcontract, phasing. Subcontract costs should include on apportionment of main contractor's attendance, prelims, profit allowance and fluctuations.

Percentage fees are best used for straightforward landscape projects where the standard services (Stages C–L) are to be used.

Available data

- *Engaging a Landscape Consultant: Guidance for Clients on Fees* contains a fee graph which shows four curves as a range of percentage fees at differing complexity ratings for works of £22 500 to £10 million. This indicates the fee costs that may be incurred by the client for landscape consultants' basic services expressed as percentages of the contract sum. Lower fee percentages may be expected with higher contract sums and vice versa. Projects below the £22 500 threshold should be agreed on a time charge or lump sum fee basis.

- Four different classifications of landscape work are identified depending on degrees of complexity. The four curves on the fee graph correspond to these four classifications and show the nominal percentage fee curve (complexity rating 1 for soft landscape design and implementation services) and three other curves (rating 2–4 for comprehensive hard and soft landscape design and implementation services for differing scales of complexity as set out in the document).

NB The graphs are indicative only and are intended to act as a guide.

How applied

- Conventionally on the latest approved revision of the budget until the contract is let and then on the contract sum until the total construction cost is established.

Advantages

- If the budget/tender price is high the consultant will achieve a high fee.

Disadvantages

- A method vulnerable to market forces and their influence on contractors tendering. If the tender figure is lower than estimate the consultant loses out.
- Working to an agreed figure means cost control is important. There is no flexibility and if the landscape architect budgets incorrectly he loses money.

Time Charges

Time charge fees are when all time expended on the project by principal and technical staff is charged at previously agreed rates and revised at stated intervals.

Time charge fees are best used where the scope of work cannot reasonably be foreseen or where services cannot be related to the amount of landscape construction costs. Preliminary, additional or varied services on an otherwise basic service such as open-ended or protracted planning negotiations are examples of where time charges are appropriate.

How applied

- The rates should be calculated in advance for individuals within the office or bands of staff e.g. principals, associates, senior professionals, junior professionals, technicians.
- The charge-out rate will depend on each individual's wage plus overheads. Often 2.5–3.0 × salary, it should also include a method of revision to reflect subsequent changes in salaries and costs. Secretarial and administration staff's time is not usually charged for, but there are

times when it should be, for example when staff are directly engaged to do semi-technical work on a specific project.

Advantages

- The landscape architect is paid for all the hours worked on the project, including work not anticipated at the outset or abortive work.
- The client pays only for the work done (as opposed to fees as a percentage of the contract sum regardless of how much work the consultant is involved in).

Disadvantages

- From the client's point of view, this method of charging may seem open ended with uncertainty regarding his total financial commitment until the job is complete.
- It also may seem that the landscape architect has no incentive to work efficiently.
- It is advisable to keep the client informed on the progress of time-charged work, and to agree a figure that is not to be exceeded without prior permission.

Lump Sum Fees

Lump sum fees are when a total sum of money is agreed for a defined package of services. Lump sums are common where the scope of work can be clearly defined from the outset. It is necessary to define the parameters of services, i.e. time, project size and cost, where applicable so that if these are varied by more than the stated amount the lump sum itself may be varied. It is unwise to agree a lump sum with no provision for variation except in the case of a highly focused service to be undertaken over a very short period.

Lump Sum Fees

How applied

- At agreed payment intervals and at agreed proportions.
- Time charges are often converted to lump sums when the project become sufficiently defined.
- Percentage fees may similarly be converted to lump sums when a firm budget or contract sum is known.

Advantages

- The limit of spend is known by both parties.

Disadvantages

- A lump sum is a risk. If anything goes wrong the practice may lose money yet have no justification for revision of the sum.

Other Methods of Charging Fees

Retainer/Term commissions

The client retains the services of a consultant for piecemeal work over a period of time at agreed rates or on an 'as needed basis'. This client has priority over another. This basis is also applicable to term commissions. Fees are calculated as a sum additional to any fees calculated by other methods or on a time basis. If agreed fees may be recalculated on a monthly, quarterly or yearly basis.

Ceiling figure

Similar to lump sum, but a ceiling figure is agreed and is often for a defined type of work.

Unit price fees

Fees agreed on a unit price, e.g. per room, per building or per area of hard paving. Used only for repetitive work and more common on architectural commissions.

Incentive fees

Additional to another fee; payable if certain criteria (often time related) are achieved.

Methods of Charging Expenses and Disbursements

The consultant's direct expenses to carry out the job can be calculated and recharged to the client. Recoverable expenses usually include reproduction or purchase costs of all documents, hotel and travelling expenses, and rental and hire charges for specialized equipment.

Disbursements are charges properly borne by the client. Examples of disbursements are planning application fees, expenses incurred in advertising for tender and resident site staff, and any fees and charges for specialist professional advice, including legal advice, which have been incurred by the landscape architect with the specific authority of the client.

Expenses can be recovered in a number of ways:

> **• AT COST •**

> **• AT MARKET RATES •**

> **• ROLLED UP •**
> Included in the fee without being separately
> expressed.

> **• CONVERTED TO A PERCENTAGE •**
> Included in the fee without being separately expressed.

> **• LUMP SUM •**

Payment of Fees

Programmed Instalment

To maintain a healthy cash flow a practice must be able to depend on the fees that arise from commissions being paid on a regular, preferably monthly, basis. This can be encouraged by suggesting that the client pays according to a plan of programmed instalments. The certainty of this arrangement is welcomed by most clients since payment can be budgeted over a period.

The Landscape Institute offers guidance on programmed instalments in *Engaging a Landscape Consultant: Guidance for Clients on Fees*. Services outside the basic services will probably be negotiated on a time-charge or lump sum basis.

Apportionment of Different Methods of Fee Calculations

Engaging a Landscape Consultant: Guidance for Client on Fees recommends the following:

- **Part 1: Preliminary services: Stages A–B**: time basis, Stages C–D can also be on a time basis if complex approvals are sought or numerous options are being considered.
- **Part 1: Basic services: Stages C–L**: percentage or lump sum fee.
- **Part 2: Other services**: time-charged or lump sum.

Non Payment of Fees

The simplest approach is to be clear as to your terms with you client and agree them in writing.

- The Landscape Institute's Code of Professional Conduct and Practice, Standard 9 states that 'a landscape architect shall not undertake professional work unless the terms of the contract have been recorded in writing. An offer and acceptance = an agreement, which signifies a contract. If it is breached, i.e. through unpaid fees, the landscape architect can seek remedy through the courts.

- The Landscape Institute's Landscape Consultant's Appointment Memorandum of Agreement added specific clauses regarding adjudication and payment as a result of The Housing, Grants, Construction and Regeneration Act 1998. Landscape architects can go to adjudication to resolve a dispute including non payment of fees.
- The Late Payments of Commercial Debts (Interest) Act 1998 covers commercial contracts for the supply of goods or services where the supplier is a 'small' business and the purchaser is a 'large' business or a UK Public Authority. The rate of interest is currently 8% above base rate.
- Case law: Dinkha Latchin v. General Mediterranean Holding SA 16.12.03. The judge held 'The giving of instructions to a professional to carry out work usually gives rise to an implied promise to pay'.

Fee Tendering

In addition to the straightforward method of being offered a commission by a client (based on a recommendation or on the existence of a good working relationship), many official bodies/agencies and local authorities look for competitive tenders from consultants. As a result of this the Landscape Institute produced *The Guide to Procedure for Competitive Tendering*. This document advises landscape consultants and their clients in the commissioning of landscape consultancy by tender. It seeks to ensure that the procedure followed is fair and equitable to all parties, and allows the client to make a valid judgement between tenders received.

Fee Submissions

Major or complex public sector projects are procured in accordance with the rules contained within The Public Contracts Regulations 2006 that require contracts for services to be advertised due to project size/value thresholds in the *Official Journal of the European Union – OJEU*.

There is usually a 3-stage submission procedure of:
- Submission of expression of interest.
- Tender submission on the basis of a standard detailed brief that could include a 'two envelope' submission.
- Final selection by interview.

Standard brief

- Description of the proposed project.
- Background information.
- Client's requirements: the project.

- Client's requirements: consultants services.
- Financial proposal.
- Tender procedure: timescale, assessment of tenders and notification.

Where public projects are of small nature and under the EU threshold, or it is a private project, a standard brief may not be available and fee submissions can be made in the form of a report that could contain the following information:

Fee submission

- Response to the brief.
- Proposed design team.
- Relevant experience.
- Proposed methodology and possibly initial design ideas.
- Services offered and conditions of appointment.
- A breakdown/outline of the anticipated stages of work, time involved and fees.
- Programme.

Appendices

- Examples of similar projects undertaken by the firm.
- CVs of the staff and consultants who may be involved.

Fee Calculation

When calculating fees on a competitive basis there are a number of points to take into consideration concerning both the nature of the project and the landscape architect's own organization:

The Project

- Project type (hard/soft landscaping).
- Project location.
- Project value.
- Services required including unusual services.
- Stages of work the landscape architect will be involved in.
- Level of appointment (main or sub-consultant).
- Other consultants required.

The Landscape Architect's Organization – fee calculation

$$\frac{\text{Overhead costs} + \text{salary costs/person}}{\text{number of hours available for work on the project}} + \text{profit}$$
$$= \text{hourly rate for a member of staff}$$

NB. The profit margin is the only flexible aspect in calculating your fee in a tender.

Appointing Sub-Consultants

Refer to the Landscape Institute's *Professional Practice Note 03/00: Sub-Consultant Appointments: Guidelines and Checklist of Heads of Agreement*. This is issued as guidance and as a checklist to assist members when entering into traditional sub-consultant appointments.

This document is under review for The Landscape Institute (Refer to www.landscapeinstitute.org.uk).

Current Key headings are:

Selecting Sub-Consultants

- Tendering procedures: only required if the project is of a substantial size or specialist nature. The Landscape Institute recommend using *Guide to Procedure for Competitive Tendering*.
- Project description: this should be set out in the letter of appointment and cover:
  - Work stages undertaken
  - Schedule of fees
  - Programme
  - Services provided within the main consultant's offices at the sub-consultant's base.

Obligations of the Parties

Sets out:
- The main roles of the parties including parts of the main consultant's brief that require performance by the sub-consultant.
- Programme, output required, attendance at meetings.
- Copyright requirements.

Liabilities, Insurances and Management

Covers:
- Professional indemnity and other insurances to be maintained by sub-consultant.
- Health and safety policy to be provided by sub-consultant.
- Quality management systems required either to comply with main consultant or sub-consultant to provide proof of their own.
- Format of outputs and quantity.
- Methods of communications.
- Agreement of revisions required.

Fees and Expenses

- Calculation basis.
- Expenses.
- Additional work and rates.
- Basis for paying fees.

Collateral Warranties

- Whether they are required.
- Advise from professional indemnity insurers and lawyers on content of document.

CDM: Regulations and Dispute Resolution

- Responsibility of sub-consultant regarding CDM Regulations and Health and Safety.
- Agreed method of dispute resolution.

Quality Assurance

ISO 9000:2000 is an international quality standard. It has three sections (9001–9003) and the requirements cover all the basic management principles of both product-based and service-based organizations. It is a conceptual document that can be tailored to develop the quality standards of any business.

Accreditation is determined by an external assessor/certification body that will be a member of the National Accreditation Council for Certification Bodies.

A firm whose management system has been successfully assessed by a certification body against the requirements of BS EN ISO 9000:2000 is entered on a register, and becomes a Registered Firm of Assessed Capability. Once accreditation is achieved by a business it is a sign of management quality assurance.

Quality Management

Quality assurance is about consistent everyday management involving evaluation, monitoring, feedback, developments and correction to assist directors, partners and sole principals in the control of their own business and in the achievement of their long-term business/management plan objectives.

Quality management refers to systems not products. Good quality management allows the landscape architect to provide expert advice and creative expression, safe in the knowledge that defined systems for all operational areas of business systems are in place to facilitate the project.

Quality Assurance is Recorded through the organizations

Quality manual

This is the firm's statement of its commitment to maintaining and operating a quality management system including its own record of the way it works. It should include the:

Organization profile

Quality policy: a statement as to the organization's long-term intentions regarding quality of service and their commitment to such intentions.

Quality Procedures Manual

Sets down the organization's profile and both overall policies and detailed requirements in relation to ISO 9000:2000 such as the firm's management systems and responsibilities, documentation, resource management, service realization and measurement, analysis and improvement. This must clearly document how the organization works and is set at under the following readings:

- Document control and records.
- Client requirements and satisfaction.
- Measurement and improvement.
- Management review.
- Resource management.
- Project control.
- Design control.
- Purchasing.
- Process control.
- Measurement and improvements.
- Internal audit.
- Control of non conformities.
- Corrective and preventive action.
- Measurement and Improvement.

Auditing

Internal audits as well as third party assessments using the criteria of BS EN ISO 9000 against the office quality manual enable a firm to assess whether its business plan objectives are being achieved.

Why Become Quality Assured?

Standard 9 of The Landscape Institute's Code of Professional Conduct and Practice: '*LAs shall have appropriate and effective internal procedures, including monitoring and review procedures, and ensure qualified and supervised staff to enable it to function efficiently.*'

Possible benefits

Enhanced credibility
- An internationally recognized benchmark reassures clients and places landscape architects on the same level as other disciplines.

Improved efficiency and consistency
- Good management practices reduce unproductive time, which means greater gains in revenue.

Wider marketing opportunities
- Many client bodies are making certification a prerequisite when drawing up tender lists. The number and type of clients may increase.

Reduction in claims
- A well-managed office is less likely to experience claims and, in the event of a claim, will have a clear record of the event.

Feedback
- Auditing ensures that lessons are learnt for the benefit of future work.

Copyright

• Copyright Designs and Patents Act 1988 •
The Duration of Copyright and Rights in Performance Regulations 1995
Copyright Rights in Databases Regulations 1997
Copyright European Directive (2001/29) 2003

Protected Works

Copyright exists only in material that falls within one of the work categories which is described by the Act as having copyright protection. Works of architecture are included in the definition of 'artistic works' for copyright purposes. This includes any graphic works, models, photographs, fixed structures (defined in 1956 to also include an elaborately laid out garden).

Duration of Copyright

The Duration of Copyright and Rights in Performance Regulations 1995 defines the duration of copyright in each category. For literary, dramatic, musical and artistic – which includes architecture/landscape architecture – the duration of protection is 70 years from the end of the calendar year in which the author dies.

Effect of Copyright

If material is protected by copyright the owner has rights to prevent certain 'restricted acts' being undertaken. Each category of work has different restricted acts. For artistic works this includes copying the whole or substantial part of the work (this refers to quality not quantity) or issuing copies of the work to the public.

Ownership of Rights

Ownership of copyright resides with the landscape architect who prepared the designs unless they are employed to produce the design in which case copyright rests with the employer. Employees do not own rights, however, a freelance agent commissioned to produce a design will own its rights unless agreed otherwise in writing. Partners are not employees and therefore own the copyright of any work they prepare in the course of the business unless the partnership agreement states otherwise.

Upon payment of the landscape architect's fees the client is entitled to possession of the drawings prepared for the project but in absence of agreement to the contrary copyright remains with the landscape architect. If copyright is assigned to the client the landscape architects is still allowed to reproduce in subsequent work part of their original design provided the main design is not repeated. This enables the landscape architect to freely repeat standard details.

2 Liability and the law

The Importance of the Law

Ignorance of the law is no excuse! Everyone who offers a service to others and claims expertise in that service, such as professional people, has a duty to have a sound working knowledge of the law in every aspect of the services they give.

A landscape architect is not expected to know all the law in areas relevant to their field of work, which includes the law of contract, construction contracts and statutory regulations such as planning law and health and safety law. However, they are expected to ensure that a client does not suffer due to an absence of legal knowledge and to know enough about the law to be aware when specialist legal advice would be required.

The Legal Systems of the United Kingdom

The UK has two traditions of law and three principal legal jurisdictions. English law prevails in England and Wales. The basis of the legal system in Northern Ireland is English common law but it has its own law courts and its own statutory provisions. Scotland has its own courts and has always had its own legal traditions, which were preserved under the Treaty of Union in 1707. This results in the Scottish legal system being entirely different from English law particularly in the fields of property, constitutional and administrative law, and criminal law. The main sources of Scots law are legislation (including EC law), judicial decisions and 'institutional' writings, which together make up the Scots common law.

The House of Lords is the unifying legal system of the UK and is the supreme court of appeal for all three jurisdictions of England and Wales,

Northern Ireland and Scotland. The 12 law lords or lords of appeal include Scottish and Northern Ireland judges. The Government's recent bill to establish a new Supreme Court is currently being reviewed by a select committee.

This book covers the principles of English Law but highlights where Scotland and Northern Ireland differ.

English Law

English law can be divided into two main parts – unwritten and written, namely common law and enacted law.

Common Law – The Unwritten Law

- Common law includes the early customary laws assembled and formulated by judges. It means all other than enacted or written law.
- Rules derived solely from custom and judicial precedent are rules of common law. It is the unwritten law of the land because there is no official codification of it.

Legislation – The Written or Enacted Law

- Legislation comprises the Statutes, Acts and Edicts of the sovereign and her advisers.
- Legislation by Acts of Parliament takes precedence over all other sources of law and is absolutely binding while it remains in the statute books.

European Union Law

Since 1973 there has been an additional source of law – the law of the European Community, which is enacted under the European Communities Act 1972. This grants that all directly applicable provisions of the treaties establishing the European Communities become part of English law, and also all existing and future community secondary legislation. European law is now of great significance as it takes precedence over domestic law where the two conflict.

Most main decisions are taken in the form of 'directives', 'regulations' and 'decisions' which require member states to achieve stated results but leave it to the member state to choose the form and method of implementation. Today there is an ever-growing corpus of EC decisions incorporated into UK law that have an impact on landscape architects, for example, Environmental Assessment Regulations and CDM Regulations.

The European Convention on Human Rights

The Human Rights Act 1988 accorded some standing to the European Court of Human Rights in English law without derogating from the supremacy of Parliament. This allows for enacting legislation to be interpreted in accordance with the convention rights where possible. If not it can be declared incompatible with English law.

Branches of English law with the greatest general effect for landscape architects are civil and criminal law.

Civil Law

- Civil law is related to the rights, duties and obligations of individual members of the community to each other, and it embraces all the law to do with family, property, contract, commerce, partnerships, insurance, copyright and the law of torts.
- Civil law determines the liabilities that exist between parties. The sanctions of civil law are not punishments but rather remedies either through awarding damages or ordering one party to do or refrain from doing something.

Criminal Law

- Criminal law sets out limitations on people's behaviour. It deals with wrongful acts harmful to the community and punishable by the State.
- A criminal legal action is between the State (Crown) and an individual.

The Law of Contract

Two of the biggest areas of civil law are contract and tort. For the law of contract to be relevant a contract must be in existence and the parties must have agreed what their legal obligations to each other are. This is distinctly different from the law of tort where no contract exists between the parties.

What is a Contract?

- A contract is an agreement between individuals that can be enforced by law.
- It is the legal relationship between the parties and if it is breached the law gives remedy.

Landscape architects can have direct contractual obligations, such as contracts for services to clients (employers), partnership agreements and contracts of employment (between employers and employees) however, they are not directly party to construction contracts which are between the client and the contracter.

For a contract to come into force and be valid there are three essential ingredients that need to be in place.

> **ESSENTIALS OF A VALID CONTRACT**
> • **INTENTION TO CREATE LEGAL RELATIONS** •
> • **CONSIDERATION** •
> • **AGREEMENT** •
> **(Offer and Acceptance)**

Intention to Create Legal Relations

The parties must intend their promises to be legally binding. A moral obligation is not enough.

Consideration *(Not applicable in Scotland)*

To bind the parties there must be some 'consideration' involved. This means that something must be paid or exchanged for the contract to be binding and enforceable in law, such as money or a service. This is known in legal terms as '*Quid pro quo*' – 'something for something else'.

Agreement

The courts apply the simple formulae of 'offer and acceptance' to determine if an 'agreement' has occurred.

Offer

An offer is a promise made by the 'offerer' to be bound by a contract if the 'offeree' accepts the terms of the offer. The offer matures into a contract when it is accepted by the other party.

Acceptance

The acceptance of the offer can by word (written or oral) or by conduct and must be communicated to the offerer. Silence is not sufficient to accept an offer. The acceptance must be unequivocal and unqualified and it must be a complete acceptance of every term of the offer.

Revocation

An offer may be withdrawn or revoked up until such times as it is accepted. An acceptance is effective when it is received by the offerer – but if it is by letter and posted the acceptance takes effect when it is posted. Revocation by post takes effect when the offeree receives the letter.

Offers are not indefinite. If a time for acceptance is stipulated then the offer must be accepted within that time. If no time is stipulated, the offer remains open for acceptance within a 'reasonable' time – except in the case of death, bankruptcy or insanity.

Other criteria will automatically apply for a contract to be considered valid:

Capacity to Contract

The parties must have proper capacity to enter into legal relations. This condition offers protection to infants (in law under 18), the mentally disordered, and persons under the influence of drink/drugs against committing themselves to binding agreements.

Consent

Consent to the agreement must be genuine and freely given. It must not be obtained by fraud, misrepresentation of fact, or under duress.

Legality of Object

The object of the contract must not be for any purpose that contravenes the law such as agreements to commit crimes or torts. If an agreement occurred between two parties to commit a murder and one party failed to perform his obligations by not paying for the crime when it was committed, the courts would not accept an action for breach of contract as the contract was unenforceable in the first place.

Object of the Contract

The object of the contract must be possible. For example, a contract to build a rocket to fly to the moon in 5 seconds would not be considered a possible object.

Necessary Formality

The necessary formality must be carried out. For example, sometimes the law requires that a contract has to be written in a certain order for it to be enforceable, e.g. contracts for the sale of land, contracts of carriage – air, land or sea.

In the absence of any of the above criteria a contract may be considered invalid – either void, voidable or unenforceable.

How are contracts discharged?

Agreement
- A mutual decision by both parties to bring their relationships to an end.

Performance
- Each party has fulfilled its obligations under the contract.

Breach or repudiation
- Either because one party fails to perform its part of the agreement or repudiates its liability (e.g. continual refusal to comply with an instruction to rectify defective work). The injured party may request damages or treat the contract as discharged.

Frustration
- When performance of the agreement proves to have been impossible after its inception and is therefore discharged as a frustrated contract, such as illness or death of one party or the property that one party is to carry out work on burns down.

By contractual stipulation
- The parties may expressly stipulate the circumstances which extinguish their obligations, e.g. when a contract is entered into for a specified period of time it is discharged at the end of that period.

By lapse of time
- Parties who have contracts of indeterminate duration (employment or partnerships) have a contract at will. Either party may determine such contracts by giving reasonable notice. The contract is discharged by the lapse of this time.

Terms of Contract

Terms of a contract establish the extent of the parties' obligations by which they have agreed to be bound. Terms are expressed or implied.

Express terms

The terms of a contract are those that the parties expressly agreed. With written contracts the terms are the written evidence within the document and each party is bound by what is recorded and signed save in exceptional circumstances.

Implied terms

Three types of implied terms exist:

- **Terms implied by the court**

The courts will imply into established categories of contract – employment, agency, partnership, etc. – standard terms which have been established in precedents as normal **unless** express agreement exists to the contrary.

- **Terms implied by custom**

If a custom in a particular trade or profession is reasonable, certain and well known, it is binding upon the parties whether or not they knew of it, such as trade fairs or confidentiality by employees. Local or regional as well as general customs may be so implied, but not if the custom conflicts with the express terms of the contract.

- **Terms implied by statute**

Many terms are implied directly by statute without any express statements by the parties and are often superseded by express statements of the parties. Two statutes exist which may automatically incorporate terms into a landscape architect's contract.

a) *The Sale of Goods Act 1979 and the Sale and Supply of Goods Act 1994*
'Where the seller sells goods in the course of a business there is an implied term that the goods supplied under the contract are of satisfactory quality'. This will include fitness for their purpose, freedom from minor defects, safety and durability.

b) *Supply of Goods and Services Act 1982*
'In a contract for the supply of a service, where the supplier is acting in the course of a business there is an implied term that the supplier will carry out the service with reasonable care and skill' and 'within a reasonable time'.

Standard Term Contracts (STCs)

The use of standard term contracts such as JCT and JCLI (see Chapters 6 and 7) ensures that misunderstandings over interpretation of terms are avoided as case law has definitively settled their meaning. In addition, insurance companies will be familiar with STCs and extra premiums on uncertain risks will be avoided. Modifications to STCs should be avoided as often clauses are interlinked and one modification will affect many clauses.

Contracts in Writing

Verbal agreements are recognized by law as contracts. However, it is easier to decide the terms of the contract if it is written. The Housing Grants Act (refer to Chapter 6) imposes adjudication as the first-tier dispute resolution process on all construction contracts. The Act states that parties can only have recourse to adjudication if the contract is in writing.

However, the Act defines that an agreement can be a 'contract in writing' regardless of whether it is signed if it is made by exchange of written communications or if it is on oral agreement evidenced in writing even by a third party. The use of the word 'subject to contract' in written agreements should be avoided, as the fact that the agreement is written may be the overriding provision. The Landscape Institute's Code of Professional

Conduct and Practice Standard 9 requires landscape architects to agree their terms in writing with the client.

Letters of Intent

Letters of intent are often used in the construction industry when a strict programme has to be adhered to and the setting up of a formal contract will eat into that programme.

A letter of intent may create a binding contract but that is unusual. Putting in place a letter of intent suggests that the partners intend to create a contract at a later stage and not by way of the letter. However, if the contract is not created at a later stage and dispute arises, the court will seek to enforce whatever the parties 'intended' to agree. It therefore follows that clarity and consistency in written negotiations and any letter of intent are very important.

Letters of intent should include as a minimum:

> • **CERTAINTY AS TO THE KEY TERMS** •
> • **AN OFFER AND ACCEPTANCE** •
> • **INTENTION TO CREATE LEGAL RELATIONS** •

The London Law Society has now created a template for letters of intent that includes:

- The works to be covered
- Areas still to be agreed in the formal contract
- The time frame for the letter to be valid
- The financial limitation including VAT
- No quantum merit payments
- Dispute resolution
- The name of the authorized person to instruct the works.

The letter must be signed and issued by the employer.

Electronic Documents

Under the Electronic Communications Act 2000 the British legal system has accepted that electronic documents have the same legitimacy as paper documents. This covers faxed and emailed documents including electronic signatures. Project extra net systems have to comply with ISO/IEC 17799 for them to be admissible in court.

Privity of Contract, The Contracts (Rights Of Third Parties) Act 1999 and Collateral Warranties

The principle feature of contract law is that it defines the rights and obligations between the parties of a contract. A party must have provided consideration in order to enforce its rights or the obligations of the other party. Without that consideration the party will not have earned the rights to the benefits of the contract. This is called privity of contract and it governs whether a person can sue or be sued in respect of that contract.

A person who is not party to a contract cannot gain any benefit by suing on it, nor can they suffer any detriment by being sued on it. This rule affected third parties who stood to gain by the contract but until recently had no redress.

The Contracts (Rights of Third Parties) Act 1999

Legislation was introduced to resolve the privity problem for the third party who benefits form a contract. The Contracts (Rights of Third Parties) Act 1999 applies to all contracts entered into after 11 May 2000 (e.g. JCLI and JCT Forms of Agreement, The Landscape Consultant's Appointment, Collateral Warranties, etc). The terms of the act may be excluded by the parties but where they are not it alters the doctrine of privity of contract (the principle that only a party to a contract may sue) and allows a right of action for non parties.

There are many parties who can suffer loss as a result of defective design or negligent administration. Obvious examples would be tenants, purchasers or funders of buildings. At present, collateral warranties create a contractual link with third parties. The Act, where it applies, gives the third party the right to sue under the original terms of the engagement.

The act allows a third party to enforce a term of a contract:

- If the contract so provides expressly, or
- If a term of the contract purports to confer a benefit on them provided that the parties intended the term to be enforceable by a third party.

The third party need not be in existence at the time the contract is made. In other words the third party could be a future tenant.

Landscape architects (and their insurers) currently control the right of third parties to sue by limiting the terms and number of collateral warranties that they will confer. The Act, where it applies, will be more unlimited in nature thus preventing landscape architects from properly evaluating the risk that they are undertaking. New forms of Standard Forms of Agreement, including JCLI, JCT and Landscape Consultant's Appointment have been redrafted to expressly prohibit/exclude the Act from the agreement, which means that traditional common law rules will still apply or the collateral warranty method is used.

Collateral Warranties

A collateral warranty or 'duty of care' is a legal agreement which stands alongside the agreement between the client and the landscape architect. It forms a legal responsibility to the client and funder/tenant/purchaser and can be very onerous. Professional indemnity insurance companies will now accept standard RIBA forms and ICE forms. There is also a standard JCT form for contractors' warranties.

The pertinent matters, which must be **no more** and **no less** onerous for the designer than that which legally prevails between designer and client, are as follows:

- The exercise of reasonable skill and care of a professional landscape architect and no other statement.
- If the client ceases to be involved with the project, i.e. novation to another purchaser or the funder, the necessary safeguards for the landscape architect's fees are provided for.
- A controlled list of deleterious materials that the landscape architect has not and will not use (be guided by the list in the approved warranty).
- Copyright license in favour of the warranty subject to payment of due fees, and only for the purposes of the development.
- The obligation on the landscape architect to maintain professional indemnity insurance cover, in so far as this is available on the market at reasonable terms.
- A right of assignment by the warrantee of the agreement to another, by absolute assignment but not more than two times.
- An undertaking of the client that collateral warranties in similar terms have been or will be entered into by others involved in the design and construction of the development.

The Law of Agency

The term 'agency' implies the relationship which comes into being when one party (the agent) is employed by another (the principal) to make legally binding contracts on behalf of the principal with a third party. The extent of authority is governed by the type of agency. 'Special agency' is usual with landscape architects where the agent and principal contract for one particular commission.

An agent's duty is to apply reasonable skill and diligence to all he has been employed to do. The degree of liability depends on the type of agency. As a rule, the principal is bound only to the extent that the agent acted within the scope of his authority, whether that authority was express, usual or implied. The agent owes to the principal the following duties:

- to act in the principal's interests (not his own).
- not to make secret profits or take bribes; and
- not to delegate his authority.

Every act the agent performs on behalf of the principal must be within the scope of his authority and is binding in law on the principal.

Within the JCLI Form of Agreement, the 'agent is named, and the scope and extent of his authority is set out clearly in cl 1.2 (and in addition cl 2.2 – extensions; cl 2.4 – practical completion; cl 2.5 – defects; cl 2.7 – failures of plants; cl 3.5 – instructions; cl 3.6 – variations; cl 3.7 – PC and provisional sums; cl 4.2 – payments, cl 4.3 and 4.4 – certificates).

Law of Tort ('delict' in Scotland)

Introduction

The law of tort is to do with civil liberty in the absence of contract.
It is concerned with:
- **Infringement** of a **right**.
- Resulting in a **loss** recognized by the law.
- To which the plaintiff seeks remedy.

A 'plaintiff' is one who commences a suit against another.

For the law of tort to apply, the three elements in bullets above must exist in a condition recognized by the law. The 'right' is often a judgement that people have a legally enforceable 'duty of care' to others. A plaintiff would complain that someone had breached their duty of care. In general terms tort is concerned with where and how liability can be attached and the reallocation of the burden of losses suffered.

The sorts of situation for which remedy or compensation may or may not be available are never finalized and may change very rapidly depending on current case law.

The law of tort covers many areas and these notes only cover the areas that relate to landscape architects.

What kinds of torts are there?
- Negligence.
- Strict liability.
- Nuisance.
- Trespass.
- Libel.

Negligence

Negligence can be described as the breach of a legal duty to take care, which results in damage to the person or property of a person.

Negligence

Three essential conditions must exist for negligence to be proven:
- A legal duty of care.
  You must not injure your neighbour
- Breach of duty.
  Negligence is the omission to do what a reasonable person would do or to do something that a prudent and reasonable person would not do.
- Damage.

Duty of care

Does the defendant owe a legal duty of care to the plaintiff?

Case law: Donaghue v. Stevenson 1932. The plaintiff found a snail in a bottle of ginger beer, but had no contract with the retailer or the manufacturer and so was forced to sue the manufacturer in tort. Whether a duty of care exists is ultimately a question of fairness. It involves a weighing up of the relationship of the parties and the nature of the risk to the public. Common examples of duty of care include that of an employer to employees or one road user to another.

For landscape architects, assessing duty of care may include detailed information about sites. For example: How safe was it? Was a risk assessment done? What documentary evidence is there of risk assessment? What particular hazards had the site, particularly for children and other vulnerable or at-risk people?

Breach of duty

Has the duty of care been breached? In deciding whether a particular Act breaches the standards of a reasonable man the courts will have to decide two main factors:

(i) the likelihood of injury occurring.
(ii) the seriousness of the injury that is being risked.

A civil claim of negligence may be judged to be criminal negligence if the breach was so grossly negligent that it constituted a criminal disregard for life. There is no formula for this: it is assessed by the jury on the facts of each case.

Damage

Has damage resulted as a breach of the duty of care? The plaintiff must prove he or she has suffered loss as a result of the defendant's breach of duty of care, that is, damage to property or personal injury.

Economic loss as a result of negligent misstatement is of direct relevance to landscape architects who give professional advice. If no express disclaimer of responsibility is made a person will be liable for the consequences of a statement which they make in circumstances where they are deemed to have assumed responsibility for the outcome.

Recent case law about property and negligence indicates that property owners may have a duty of care to warn neighbours of risks associated with the land that may affect the neighbour, e.g. Scarborough BC v. Holbeck Hall Hotel. This was the case arising from the cliff-top hotel on the crumbling cliff that fell into the sea.

'Gross negligence' occurs if a breach of a duty of care was the substantial cause of death (of people) and showed a criminal disregard for life.

Strict Liability: the Rule in Rylands v. Fletcher 1866

> **Strict liability**
>
> Also called the 'Fletcher v. Rylands' rule.
>
> Four essential conditions that together create a duty of care:
> - An accumulation.
> - A non-natural user.
> - An escape from the defendant's land.
> - Damage.

The rule has its origins in the tort of nuisance but has developed into a separate tort of its own. It applies in England and Wales, but has less authority in Scottish law. In Scotland the liability is not strict and fault must be both alleged and proved.

The rule is that a person, who in the course of a non-natural use of their land accumulates on it anything likely to do harm if it escapes, is liable for all the damage that is the natural consequence of its escape. A landscape example could be a refuse tip with noxious discharge.

The combination of an 'accumulation' and the non-natural use are deemed to create a duty of care on the part of the land-user. For a plaintiff to be able to use the rule he or she must establish that all four essential conditions apply. In recent case law it was established that the accused is not liable if the 'escape' could not reasonably have been foreseen.

Note that this law is relevant to designers under the CDM Regulations. For instance, a landscape architect would need to be able to demonstrate that he or she made an assessment of risk during design, construction and maintenance. This assessment would have been recorded in the Health and

Safety Plan and File. Assessing risk means evaluating the *likelihood* of injury and damage and the *seriousness* of such harm. During the Defects Liability Period the Health and Safety File will have been handed to the client.

Nuisance

> **Nuisance**
>
> Is concerned with protection of:
> - The environment.
> - A person's use of their own land.
> - Land over which there is a public right of way.
>
> In England and Wales there are two types of nuisance:
> - Public nuisance.
> - Private nuisance.
>
> In Scotland this distinction is not made.
> - Anything noxious, obstructive, unsafe or that makes life uncomfortable may be a 'nuisance'.

Public Nuisance

> **Nuisance in England and Wales**
>
> Public nuisance
> - An act or omission that inflicts damage, injury or inconvenience for all members of the public.
> - This is criminal law, recently strengthened by the Environmental Protection Act 1990.
>
> Private nuisance
> - Unlawful interference with a person's use of their own land or enjoyment of some right in connection with it.
>
> Three essential conditions:
> - Interference.
> - Unreasonable interference.
> - Damage.

The activities covered by public nuisance range from operation of rubbish tips, disorganized festivals, oil pollution or emissions of noxious fumes. It is a *crime* to cause such a nuisance; it is not actionable by the public, but is generally dealt with by criminal prosecution. In addition, a civil action may be brought by the Attorney General to obtain an injunction to prevent the nuisance from continuing or re-occurring.

However, if a person has suffered some special damage over and above that suffered by members of the public as a whole they are able to bring an action in nuisance to recover that damage (Halsey v. Esso Petroleum).

Nuisance claims may also be pursued under the Human Rights Act 1998. In Marcic v. Thames Water 2002, the public authority had to pay compensation to an individual adversely affected by the carrying out of its tasks, even though those tasks were properly carried out for the benefit of the community as a whole.

Definition of nuisance has been sharpened by statute in the Environmental Protection Act 1990 and the Clean Neighbourhoods and Environment Act 2005 (refer to Chapter 4).

Private Nuisance

Private Nuisance in England and Wales

Interference may be of two types:
- Physical injury – material damage to property.
- Substantial . . . discomfort to normal modes and habits of living.

It may be agreed that interference has been unreasonable, but courts also consider:
- Community benefit.
- Suitability of locality.
- Temporary nature of the injury.
- Malice.

Damage must actually occur.

Private nuisance may be described as 'unlawful interference with a person's use of his land, or enjoyment of some right over or in connection with it'. The purpose of the tort of nuisance is to preserve a balance between the right of the occupier to use their land as they think fit and that of their neighbour not to be interfered with.

There are three essential requirements for an action for nuisance:

1 Interference.
2 The interference must be unreasonable.
3 Damage.

Unreasonable Interference

Not every kind of interference with use or enjoyment will constitute a nuisance. Only if the act becomes unreasonable will it be classified as a nuisance. The test whether an act becomes unreasonable is objective – namely the view with which a disinterested member of the public would take of the situation. A number of factors are taken into account when deciding on the nature of unreasonableness.

Several factors are taken into account when deciding on the nature of unreasonableness:

- Community benefit. Does the nuisance benefit the community? For example, emergency sirens.
- Suitability of locality. Where substantial interference with enjoyment of the land is alleged, then the suitability of the locality of the defendant's use of the land is relevant. It was established in case law (St Helens Smelting Co. v. Tipping 1865) that if one lives in a town, then one should accept the consequences of trade carried out in that locality.
- Temporary nature of the injury. A temporary interference arising out of a normal use of land will not normally amount to unreasonable interference in the absence of reasonable and proper care. However, if the injury in itself is serious it may be sufficient to establish a nuisance regardless of whether it is only temporary.
- Malice. For example, if a defendant intentionally makes a noise in order to annoy a next-door neighbour, it may constitute a nuisance because it has been done deliberately. If an action were committed without malice and totally innocently it would not be classified as a nuisance.

Damage
Causing annoyance is insufficient harm; actual damage must be demonstrated for nuisance to be proved.

Nuisance in Scotland
A distinction between public and private nuisance is not made in Scotland. Anything noxious, obstructive, unsafe or which makes life uncomfortable can be a nuisance. Any affected person may act in the interest of all. The remedy is 'interdict' with or without damages.

In addition, local authorities have a duty to seek out and deal with 'statutory nuisances' such as noise. Also, a member of the public can complain to the relevant agency, requiring it to use its powers.

Trespass ('interdict' in Scotland)

Trespass

Trespass to land is 'the intentional or negligent entering or remaining on or directly causing any physical matter to come into contact with land in the possession of another.'

Trespass may be committed in three ways:
- Entering upon land.
- Remaining on land.
- Placing or projecting any material object upon land.

In England and Wales no proof of damage is necessary.
- The Scottish equivalent of trespass is 'interdict'. In Scotland, proof of damage is required.

In the tort of trespass, 'land' is given a wide meaning and includes not only the surface of the land but also the subsoil and the air space above the land. However, for trespass to occur, interference with the land must be 'direct' and not 'indirect'. Case law (Esso Petroleum v. Southport Corporation 1956) established that the discharge of oil from a ship, which was carried on to the plaintiff's foreshore, did not amount to trespass because the interference was consequential and not direct. For the same reason in Lemmon v. Webb (1895) the House of Lords held that the growth of overhanging branches from a neighbour's tree did not amount to trespass.

It is no defence that the trespasser intended no harm or did not know that they were trespassing, as an occupier's rights should not be violated.

A trespass is only a civil wrong, but it may become a crime if damage also occurs.

Defamation/libel

Defamation or libel is the publication of a false statement that tends to injure the reputation of another. It must be published and it must be written to a third party. Slander is a verbal false statement and applies in England and Wales only.

Delict

The law of 'delict' is the Scottish equivalent of the law of tort. It is that part of law that deals with the righting of legal wrongs in the civil court (as opposed to the criminal court). The reasoning is slightly different, with Scottish delict concentrating more on general theory and less on specific wrongs. Most actions based in delict arise out of negligence.

Liability

Introduction

What are a landscape architect's legal responsibilities (or liabilities)?
- Professional liability.
- Liability in tort.
- Liability in contract.
- Liability as a member of a practice.

- Liability as an officer in a public authority.
- Vicarious liability.
- Statutory liabilities.

'Liability' refers to the obligation to pay damages when things go wrong. As indicated in the box, there are several types of liability that may concern the landscape architect.

Three of these – liability in tort, strict liability and breach of contract – relate to sections 2.0 and 3.0 above but, in addition, landscape architects need to be aware of professional, employer's, occupier's and vicarious liability, liability as a member of a practice and statutory liability.

It is possible that a landscape architect could be simultaneously liable both in tort and contract (and indeed in other forms of liability) for a single offence. For example, incompetent design could be in breach of contract and constitute negligence (*subsequent defects*) and, say, implicate the practice as a whole (*partnerships and companies*).

Liability in the Tort of Negligence

The fundamental principle of the law of tort is that 'you owe a duty to all persons you can reasonably foresee would be directly or closely affected by your actions, for it is assumed that you ought reasonably to have them in mind when you commit your acts'.

Professional designers, including landscape architects, have a specific and wider responsibility and duty of care than the general case in the paragraph above (or than in contract) and that is to all those who will use that which he or she designs, though this may include others than the client.

Specific aspects of the landscape architect's activity may give rise to liability claims if not carried out with reasonable care (failure to perform). These include:

- Personal injury: a landscape architect may be liable if their negligence causes foreseeable personal injury to any foreseeable victim, e.g. where he or she orders something to be done which is dangerous and causes injury. Note that the landscape architect is not liable if they order something to be done that is dangerous only if done in the wrong way (for example, on the contractor's mistaken direction).
- Liability to subsequent purchasers for defects in the building works arising out of faulty design or inspection of construction works, but only if the defect could not have been known about at the time of purchase.
- Liability to the builder for economic loss that is the direct result of the professional's advice.

Professional liability

Both the law of contract and the tort of negligence require the professional to exercise 'reasonable care'. What is the meaning of 'reasonable care'?

The meaning of reasonable care

- For ordinary citizens the standard of care is that of a 'reasonable man'.
- For professionals, the standard of care is that of a skilled man exercising and claiming to have that special skill.
- For landscape architects, this is restated in the *Landscape Architect's Appointment*: 'The landscape architect will use reasonable skill, care and diligence in accordance with the normal standards of the profession'. In the case of a landscape architect this is restated in the *Landscape Consultant's Appointment (Part 3 Conditions of Appointment)*: 'The landscape consultant will use reasonable skill, care and diligence in accordance with the normal standards of the profession'.

The liability of the professional landscape architect in contract and negligence is described more fully below.

Liability for breach of contract

For this to apply there must be a contractual relationship with another party.

Liability in breach of contract

A party without lawful excuse refuses or fails to perform, performs defectively or incapacitates himself or herself from performing the contract.

When a landscape architect enters an agreement with a client, they make a commitment to exercise professional skills competently and with care for the client's interests. So if the landscape architect neglects to do what they undertook to do, or bungles it, they commit a breach of contract, making them liable to the person who engaged them.

Specifically, duties in contract are of two kinds: duties of care and strict duties (duties of result). A duty of care is a duty to make reasonable efforts to produce the desired result. A strict duty (or duty of result) is a guarantee that the desired result will be produced, making the person who promises liable even if the failure to produce it cannot be shown to be their fault.

Usually a landscape architect's duties are duties of care, but liability may be strict either when a landscape architect delegates part of their work to someone else or is brought in to solve a particular problem.

The landscape architect's liability in breach of contract

Specific aspects of a landscape architect's work may give rise to liability claims:
- Negligent survey.
- Incompetent design.
- Inadequate inspection.
- Negligent financial advice.
- Negligent legal advice.
- Negligence in certifying payments.

Incompetent design refers to errors or omissions in plans, drawings or specification, and also in choice of materials, 'build-ability' and 'supervise-ability'.

The landscape architect is required to inspect the works to ensure that the standard is in line with that originally conceived. Reasonable inspection does not mean a 24-hour presence, but it does mean overseeing the principal parts of the works especially if these are subsequently hidden, e.g. drains or foundations. Inadequate inspection would be a failure to do this.

Negligent financial advice could be for example on likely building costs. While negligent legal advice would refer to aspects of the law relevant to the business of landscape architecture. Negligence in certifying payments may include over-certifying or issuing certificates for work inadequately done.

Case law in 2004 established that people providing services to an organization owe a duty of skill and care to that organization to give it a warning about harmful situations or potentially harmful consequences of actions of which they are aware.

Collateral warranty

A landscape architect may have a contract of appointment with a client. The purpose of a collateral warranty is to bind a third party (usually a developer or financial institution which is backing the client) into a contract where no contract would otherwise exist. Without a warranty the third party would have to establish a claim in tort.

Liability as a member of a practice

Partnerships (Unlimited)

In addition to all their normal individual liabilities, each partner has added responsibilities as a member of a partnership. The nature of the liability for contract debts and torts (including professional negligence) is defined by the Partnership Act. (Refer to Chapter 1.)

Any partner in a partnership (in England) who makes any admission, representation or action in the course of carrying out the firm's business binds the firm and his fellow partners, unless it is outside their authority to act for the firm in that particular matter. Any torts, where it may be inferred that the partner was acting as a member of the firm, would be considered as being committed by all in the partnership.

Limited Liability Partnerships (LLPs)

LLPs are governed by their members. For an LLP to be incorporated, two or more persons associated for carrying on a lawful business with a view to profit must be named in the incorporation document. These are classified as designated members and are not employed by the LLP, which is a separate legal entity.

- Every member of an LLP is the agent of the partnership. The LLP is bound by what a member has agreed unless he or she acted outwith the scope of their authority.
- A member is not liable for the torts or obligations incurred by the LLP, other than in tort for their own negligence. Therefore it is only possible to sue the LLP in contract and not the member. However, the member can be sued under the law of tort.
- A member is liable for the debts of the LLP in the event of it being wound up to the amount that he or she has contributed to the LLP as capital.

Companies

A company is owned by its members or shareholders and is governed by its directors or managing director with the supervision of its shareholders.

Shareholders

- Are liable personally in tort for their own negligence.
- Are only liable for the debts of the company to the amount unpaid on their shares if the company is limited.
- Are fully liable for torts and obligations if the company is unlimited *only* on the winding up of the company, otherwise it rests with the company itself.
- If a company is dissolved by winding up, both members and past members (within past 12 months) will be liable to contribute towards the assets of a company so it can meet its liabilities.

Directors

Directors are not servants/agents of the company and cannot be liable for the company's debts or torts. However they are liable for their own torts.

Personal Liability of Employees

Case law since 2003 has established that the concept of 'controlling mind' applies to both private companies and public practice. In a charge of 'corporate manslaughter' it is necessary to prove that:

- The defendant is a company or corporate body, rather than a partnership or other form of enterprise
- An individual within the organization is of such seniority that they can be said to be the 'controlling mind' or 'directing mind'
- The individual is guilty of manslaughter through gross negligence.

The controlling mind will usually be a senior manager, or if the task has been delegated to an individual with full discretion to act independently that delegate may also be regarded as a controlling mind. In this context, others engaged to provide services to an organization, who see that a situation is clearly dangerous, have a duty to warn the organization about the danger as part of the skill and duty they owe to that organization.

Liability in local authority

In law the 'corporation' has a legal identity and can be sued.

Local authorities were originally set up to safeguard public health and safety. Therefore, to succeed in a claim against a local authority a claimant must establish imminent danger to health and safety. This may be difficult to prove, therefore the claimant is more likely to sue the individual professional.

In the case of local authorities, identifying a risk and having the power to do something about it does not necessarily create a duty, but each case would be assessed individually. Were such a duty to exist, it would place a heavy burden on authorities in staffing, training and budgets. (Sandhar v. Dept. of Transport 19.1.1994)

Legal actions relating to civil wrongs committed by a 'servant' (officer) can be raised against the officer and the authority. Local authorities specify the area of decision-making delegated to specific officers – an officer may only make a decision on behalf of the authority or council, if clearly delegated to do so – otherwise he or she is acting *ultra vires* (outwith their or the authority's powers laid down by Parliament). The local authority will be held liable for the act of an employee if the act was committed by a 'servant' engaged in the work of the authority and during the course of their employment. However, an authority cannot be sued if the officer acted outwith the scope of their authority

An officer has a duty to take care in giving advice. If an officer is negligent and loss is suffered due to faulty advice, both the authority and the officer may be sued for damages. A negligent though honest mistake may still lead to legal action as the officer is held to be in possession of specific skills (i.e. a professional) and that officer should know that reliance is being placed on their skills.

Vicarious liability

A person is liable for their own torts. He or she may also be liable for those of another.

> Vicarious liability arises from the 'master–servant' relationship, that is, the master directs exactly how work should be done.
>
> This is in contrast to the relationship between an employer and an independent contractor, in which the contractor undertakes to perform work or services, but has discretion how that work is done.
>
> The difference is the degree of control that the employer is entitled to exercise over the acts of the employee.

Generally the employer is not liable for the torts of an independent contractor. However he becomes liable if he interferes and assumes control, because by doing so, the master–servant relationship arises. An employee or servant is always liable for their own torts, and their employer is also jointly and severally liable if the tort is committed in the course of their employment.

Statutory liability

This liability refers to duties imposed upon landscape architects and others by Acts of Parliament.

> **Statutory liabilities of landscape architects**
> * Suppliers of services.
> * The Defective Premises Act 1972.
> * The Supply of Goods and Services Act 1982.
> * Construction (Design and Management) Regulations 1994.
> * Employer's liability.
> * Equal Pay Act 1970.
> * Employment Rights Act 1996.
> * Occupier's liability.
> * Occupier's Liability Act 1954.
> * Offices, Shops and Railway Premises Act 1963.
> * Health and Safety at Work Act 1974.

The Statutory Liabilities of Suppliers of Services

The Defective Premises Act 1972

'A person taking on work for or in connection with the provision of a dwelling…owes a duty…to see that the work which he takes on is done in a workmanlike or, as the case may be, professional manner, with proper materials, and so that…the dwelling will be fit for habitation when completed.' This does not apply to factories, offices and warehouses.

The Supply of Goods and Services Act 1982

This Act (section 13) says that in a contract to supply services (such as those provided by an architect for an employer) there is an implied term that the architect will carry out the service with reasonable skill and care.

Construction (Design and Management) Regulations 1994 SI No. 1994 3140

These regulations were a reaction to unacceptably high rates of death, injury and ill health associated with all types of project ranging from new works through to subsequent maintenance repairs, refurbishment and demolition. Infringement may be a criminal offence. This is discussed in detail below.

Employer's Liability

This is based on a mixture of rules developed in common law and those set down by Parliament. The basic relationship between employer and employee is defined by the contract of employment. These rights have been brought together into the Employment Protection (Consolidation) Act 1978 amended by the Employment Act 1980 and the Employment Rights Act 1996.

These statutory rights are mostly to do with fairness and are enforced in industrial tribunals, not courts as in the normal way.

Also binding on employers are the Equal Pay Act 1970; National Minimum Wage Act 1998; the Race Relations Act 1976; Sex Discrimination Act 1975; Employment Relations Act 1999; the Health and Safety at Work Act 1974; the Offices, Shops and Railway Premises Act 1963; Employer's Liability (Compulsory Insurance) Act 1969; the Disability Discrimination Act 1995; the Asylum and Immigration Act 1997; the Employment Relations Act 1999; and the European Community Work Directive 2000.

Occupier's Liability

Occupiers (and employers) also have liabilities for Health and Safety set down under:

Health and safety at Work Act 1974

The Health and Safety at Work Act concerns the general responsibility of employers, employees and the self-employed with respect to both each other and third parties. Infringement is a criminal offence. The COSHH Regulations and Control of Pesticides are related issues.

Offices, Shops and Railway Premises Act 1963

The Offices, Shops and Railway Premises Act 1963 is concerned specifically with the obligations of the occupier for health and safety. Infringement is a criminal offence.

Occupier's Liability Act 1954

This imposes a duty of care on occupiers of premises to all those lawfully entering their premises (public liability).

Health and Safety Legislation

Background to the Health and Safety Regulations

The mainstay of Health and Safety Legislation was brought into force in 1974 with the introduction of the Health and Safety at Work Act 1974, which remains to this day the foundation of all related legislation. This is a general document and it places duties on employers, the self employed, people in control of premises and designers, manufacturers, importers and suppliers of articles for use at work.

The general duty is:

> *'To ensure as far as reasonably practical that the article is so designed and constructed that it will be safe and without risks to health at all times when it is being set, used, cleaned or maintained by a person at work.'*

Health and Safety legislation covering construction sites through both general regulations and construction specific regulations is quite substantial, but in spite of this the record of death, permanent disability and serious injury in the construction industry is second to none. A new strategy was introduced which put the emphasis on management of risks. In 1992 the European Union's Construction Directive was published which lead to the introduction of the 'six pack'.

- Management of Health and Safety at Work Regs 1992 (amended 1999).
- Workplace (Health, Safety and Welfare) Regs 1992 (not construction sites).
- Provision and Use of Work Equipment Regs 1992.
- Personal Protective Equipment at Work Regs 1992.
- Manual Handling Operations Regs 1992.
- Health and Safety (Display Screen Equipment) Regs 1992.

Since then a raft of other legislation has emerged, all aimed at reducing or managing risks, which includes:

- The Construction (Health, Safety and Welfare Regs) 1996 (being reviewed at the time of going to press).
- The Provision and Use of Work Equipment Regs 1998.
- The Lifting Operations and Lifting Equipment Regs 1998.
- The Control of Asbestos at Work Regs 2002.

The Construction (Design and Management) Regulations 1994 (CDM Regs) (At the time of going to press these were due to be revised October 2006)

The implementation of the EU's Construction Directive introduced the Construction (Design and Management) Regulations 1994 in the UK. The aim of the CDM regulations is to promote good management in the construction industry, prompting all parties involved to rethink their approach to Health and Safety.

The regulations place specific duties on clients, designers and contractors as well as on the new roles of planning supervisors and principal contractors. Each member of the team is required to contribute to the overall management of health and safety by working and co-operating with the other members to produce a co-ordinated strategy for managing health and safety throughout the execution of work on site and subsequent maintenance, alteration or removal of the structure.

In all there are 24 regulations and listed below are the ones of particular importance to landscape architects, although understanding or awareness of all the regulations is required:

- Regulation 2   Interpretation
- Regulation 3   Application of the regulations
- Regulation 4   Clients and agents of clients
- Regulation 6   Appointment of planning supervisor and principal contractor
- Regulation 7   Notification of project
- Regulation 8   Competence of planning supervisor, designers and contractors
- Regulation 9   Provision for health and safety
- Regulation 13   Requirements on designer
- Regulation 14   Requirements on planning supervisor

Application of the Regulations

Regulation 3 defines when the regulations apply, but in simpler terms the following can be applied to check if the regulations are applicable to projects.

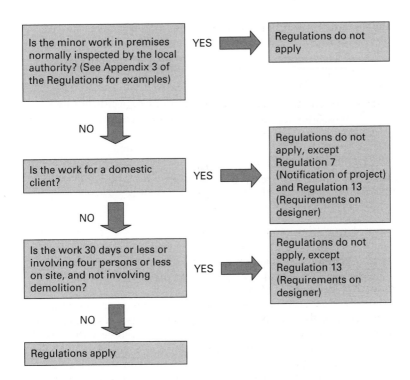

Regulation 2 defines the various words and terms used throughout the regulations. Particular attention should be given to the definitions of 'construction work', 'design', 'designer' and 'structure'. The definitions of construction work and structure are fairly all-encompassing, with the intention probably being to include any situation which is potentially dangerous to employees or the general public.

Duties of the Parties
Each party has specific duties placed on them by the regulations and these parties include:

- **DESIGNER**
- **CLIENTS**
- **PLANNING SUPERVISOR**
- **PRINCIPAL CONTRACTOR**
- **CONTRACTORS**

Requirements on designer (Regulation 13 generally)
HSE have produced an information sheet 'Construction (Design and Management) Regulations 1994: The role of the designer'. At the end of

the sheet they state: *'Following the guidance is not compulsory. But if you follow the guidance you will normally be doing enough to comply with the law.'*

Duties of designers

- Make clients aware of their duties (Note: there have been prosecutions of designers who did not inform a client of their duties under the regulations).
- Give due regard to health and safety in your design.
- Provide adequate information about the health and safety risk of the design to those who need it. (This includes any variations in designs that are required during works on site.)
- Co-operate with the planning supervisor and, where appropriate, other designers involved in the project.

Requirements on Clients (Regulations 4, 5, 6, 8, 9, 10, 11 and 12)

As a designer it is your duty to know what these are.

Duties of clients

- Appoint a planning supervisor.
- Provide information on health and safety to the planning supervisor.
- Appoint a principal contractor.
- Ensure those you appoint are competent and adequately resourced to carry out their health and safety responsibilities.
- Ensure that a suitable health and safety plan has been prepared by the principal contractor before construction work starts.
- Ensure the health and safety file given to you at the end of the project is kept available for use.

Requirements on Planning Supervisor (Regulations 14, 15)

It is important to note that the planning supervisor has no specific responsibility for ensuring site safety or that the principal contractor's health and safety plan is followed.

Duties of planning supervisor

- Ensure HSE is notified of the project.
- Ensure co-operation between designers.
- Ensure designers comply with their duties.
- Ensure a pre-tender stage health and safety plan is prepared.
- Advise the client when requested to do so.
- Ensure a health and safety file is prepared.

Requirements on Principle Contractor (Regulation 8, 9, 15–19)

Duties of Principal Contractor

- Ensure a health and safety plan is prepared for construction work and kept up to date.
- Take reasonable steps to ensure co-operation between contractors.
- Ensure compliance with rules if these are made, take reasonable steps to ensure only authorized persons are allowed on site and display notification form.
- Provide planning supervisor with information relevant to health and safety file.
- Give directions to contractors where required.
- May make rules in the health and safety plan, which should be in writing.
- So far as reasonably practical provide information to contractors.
- So far as reasonably practical ensure contractors provide training and information to employees.
- Ensure views of people at work are heard and incorporated into health and safety plan where appropriate.
- Ensure when arranging for designers to carry out design they are competent and make adequate provision for health and safety in their design.
- Ensure when arranging for contractors to carry out or manage construction work that they are competent and make adequate provision for health and safety.

Risk Assessments

For every project a risk management plan has to be established which has to consider methods of *identifying, assessing* and *minimizing* hazards, as well as methods of *reducing* the loss. We have to accept that there are risks in everything we do but must work to minimize these and take all *reasonable* precautions against foreseeable hazards.

Risk assessments

Hazard: a physical situation with **the potential** for human injury, damage to property, damage to the environment or some combination of these (i.e. the potential to cause harm).

Risk: the *chance*, great or small, that someone will be harmed by a hazard.

The Pre-Tender Health and Safety Plan

The pre-tender health and safety plan is essentially a collection of information about *significant* health and safety risks of the construction project that the principal contractor will have to manage during the construction phase. It is important to note the use of 'significant' here, as the intention is not to turn out vast piles of paper covering everyday risks such as the use of cement or pesticides. The purpose is to highlight risks specific to the site, type or method of work that a competent contractor may not be aware of. This information will mainly come from the client and the designers.

The contents of the pre-tender health and safety plan will depend on the nature of the project itself.

Pre-tender health and safety plan: purpose

- To provide a focus at which health and safety considerations of the design are brought together under the control of the planning supervisor.
- It enables prospective principal contractors to be fully aware of the project's health, safety and welfare requirements.
- It provides a template against which the tenders can be measured.

Construction Phase Health and Safety Plan

This is developed by the principal contractor from the pre-tender health and safety plan and should set out the arrangements for securing the health and safety of everyone carrying out the construction work and all others who may be affected by it. It should deal with the arrangements for management of health and safety for the work, with monitoring systems for checking that the plan is followed and with the management of the risks to those at work arising from the work or other work that may be going on in the premises.

As a minimum the plan should include:

- General information about the project including a programme.
- Specific procedures and arrangements for the early work.
- Procedures and arrangements for the construction phase including management and monitoring of health and safety.
- Welfare arrangements.
- Emergency procedures.
- Arrangements for communication.

The Health and Safety File

Information in the file needs to include that which will assist persons carrying out construction/maintenance work on the structure at any time after completion of the current project. It amounts to an enlarged maintenance manual with information to alert those who will be responsible for a structure after handover to avoid risks that must be managed when the structure and associated plant is maintained, repaired, renovated or demolished. It is a record of information to inform future decisions on the management of health and safety.

The file is a record of information to inform future decisions on the management of health and safety.

Health and safety file

Record of information for future risk management

- As built drawings.
- Service information.
- Construction methods and materials.
- Operating and maintenance manuals.
- Risk assessments.

The Landscape Institute has produced two advice notes:

- Advice note 02/99: Landscape Construction Work: CDM Regulations 1994.
- Advice note 03/99: Landscape Maintenance Work: CDM Regulations 1994.

The advice notes sets out the LI's current interpretation of the regulations with regard to landscape construction and maintenance work. This is based on current advice from the HSE and has not been tested in law.

CDM Regulations: Breach and Prosecution

There are four principal areas of potential liability for the landscape architect in failing to comply with obligations relating to health and safety.

Criminal Law

- Failure to comply with HASAW and its associated legislation is regarded as a crime as the acts are criminal law. This may result in criminal prosecution with unlimited fines and/or a maximum of two years' imprisonment.

Civil Law – The Law of Tort

- Civil action based on a breach of a statutory duty (in limited circumstances) or based upon the tort of negligence by injured workers.

Civil Law – Breach of Contract

- Contractual claims regarding health and safety are civil law and failure to comply with a contract can only be redressed by an action for breach of contract. This may occur when the regulations are incorporated into the landscape architect's appointment or referred to in a collateral warranty.
- In addition, in order to ensure that all breaches of the CDM regulations can confer on the parties the right to civil proceedings, amendments have been produced to the various versions of the standard forms of contract to provide that compliance with the regulations is a contractual obligation and that failure to comply can therefore also be a breach of contract.

Prosecution

- For the same accident on site it is possible for there to be a prosecution under criminal law for failure to comply with statutory law and a separate action under civil law for breach of contact and/or negligence.

Revisions to the CDM Regulations – October 2006

The Health and Safety Commission commenced a 4-month consultation process at the end of July 2005 to review and consolidate the following CDM regulations into one CDM piece of legislation:

- The Construction (Design and Management) Regulations 1994.
- The Construction (Health, Safety and Welfare) Regulations 1996.

The new legislation is due to be released in October 2006. (Refer to www.hse.gov.uk). The proposals focus on achieving effective planning and management with the minimum of bureaucracy, concentrating on the provision of necessary and relevant information rather than on generic documents adding to bureaucracy without adding value.

New proposals that are being considered aim to:

- Simplify the regulations, including the application and notification process, to improve clarity and make it easier for everyone to know what is expected of them.
- Maximize the flexibility to fit the vast range of contractual arrangements.
- Focus on planning and management rather than 'The Plan' and other paperwork.
- Encourage co-ordination and co-operation between designers and contractors.
- Restructure risk assessments to reduce generic documents and provide site specific information.
- Simplify the assessment of the competency of organizations.

In addition, revisions to the following roles are being considered:

- Role of client – duties extended to ensure that suitable project management arrangements for Health and Safety are in place including appointment of a co-ordinator prior to design work commencing and ensuring allocation of resources.
- Role of planning supervisor replaced with a new role – 'the planning co-ordinator' – to advise and assist the client in undertaking measures to comply with the regulations.
- Role of the designer – duties now also to ensure their professional judgement is used when designing to reduce/eliminate risks or hazards for construction, demolition and maintenance.
- Principal contractors: an emphasis is placed on their role to manage Health and Safety efficiently during the construction phase and promote worker consultation.

The Management of Health and Safety at Work Regulations 1999

These regulations came into force in December 1999 and re-enact the 1992 regulations and amend The Construction (Health, Safety and Welfare) Regulations 1996, which is now also under review. These regulations deal with employers' and employees' obligations regarding minimum health and safety requirements in the workplace. They require:

- Employers/self employed people to carry out an assessment of risks that employees are exposed to while at work and of any people affected by their operations.
- Employers of more than five employees to record the findings of the assessment and record any groups of employees identified as being especially at risk.
- Employers to implement preventive and protective measures on the basis of the schedules contained within the regulations.
- Employers to provide employees (including temporary employees) with relevant information on the risk assessment and the preventive and protective measures, and also provide adequate health and safety training.
- Employees' duties are to comply with the training and they should inform employers of any situations that are dangerous to health and safety or any shortcoming in existing protection arrangements.
- Special provisions apply to new or expectant mothers and also to young people.

Refer also to the *Landscape Institute Practice Note: Health and Safety and the Landscape Architect*, which gives guidance on the landscape architect's responsibilities for Health and Safety. This is due for review by The Landscape Institute. (Refer to www.landscapeinstitute.org.uk for updates).

Limitations Act 1980

Loss, damage or injury from landscape works (building or engineering) may not occur for many years until after the negligent act that caused them. It is then that a claim may arise. However, there is a statutory limit on the period within which claims may be made.

For how long is anyone liable in contract or tort?

For actions in contract or tort – 6 years with the exception of:
* Actions 'under seal': 12 years.
* Actions for personal injury: 3 years from the date at which the cause of action accrued or the date at which the person injured knew that they were injured.
* Actions for latent damage: 15 years (except personal injury).

Latent damage refers to cases where the damage could not reasonably have been discovered at the time when it actually occurred.

From the exceptions listed above, it is clear that it is important to establish the date at which the cause of action 'accrued', that is, the date on which the cause of legal action occurred.

There is a good deal of case law about limitations and while the summary above describes the basic rules, legal advice or a specialist legal text should be consulted for advice in specific real-life cases.

Civil Liberties Contribution Act 1982

Under the Civil Liberties Contribution Act 1982 a person sued may join in the case further parties and the judge will have to decide the portion of blame attributed to each. (Ann's v. Morton LBC 1978).

Allocation of blame

In cases of tort, even though the judge decides the percentage of blame attached to each of the conjoined defendants, the claimant may look to any one of them for the whole of their loss. If their parties have no resources, one or more of the parties may have to make full contribution even if the adjudication ascribed to them only part of the blame.

Insurances

What Types of Insurance Should a Landscape Architect be Aware of?

• PROFESSIONAL INDEMNITY INSURANCE •

• EMPLOYER'S LIABILITY INSURANCE •

• PUBLIC LIABILITY INSURANCE •

• MOTOR INSURANCE •

• CONTRACTUAL INSURANCE •

Professional Indemnity Insurance

Why insurance?

The Landscape Institute requires registered practices to take out PII (as do local authorities). This insurance ensures that practices have sufficient funds to meet their financial obligations should an action for negligence be brought against them. It is a Landscape Institute rule that practices have evidence of adequate insurance to be registered with the Institute.

How much insurance?

Premiums are now in excess of 10% of gross fee income. The Landscape Institute will be issuing a policy on minimum cover for PII. (Refer to www.landscapeinstitute.org.uk for updates).

What is the premium calculation based on?

- Largest commission in the past five years.
- Projected schemes in detail, including the nature of the work at home and abroad.
- What forms of contract (e.g. JCT) and what conditions of engagement are used.
- Turnover of practice.
- Number of employees.
- Pollution liability.

The larger the organization, the greater the chance of failure, therefore the higher the premium.

How Long Does It Have To Be Taken Out For?

For life and beyond since an architect's colleagues and family can be pursued for settlement of a claim. The practice will continue to indemnify a landscape architect after they have left or retired. If the practice ceases, e.g. retirement of partners or death, PII is paid generally for a maximum of 12–15 years after the completion of the last project, with a decreasing scale.

Watch points for PII

- Multidisciplinary practices will have separate insurance policies for each profession. You may wish to consult insurers to check you are covered for the skill required in a job, e.g. a small amount of quantity surveying work.
- Give insurers early warning of a crisis. They may instruct you how to proceed. You must obey. If issued with a writ, do not answer it immediately but consult your insurers.
- Additional insurance cover is required in relation to pollution and contaminated land.
- PII will cover the obligations of the designer set by CDM Regulations under civil law for breach of contract or negligence. However, PII companies may require the designer to take out additional insurance to cover the cost of defending a criminal prosecution. (It is not possible to insure against fines or imprisonment for a breach of criminal law.) This prevents designers avoiding set fines by pleading guilty and allowing PII being claimed against them.
- If a landscape architect intends to perform the role of planning supervisor then extra insurance is required.

Dealing with Liability Claims

A claim against a professional may happen at any time. It could happen at the end of a demanding day when resistance is low: you need to be prepared for what to do.

Notification of claims

All PII policies include the following conditions:
- Notify all claims and potential claims as soon as you are aware of a problem.
- Do not admit liability to anyone.
- Co-operate fully with your insurers, who will be entitled to take over the conduct of the claim.

Any delay in notifying your insurers could:
- Adversely affect your defence to the allegations.
- Put you in breach of your policy conditions.
- Amount to a breach of your duty to disclose material facts to the insurers.

Any of these could prejudice your entitlement to indemnity.

The legal conduct for professional indemnity claims is governed by protocols under the Civil Procedures Rules. There are very short timescales in which to investigate and formally respond to claims if legal action is taken against you. Special and very urgent reporting requirements apply to claims bought under the adjudication provisions of the Housing Grants, Construction and Regeneration Act 1996, which will be set out in your policy.

Employer's Liability Insurance

Under the Employer's Liability (Compulsory Insurance) Act 1969 all employers in the UK are required by statute to take out specific insurance to meet their obligations for liability against bodily injury or disease sustained by employees arising out of and in the course of their employment; this includes work abroad for a continuous period of 14 days. Cover must extend to £2 million for any one occurrence.

Public Liability (Third Party) Insurance

An owner or lessee of premises or occupier may be legally liable for personal injury or damage to property of third parties caused by their negligence or that of their staff. Cover must be:

- Appropriate to the status of owner, lessee or occupier.
- Extended to cover the actions of employers and employees anywhere while on business.
- Extended to cover overseas if employees are likely to be on business abroad.

Motor Vehicles

Third party insurance is a legal requirement under the Road Traffic Act 1972 in respect of death or personal injury to third parties or damage to a third party's property. Cars owned and operated by a practice must be covered for business use and cars owed by employees and used by them in the course of their duties must be covered by occasional business use.

Contractual Insurance

This refers to insurance between the employer and landscape contractor for works undertaken as part of a landscape contract. (Refer to Chapters 6 and 7.)

3 Planning legislation

Introduction to the Planning Framework

Planning is a mechanism for controlling and guiding the use of all land and buildings and the process of change in the environment. The UK government summarizes the role of the planning system:

> Planning shapes the places where people live and work and the country we live in. It plays a key role in supporting the Government's wider social, environmental and economic objectives and for sustainable communities.

The current system of planning originated in the Town and Country Planning Act 1947. This Act introduced the basic system of development plans, development control and enforcement. It brought all development under control by making it subject to planning permission, and development plans had to be prepared for the whole of the country that outlined the way in which areas were to be developed or preserved. In addition, the Government had to provide policy guidance to local planning authorities on how to administer and operate the planning system.

The following elements are still central to the system that is current in the UK today:

> **Primary legislation**
>
> In the UK primary legislation sets out the basic framework for the operation of the system.

National planning policy

National planning policy sets out the basic objective of the planning system and forms the policy framework for the day-to-day administration of the planning system including the preparation of development plans and the way in which planning applications should be assessed, which is undertaken by local planning authorities.

Development plans

Development plans are the main documents for guiding development control decisions and also for setting out decisions for future development.

Development control and enforcement

'Development control' is the term used to define the system for issuing permits for land use development and for taking actions against unauthorized development.

The Hierarchy of Planning Policy and Development Plans

Primary Legislation and European/National Planning Advice

In the UK primary legislation sets out the basic framework for the operation of the system and the Secretary of State and the government minister for planning, environment, and transport for each country fill in the details in the form of orders and regulations which guide the planning authority on how it should operate within the limits set by the law. In order to achieve uniformity in decision-making, planning control is heavily influenced by policy guidance. The format of this varies for each country in the UK.

England

Primary legislation
- Planning and Compulsory Purchase Act 2004.
- Town and Country Planning Act 1990.
- Planning (Listed Building and Conservation Areas) Act 1990.

Government departments and planning guidance
- Department for Communities and Local Government (DCLG).
- Department for Transport (DFT).
- Department for Environment, Food and Rural Affairs (DEFRA).
- Department for Productivity, Energy and Industry (DPEI).

Planning Policy (www.communities.gov.uk)

Planning policy is issued by the DCLG through the following formats that are intended to provide concise and practical guidance on planning policies in a clear and accessible form.

- **Planning Policy Statements:** PPSs are being prepared to eventually replace all PPGs.
- **Planning Policy Guidance:** PPGs explain statutory provisions and provide guidance on policies and the operation of the planning system. They are being used increasingly to set out general policy guidelines and currently cover many topics, e.g. PPG3 – Housing.
- **Mineral Policy Guidance:** MPGs provide general guidance on policies relating to mineral planning.
- **Mineral Policy Statements:** MPSs are being prepared to replace MPGs.
- **Regional Policy Guidance:** RPGs provide general guidance on planning issues affecting a particular region and provide the framework for the preparation of the strategic element of the development plans.
- **Marine Mineral Guidance:** MMGs
- **Circulars:** These are still issued but are confined to the provision of advice on legislative changes and procedural matters.

Wales

Primary legislation

- Planning and Compulsory Purchase Act 2004.

Government departments and planning guidance (www.wales.gov.uk)

- National Assembly for Wales (NAW).
- Department for Environment Planning and Countryside.
- Department of Economic Development and Transport.
- Department of Culture, Welsh Language and Sport.

NAW was inaugurated following devolution in July 1999 under the Government of Wales Act 1998. NAW does not have primary legislative powers but can create secondary legislation and develop policy for Wales.

Planning policy (www.wales.gov.uk)

NAW provides the following national planning guidance through the Department for Environment Planning and Countryside:

- **Wales Spatial Plan 2004:** sets out the direction to enable sustainable spatial development.

- **Planning Policy Wales 2002 (PPW):** provides strategic policy framework for the effective preparation of development plans.
- **Technical Advice Notes (TAN):** support (PPW) policy documents and cover detailed topics including coastal planning; housing; design, environmental impact assessment, waste and noise. These are currently being reviewed.
- **Minerals Planning Policy Wales (MPGW):** sets out land use planning policy guidance of NAW in relation to mineral extraction.
- **NAW Circulars:** national guidance is also provided through the medium of circulars.

Scotland

Primary legislation
- The Town and Country Planning (Scotland) Act 1997.
- The Planning (Scotland) Bill 2005 – due for adoption the end of 2006.
- Planning (Listed Buildings and Conservation Areas) (Scotland) Act 1997.

Government departments and planning guidance (www.scotland.gov.uk)
- Scottish Executive.
- Environment and Rural Affairs Department.
- Development Department.
- Enterprise, Transport and Lifelong Learning Department.

The new Scottish Parliament was formed following devolution in July 1999 under the Scotland Act 1998. The Scottish Parliament has primary and secondary legislative powers subject to compliance with EC law and S29 of the 1998 Act relating to 'Reserved Matters', i.e. not acting outwith the competence of Scottish Parliament.

Planning policy (www.scotland.gov.uk)
Planning guidance is issued by the Scottish Executive in the form of:
- **National Planning Framework 2004 (NPF):** sets out a vision for the development of Scotland for the next 20 years and proposes an overhaul of the current planning system.
- **Scottish and National Planning Policy Guidelines (SPPGs):** will replace NPPGs under the NPF in providing statements of government policies on nationally important topics such as land use and planning and related matters such as business and industry, natural heritage and transport. It will also provide statements of government policies on single topics such as waste management, minerals, and archaeology.

- **Planning Advice Notes (PANs):** support SPPGs and identify and disseminate good practice and provide more specific design advice of a practical nature. Subjects covered in PANs range from siting and design of new housing in the countryside to planning for crime prevention.
- **Circulars:** National guidance is also provided through the medium of circulars.

Northern Ireland

Primary legislation
- Planning (Northern Ireland) Order 1991 and amendment 2003.
- Draft Planning Reform (Northern Ireland) Order 2006 – currently at Westminster. (Check websites for updates.)

Government departments and planning guidance (www.northernireland.gov.uk)
- Northern Ireland Executive.
- Department of Agricultural and Rural Development.
- Department of Regional Development.
- Department of Environment.
- Department of Enterprise, Trade and Investment.

The system in Northern Ireland is radically different with the governing legislation being provided by way of parliamentary orders in council, a form of secondary legislation under the Northern Ireland Act 2000. This Act provides for the suspension of the operation of the devolved Northern Ireland Assembly and Executive into a power sharing government in Northern Ireland. The Act provides for executive responsibility for Northern Ireland to revert to the Secretary of State for Ireland, and for the legislative power of the Assembly (i.e. the devolved government) to be exercisable during the suspension by orders in council.

Planning policy (www.northernireland.gov.uk)
The Northern Ireland Office, Regional Development Department and Department of Environment (DOENI) Planning Service provide both regional and local planning guidance and development control. This currently comprises:
- **The Planning Strategy for Northern Ireland – Shaping our Future 2025.**
- **Planning Policy Statements (PPSs):** guidance for plan preparation and development control.
- **Development Control Advice Notes and Design Guides:** detailed guidance for development control.

The European Spatial Development Perspective (ESPD)

The ESDP prepared by the EU is a policy document based on the aims of encouraging discussion between its partners in order to encourage balanced and sustainable development, enhancing social and economic cohesion, and acting as a catalyst for action. The Government's proposed Regional Spatial Strategies will work in context with the ESDP.

Development Plans

The Role of Development Plans

The development plan is intended to provide the policy framework within which planning authorities exercise their planning powers. The plan also serves as a guide to landowners, developers and members of the public as to the local planning authorities' main policies and proposals for the future use and development of land in their areas.

The Planning and Compensation Act 1991 shifted the relationship between plans and control to a plan led system, and elevated the status accorded to development plans and secured them a positive role in decisions made by the Secretary of State and local authorities.

The New Planning and Compensation Act 2004 emphasizes this more in section 38(6) and planning applications require to accord with the development plan unless material considerations indicate otherwise:

> *The presumption is that the plan is sound unless it is shown to be otherwise as a result of evidence brought to the examination (inquiry).*

This is underpinned by the overall aim of delivering sustainable development.

Development Plans in England and Wales: Planning and Compensation Act 2004

This Act paved the way for the biggest shape up in the planning system in England and Wales since the 1947 Act with the proposal to streamline planning by scrapping structure plans, unitary development plans and local plans and leaving a two-tier system of development plans:

- **Regional Spatial Strategies (RSSs).**
- **Local Development Frameworks (LDFs)** which comprise a portfolio of **Local Development Documents (LDDs)**

This was reinforced through the publication of:

> • Planning Policy Statement 1: Delivering Sustainable Development (PPS1).
> • Planning Policy Statement 11: Regional Strategies (PPS11).
> • Planning Policy Statement 12: Local Development Framework System (PPS12).

A key aspect in the new transformed planning system is the emphasis on spatial planning and sustainable development. Spatial planning brings together and integrates policies for the development and use of land with other policies and programmes outwith the traditional land use planning system. New style development plans have to be appraised to ensure they are environmentally sound, through sustainability appraisals (SAs), and all development plans are subject to strategic environmental assessment (SEA) and Appropriate Assessment (AA) under the Habitats Directive 2000, Article 6, where development plans affect Nawra 2000 sites (refer to Chapter 4).

Regional Spatial Strategies (RSS) and the Spatial Development Strategy for London

RSSs are drawn up by regional planning bodies that include Regional Development Agencies (RDAs) and Regional Government Offices. Existing Regional Planning Guidance (RPG) where appropriate will become the new RSS. Existing regional strategies prepared by regional planning bodies and Regional Development Agencies must be reviewed and updated in accordance with PPS 11.

RSSs provide a broad development strategy for a region for a period of around 15–20 years. They provide the framework to inform the preparation of local development documents, local transport plans and regional and sub-regional strategies that have a bearing on land use activities. They will incorporate:

> • Priorities for the environment including countryside and biodiversity protection.
> • Regional transport strategies (RTS), infrastructure, housing, economic development, agriculture, minerals extraction and waste treatment and disposal.

RSSs carry statutory status. They are set out on a key diagram that establishes broad criteria but which does not identify key sites. They must contribute to sustainable development and incorporate community involvement and partnership working.

County councils are a consultative body in the preparation of RSS and they will also prepare sub-regional plans and policies that cover issues that cannot be dealt with through a joint plan, or where the detailed strategic policy context cannot be provided by a generic policy in an RSS.

Local Development Frameworks (LDFs)

A local development framework is the new non-statutory term for the portfolio of Local Development Documents (LDDs) in England that comprise the spatial planning strategy for a local planning authority area. LDDs is a collective term for the development plan documents that will replace the existing system of local, structure and unitary development plans, together with Supplementary Planning Documents (SPDs) and the Statement of Community Involvement (SCI).

LDFs are intended to streamline the local planning process and be spatial rather than purely land use plans. The aim is to set out a clear vision for an area together with a realistic implementation strategy and focus on delivery. The new system is designed so that local authorities can decide which combination of documents is most suitable for their situation. The ability to produce various documents rather than one plan is intended to make it easier to keep policies and proposals up to date.

Development plan documents (DPDs) include:

- **A Core Strategy** – setting out the spatial vision, spatial objectives and core policies of the planning authority's area (mandatory).
- **Site Specific Land Allocations** for development (mandatory).
- **Area Action Plans (AAPs)** provide a planning framework for areas where significant change or conservation is needed and focus on regeneration (optional).
- **Other DPDs** (optional) for particular topics such as affordable housing or retail development and 'Generic Development Control Policies' – policies that set out criteria against which planning applications will be considered.

In addition to the DPDs listed, the LDF portfolio will also contain:

- **A Local Development Scheme** setting out the details for each of the LDDs to be produced, the timescale and arrangements for production (mandatory).
- **A Statement of Community Involvement (SCI)** – specifying how the local authority intends to involve communities and stakeholders in the LDD process (mandatory).
- **An annual monitoring report (AMR)** – setting out the progress on producing LDDs and implementing policies (mandatory).
- **Supplementary Planning Documents (SPDs)** – providing supplementary guidance on policies in the DPDs (optional).
- **Local Development Orders (LDOs)** and simplified planning zones that have been adopted.

Local Development Frameworks will cover many areas including regeneration, housing, transport, culture and social issues at a more strategic spatial policy level than local plans. Joint Local Development Documents can be prepared by two or more LPAs.

LDFs must comply with regional spatial strategies (RSS) and are to be revised continuously. Planning Inspectors will review the soundness of development plan documents through inquiries – now examinations, which are more informal than previously. The inspectors report is binding on the LPA. The Secretary of State receives copies of LDFs and the default position will be approval of the documents; however, they can intervene.

Reform of the Welsh Development Plan System

Part 6 of the Act reforms the Welsh development plan system, which came into force in autumn 2005. The basic pattern of the existing regime will be retained (unlike in England) but the plans themselves will be simpler, more concise than the present UDPs and will be called local development plans (LDPs). They will not be split into two.

LDPs will focus on objectives for the use and development of land and will include general policies (with scope for more detailed policies in key localities). They will include specific allocations and detailed proposals, which will be illustrated on a proposals map.

Plan-making procedures will be simplified and the authority will be required to prepare a Community Involvement Scheme (CIS) and be informed by a Sustainability Appraisal (SA).

UDPs must take account of the Wales Spatial Plan (prepared by the NAW), which is the strategic context for local authority development plans. The provisions of the Act came into force in autumn 2005 with transitional arrangements.

Reform of Development Plans in Scotland and Northern Ireland

Northern Ireland and Scotland are currently reviewing changes to the existing development plans and are still to implement changes under separate legislation. (Refer to later sections *'Responsibility for Development Plans – Scotland* and *Responsibility for Development Plans – Northern Ireland'.*)

Other Changes from the Planning and Compensation Act 2004

- The reintroduction of simplified planning zones for areas of regeneration where jobs, growth and productivity are needed most. (Originally from hi-tech industries).
- Reformed compulsory purchase powers to simplify land assembly. Government regeneration agency English Partnerships and the regional

development agencies will now get the same powers as LPAs whose powers are widened in the interest of the economic, social or environmental well-being of an area.

- Section 106 Agreements. Developers are to be offered the choice of paying a fixed pre-determined charge or to negotiate with the LPA as is the current situation. Details of charges must be set out by LPA (e.g. cost per house unit or square metres of retail floor space).
- To speed up the planning of major infrastructure projects by introducing Government objectives in clear policy statements and changing inquiry processes to make them more efficient.
- Abolishing automatic renewal of planning permissions and abolishing twin-tracking and repeat applications.
- Providing provisions for a future new national standard outline planning application. This will include a design statement to ensure sufficient information is provided to meet the requirements of the EIA, such as details on massing, layout, relationship to public space, density, height, access routes, landscape strategy, mix of use and response to context – appropriate to the complexity of the scheme.
- Reducing the lifespan of outline planning applications from 5 to 3 years to prevent land banking.
- Crown immunity from planning control now removed except in matters deemed high security or urgent (e.g. asylum seeker accommodation).

Transition Period and Existing Development Plans

Local authorities by April 2005 were required to have prepared a timetable to produce their new LDFs. There is a 3-year transitionary period from when the act came into force in October 2004. Until the transitionary period is over the current adopted plans will remain in force and their policies retained for a 3-year period from the commencement of the new plan-making regime. Under the existing planning system development plans are divided into:

TYPES OF DEVELOPMENT PLANS

- **UNITARY DEVELOPMENT PLANS (PARTS 1 AND 2)** •
- **STRUCTURE PLANS** •
- **DISTRICT-WIDE LOCAL PLANS** •
- **MINERAL PLANS** •
- **WASTE PLANS** •
- **TRANSPORT PLANS** •
- **COMMUNITY STRATEGIES** •

(Refer to later sections *'Responsibility for Development Plans – Scotland* and *Responsibility for Development Plans – Northern Ireland'*.)

Unitary Development Plans (UDP): England and Wales

The introduction of a single-tier local government in metropolitan areas in England under the Local Government Act 1985, in Wales in 1996 and in other parts of England since 1993 has led to unitary development plans which replace structure and local plans.

Structure Plans (UDP Part 1)

The structure plan provides a broad planning framework at regional level over a 15-year period. Its purpose is to:

- Provide strategic policy framework for local planning and development control.
- Ensure that the provision for development is realistic and consistent with national and regional policy.
- Secure consistency between local plans for neighbouring areas.
- Provide guidance on the preparation of local plans.

The structure plan consists of a written statement and a key diagram (not on an OS base plan). The spatial development strategy for London sets out strategic policies, proposals and guidance for the unitary authorities in Greater London and supplementary planning guidance.

District-Wide Local Plans (UDP Part 2)

The local plan is the detailed expression of the planning authority policies and proposals for the development and use of land within a particular area over a 10-year period. It:

- Sets out detailed policies for the control of development.
- Makes specific proposals for the use and development of land.
- Allocates land for specific purposes.

The local plan consists of a proposal map (OS base) and a written statement.

It is now mandatory for all local authorities to prepare UDPs. They are continually reviewed and no longer require Secretary of State approval (Planning and Compensation Act 1991).

There is a statutory requirement for consultation with listed consultees including the Secretary of State, adjacent local authorities, Environment Agency, the countryside agencies and also the public. Six weeks are allowed for comment and if there are any objections the local planning authority must hold a public inquiry and allow for modifications and objections to modifications. The LPA must publish a Notice of Intention to Adopt.

Mineral Plans

The Planning and Compensation Act 1991 excludes mineral and waste policies from local plans. Mineral planning authorities are under a duty to prepare a countywide minerals plan containing detailed proposals in respect of development consisting of the winning and working of minerals or involving deposit of mineral waste.

The plan is to consist of a written statement and a map and in general conforms with a structure plan. Procedures for making a plan are the same as local plans. This mineral plans requirement does not apply in Scotland.

Waste Plans

A waste local plan contains detailed policies in respect of development involving the deposit of refuse or waste material, other than mineral waste. This was previously included in structure plans but the Planning and Compensation Act 1991 requires planning authorities in non-metropolitan areas to prepare a waste plan or include their waste policies in their minerals plan. In formulating their policies the LPA must have regard to any 'waste disposal plan' for their area made under the Environmental Protection Act 1990. Procedures for making a plan are the same as local plans.

Transport Plans

Local authorities are required to set out their 5-year strategies for transport and implement local transport plans (LTPs) under the revised transport PPG 11. These plans include policies for walking, cycling, bus, rail, motorcycling, seamless journeys, interchanges, timetables, passenger information and taxis. LTPs are currently environmentally appraised in accordance with the 'New Approach To Appraisal' (NATA) (refer to 7.5). However, they will now be assessed using strategic environmental impact assessment (SEA).

Community Strategies

Local authorities have a duty to prepare Community Strategies and a Sustainable Communities Plan that is developed in conjunction with other public, private and community sector organizations. Community Strategies should promote the economic, social and environmental well-being of their areas and contribute to the achievement of sustainable development. They must have four key components:

- A long-term vision for the area which focuses on the outcomes that are to be achieved.
- An action plan identifying shorter-term priorities and activities that will contribute to the achievement of long-term outcomes.
- A shared commitment to: implement the action plan and the proposals for doing so; to make arrangements for monitoring the implementation of the action plan; to periodically review the community strategy; and to report progress to local communities.
- ODPM Circular 06/2005 requires authorities to be able to prove that they have included consideration of the local biodiversity action plan in their community strategy.

Responsibility for Development Plans

Legislation has given local planning authorities the powers and responsibilities for the day-to-day administration of the planning system. They are responsible for producing development plans and for determining applications for land use development (planning applications).

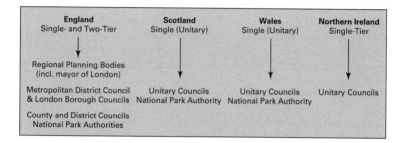

Responsibility for Development Plans in England

Two-tier system:

- Countries currently prepare the structure plan, waste and mineral plans. They will work under the new Act to help, as a consultative body, prepare RSS with regional planning bodies and will also prepare sub-regional plans and policies.
- Districts currently prepare local plans and will start to prepare LDFs during the transitionary 3-year period.

Unitary authorities:

- Currently prepare joint structure plans with neighbouring county councils and also their own district-wide local plans.
- They will start to prepare LDFs during the transitionary 3-year period and work with regional assemblies and joint county councils to help prepare new RSSs.

Metropolitan Districts and London Boroughs:

- Currently prepare Unitary Development Plans.
- They will start to prepare new LDFs during the transitionary period that must be in line with the RSS prepared by the regional planning bodies after consultation of the Spatial Development Strategy for London.

Responsibility for Development Plans in Wales

Local government reorganization created unitary councils in 1996 and the plan framework was amended to require each authority (including the national Parks) to prepare Unitary Development Plans. Under The Planning and Compensation Act 2004 these will now start to prepare Local Development Plans (LDPs).

In 2004, the NAW prepared 'The Wales Spatial Plan', the first spatial strategy in the UK. It provides a blueprint to act as a guide for local authorities for the next 15 years. It covers the traditional definition of planning through directing land use and planning, but extends into other areas with spatial implications including health, social, economic, environmental, transport and education issues. It divides Wales into four zones with a commentary and list of objectives for each area.

Responsibility for Development Plans in Scotland

The current development plan system in Scotland is similar to England and Wales. Local government reorganization created unitary authorities in Scotland in 1996 with the retention of a two-tier system, prepared by each authority, of structure plans and local plans.

Scotland's new national planning framework was published in April 2004 to guide the country's spatial development until 2025. It is a broad based document identifying:

- The key trends in Scotland's development.
- The drivers of changes.
- A vision of spatial development across the broad natural divisions of the country.
- Specific areas as economic development zones.
- This has heralded the change to the current planning system.

The Planning (Scotland) Bill was put before Parliament in December 2005 (refer to www.scotland-gov.uk for updates) and introduces a radical change to the planning system with new style development plan schemes:

Strategic Development Plans: prepared for a strategic development plan area and include:

- A broad statement of strategic development.
- A spatial strategy and vision.
- Key maps and diagrams for the area.

The plans are to consider the physical, economic, social, environmental, and infrastructure (waste, water and transport) features of an area and any changes proposed. They must be prepared in accordance with the national planning framework.

Local Development Plans include:

- The detailed statement of the policy and proposals for an area.
- Key maps and diagrams for the area.

The LDPs are to consider the physical, economic, social, environmental, and infrastructure (waste, water and transport) features of an area and any changes proposed.

The local planning authorities must prepare a development plan scheme that provides a timetable for preparing and reviewing the strategic or local development plans, with an action programme. They should include a consultation statement prior to final adoption of the plan.

The form and content of each plan will be consistent and contain model policies relevant to development control that will speed up the plan-making process. All plans will now be examined mandatorily by the Scottish Executive.

Responsibility for Development Plans in Northern Ireland

The hierarchy of planning documents includes:

The Regional Development Strategy (RDS) 'Shaping our Future'

The RDS is a strategy for Northern Ireland up to 2025 and it contains a spatial development strategy and related strategic planning guidelines that provide the planning context for:

- Social and economic growth.
- Protecting and enhancing the environment.
- Housing, transport, air and water quality, energy, waste strategies and infrastructure.
- Development plans for guiding land use.

All planning policy and plans must now be in 'general conformity' with the strategy.

Development plans

DPs are in the form of area, local or subject plans. The aim is to have complete coverage of the country by 2006.

The Draft Planning Reform (NI) Order 2006 was laid at Westminster in March 2006. Its aim is to modernize the planning system by streamlining the development plan process and to speed up the development control system. New powers include the enhancement of community involvement and greater protection of the built and natural environment. (Refer to www.northernireland.gov.uk for updates)

Development Control

The Meaning of Development

Current legislation is consolidated into the Town and Country Planning Act 1990, the Planning and Compensation Act 1991, the Planning and Compulsory Purchase Act 2004 and the Town and Country Planning (Scotland) Act 1997. In Northern Ireland, legislation is based on parliamentary orders in council, for example, the Planning (Northern Ireland) Order 1991. Detailed explanation and interpretation of development is given in the General Permitted Development Order (GDPO) 1995, revised in 2003. The current GPDO in Scotland dates from 1992.

In planning law, particular meaning is given to certain words and a number of definitions are given. In the Acts, permission is required for any development of land.

Definition

Development refers to the carrying out of building operations, engineering operations, mining operations or other operations in, on, over or under land or the making of any material change in the use of any buildings or other land.

Definition

Building operations refer to rebuilding, structural alterations or additions of buildings and other operations normally undertaken by a person carrying on business as a builder. Demolition, reconstruction and certain other similar operations are also included under building operations.

Definition

Building refers to any structure or erection and any part of a building, structure or erection, but does not include plant or machinery comprised in a building, structure or erection.

Under the Town and Country Planning Act (General Permitted Development) Order 1995 and amendments to 1999, gates, fences, walls or other means of enclosure are also expressly excluded from the definition of building.

Definition

Engineering operations refer to the formation or laying out of means of access to highways and 'means of access'.

Engineering operations include any means of access, public or private, for vehicles or foot passengers. Also included is the building of streets, bridges, functional items such as the installation of fuel storage tanks and anything that results in some physical alteration of land, i.e. an alteration that has some degree of permanence in relation to the land itself.

Definition

Mining refers to the winning and working of minerals in, on, or under land whether by surface or underground working. It includes the removal of material of any description from a:
- Mineral deposit.
- Deposit of PFA or furnace ash or clinker.
- Deposit of iron, steel or other metallic slag.
- Extraction of mineral deposits from a disused railway embankment.

Definition

Mineral refers to:
- All minerals and substances in or under land of a kind ordinarily worked for removal by underground or surface working.
- Sand, gravel, top soil, clay, peat, stone and mineral ores.

Definition

Mineral deposit refers to any deposit of material remaining after minerals have been extracted from land.

Definition

Other operations refer to operations in the context of or in association with building, engineering or mining.

Definition

Material change of use refers to activities which are done in, alongside or on the land, but which do not interfere with the actual physical characteristics of the land.

A change of use constitutes development only if it is material from a planning point of view. 'Materialness' is a matter of fact and degree and is assessed according to the following criteria:

- Will the change of use materially alter the character of land or buildings?
- Where an existing use is intensified, does this alter the character of land or buildings?
- If character is only partly affected, is the change material for some other reason? For example, the burden on services is substantial or the change of use has a major affect on the neighbourhood. Or in contrast, the purpose of the change of use is incidental to the existing use.
- Will the change of use affect only a proportion of the whole site?
- Whether or not 'established use' rights have been lost or abandoned.
- Extinguishment: if a building is destroyed use rights attached to it are also extinguished.
- Abandonment: can it be demonstrated that use has been properly discontinued?
- Change from one 'use class' to another.

'Use classes' refers to a classification of uses of all land into 16 different types. This was most comprehensively set out in the Town and Country Planning (Use Classes) Order 1987, SI 1987 No. 764 with subsequent amendment, and in Scotland under the Town and Country Planning (General Development) (Scotland) Order 1997 (SI 1997:3061).

The Use Classes Order is a detailed list of definitions accompanied by subsidiary definitions. For example, there is a basic definition of the expression 'business use' followed by even more refined definitions of 'light industrial building', 'general industrial building' and 'special industrial building'. Words like 'office' and 'shop' are also defined.

Examples of Use Classes:

A1	Shops.
A2	Financial and Professional Services.
A3	Food and Drink.
B1	Business.
B2	General Industrial Use (Since 1997 this includes special uses.)
B8	Distribution or Storage Centre.
C1	Hotel or Hostels.
C2	Residential Institutions.
C3	Dwelling house.
D1	Non-residential uses, such as medical or health services.
D2	Assembly and Leisure.

> **Example:**
> Change of use from bookshop (A1) to a travel agency (A1) will not be development unless the planning authority says it does by order. But a change of use from a bookshop (A1) to a shop for the sale of hot food may be development because the latter is in class A3.
>
> Not all uses are in a class and these are referred to as *sui generis* (unique). Examples include theatres, sculptors' studios, a students' hostel.
>
> The A3 class order was split into three separate categories in 2005: restaurants and cafes, pubs and bars, and takeaway outlets. Planning permission is required to convert any building into a nightclub. The intention was to give local planning authorities more influence over the evening economy.

Is Planning Permission Always Necessary?

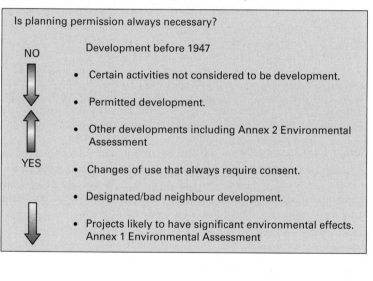

Planning permission is not always necessary. Most developments that took place before the Town and Country Planning Act 1947 and certain activities 'not considered to be development' are exempt from permission. Other activities are deemed to be 'permitted development' and no formal application is usually necessary. These distinctions are explained further below.

However, some developments always require planning permission, i.e. certain changes of use, designated/bad neighbour developments and developments covered by Annex 1 of the Environmental Assessment Regulations.

Between permitted development and those proposals always requiring consent lies a mass of developments, which a planning authority will assess individually on merit. These include proposals covered by Annex 2 of the Environmental Assessment Regulations.

Certain activities are not considered to be development

- Works to the interior of a building or works that do not materially affect its external appearance. Note that putting in windows or doors and works below ground internally may constitute development.
- Maintenance or improvement to highways by the local authority.
- Breaking open of streets for inspection, repair, etc., of sewers, cables, etc., by local authority or statutory undertaker.
- Use of land, building, etc. within the curtilage of a dwelling house for purposes incidental to the enjoyment of a house. This does not include putting up buildings in the first place, i.e. a new building does require planning permission.
- Use of land and buildings for forestry or agriculture. New buildings are not included here though they may be 'permitted development'.
- The formation of a means of access to a road which is not a trunk or classified road, except in conservation areas.
- The installation of solar panels and Velux windows on up to 10 per cent of a roof area, except in conservation areas.
- Developments in enterprise zones, simplified planning zones and special development orders (new towns).

Permitted Development

To reduce the burden on planning authorities, the government introduced the concept of developments that are permitted without the necessity of formal application for planning consent. Such development is known as 'permitted development' and is described in the General Permitted Development Order.

Permitted development includes:

- Limited enlargement or improvement of a dwelling house.
- Forming, laying out and constructing a means of access to a minor road except where this caused a hazard or obstruction.
- Painting the exterior of a building or work other than for purposes of advertisement, announcement or direction.

There are 31 classes of permitted development. Some examples are listed below.

Class I   Development within the curtilage of a dwelling house. This includes summer-houses and tool sheds, provided that they

	meet height, distance and location requirements. These would not be permitted developments in national parks, areas of natural beauty and conservation areas. However, decking may require planning consent if, for instance, it has a significant visual impact or compromises the privacy of neighbours.
Class II	Gates and fences below 1 m high, adjoining a vehicular highway; less than 2 m high elsewhere.
Class III	Change of use within the same 'use class'.
Class IV	Temporary buildings and uses.
Class VI	Agricultural buildings and works. (See note below.)
Class VII	Forestry buildings and works.

National parks, areas of outstanding natural beauty and conservation areas (including SSSIs) have special protection as permitted development rights can be withdrawn in conservation areas.

Installation of garden decking or patios may require permission if they are a substantial enlargement of a dwelling house, have a significant visual impact or compromise the privacy of neighbours.

1992 Revision to Classes of Permitted Development in Scotland
In Scotland, the principle of 'use classes' applies, but the classification differs from England. See the Town and Country Planning (General Development) (Scotland) Order 1992.

Article 4 Direction
In the UK as a whole, permitted development rights can be removed if necessary using an 'Article 4 Direction' expedited by the Secretary of State or the local planning authority. These are usually applied in areas of architectural, historic or scenic interest such as conservation areas and national parks, where stricter powers of control are desirable.

Agricultural Buildings
Under PPG7, when an agricultural building, substantial extension or alteration erected under permitted development rights since 1.4.97 ceases to be in agricultural use within ten years of completion and there is no permission for change of use within three years of cessation (and no outstanding appeal) it must be removed (unless the LPA has agreed otherwise in writing).

Changes of use that always require consent:
- Separation of a building into two or more separate dwelling houses.
- Deposit of refuse or waste material on land already used for this purpose, which enlarges the surface area or increases the height above the land adjoining the site.

- Display of advertisements on any external part of a building not normally used for that purpose. In this case you need to refer to the Advertising Regulations, Town and Country Planning (Control of Advertisement) Regulations 1992.
- Fish farms.

Designated Development (Bad Neighbour Development in Scotland)

In Scotland the term 'bad neighbour development' has been retained – see Town and Country Planning (General Permitted Development) (Scotland) Order 1992. In England and Wales these are now called 'designated developments'. For these developments, formal planning permission and advertisement, consultation and consent is required beyond the usual case. Press advertisements are mandatory and, since 1984, have been placed by the local planning authority.

What are bad neighbours?

- Public conveniences.
- Disposal of refuse or waste, scrap yards, coal yards, winning or working of minerals.
- Construction of buildings or other operations or use of land for retention, treatment or disposal of sewage, trade waste or sludge.
- Construction of buildings to a height exceeding 20 metres.
- Slaughter house, knacker's yard, any building for killing or plucking poultry.
- Casino, fun fair, bingo hall, theatre, cinema, music hall, dance hall, skating rink, swimming bath, gymnasium (not part of a school, college or university), Turkish or other vapour or foam bath.
- Zoo, breeding or boarding dogs or cats.
- Motor car, motor cycle racing.
- Cemetery.
- Construction of buildings, operations, use of land which will affect residential property with fumes, noise, vibrations, etc; alter the character of an established amenity; bring crowds to a generally quiet area; cause noise and activity between 8pm and 8am; and introduce significant change into a homogeneous area.

Special Development Areas

These are areas not classified as development. They are subject to less stringent control or have a special agency set up to promote regeneration.

> • **URBAN DEVELOPMENT AREAS AND CORPORATIONS** •

> • **ENTERPRISE ZONES/SIMPLIFIED PLANNING ZONES** •

> • **REGIONAL DEVELOPMENT AGENCIES** •

> • **BUSINESS IMPROVEMENT DISTRICTS** •

Urban Development Areas and Corporations

The Local Government Planning and Land Act 1980 empowered the Secretary of State to designate an area of land as an 'urban development area' and to establish an urban development corporation to regenerate the area. Urban development corporations have great powers to deal with matters of land assembly and disposal, planning, housing and industrial promotion. They have wide planning responsibilities and usurp local planning authorities' development control functions (except in Wales).

They have the duty of regenerating their respective areas by:

- Bringing land and buildings into effective use.
- Encouraging development of industry and commerce.
- Ensuring that housing and social facilities are available, and creating an attractive environment.

The Thames Gateway and the Clyde Gateway are the latest UDCs to be formed.

Enterprise Zones/Simplified Planning Zone Schemes

The Housing and Planning Act 1986 empowers local authorities to make Simplified Planning Zone Schemes, an extension of the Enterprise Zone concept without the financial benefit.

Power is given to local authorities to grant advance planning permission for defined types of development in specified areas. A developer will be able to carry out such development in a scheme without making an application for planning permission and paying the requisite fee. Schemes will most often be promoted to assist with the industrial regeneration in older urban areas by stimulating investment and development activity and by helping generate confidence in the area. SPZs are shown in the local authority's development plan.

Exemption exists as to the type of land that may be included in an SPZ. Examples of exemptions include land in a national park, an SSSI, a conservation area, an area of outstanding natural beauty or in green belts or in the area of the Broads Authority.

SPZs have now been extended by the 2004 Act to include all areas of regeneration where jobs, growth and productivity are needed.

Regional Development Agencies and Regional Assemblies (England)

The Regional Development Act 1998 set up Regional Development Agencies (RDA) in each of the eight English regions, with a ninth for London, e.g. One North East and Yorkshire Forward. The RDAs were set up in April 1999 as a direct furthering of the Government's White Paper '*Building Partnership's for Prosperity*' with the purposes of:

- Furthering economic development and regeneration of its area.
- Promoting business efficiency, investment and competitiveness in its area.
- Promoting employment in its area.
- Enhancing the development/application of skills relevant to employment.
- Contributing to the achievement of sustainable development in the UK.

RDA's main objective was the preparation of Regional Strategies, completed for each region in 1999. The Strategy sets out for the medium term (5–10 years) the RDA's policies and objectives for the region's economy including sustainable development through sustainable communities, protection of the environment and natural resources, and the integration of social, economic and environmental objectives. The Regional Strategy is prepared in conjunction with regional and local partners such as English Partnerships, training and enterprise councils, tourist boards, local authorities, universities and the regional chamber.

RDAs must work with the framework provided by Regional Planning Guidance issued by the Secretary of State, which sets out the land-use planning framework for the regions (PPG11) and also with local authority development plans. RDAs are governed by democratically elected regional chambers but are controlled by the Department of Trade and Industry.

The Regional Assemblies (Preparation) Act 2003 set up Regional Assemblies or Regional Government Offices, which were to become democratically elected under the provisions of the Planning and Compensation Act 2004. There are nine Regional Government Offices in England; however, the referendum in November 2004 in the North East rejected elected Regional Assemblies, which has led the Government to drop further plans for elections. The Government still retains the Regional Government Offices, which include regional functions of DTI, Department for Transport (DFT), Department for Education and Skills (DfES), DEFRA and DCMS.

Business Improvement Districts (BIDS)

The Local Government Act 2003 paved the way for towns and cities in England to regenerate urban areas. The first UK BID was established in Kingston upon Thames in early 2005 after a successful pilot scheme was run. The Act enables businesses to work with local authorities and other stakeholders on urban realm projects that benefit them and local communities both economically and socially. BIDS are financed through establishing a local tax and have to be approved by a majority of local businesses.

Heritage Planning and Special Forms of Control

Under the Planning (Listed Building and Conservation Areas) Act 1990, The Planning and Compulsory Purchase Act 2004 and The Town and Country Planning Act (Scotland) Act 1997, local authorities are empowered by legislation to preserve and/or enhance the 'pleasant' features of the town and country by formulating policies relating to conservation, townscape and landscape. In addition, other legislation exists to preserve the UK heritage.

In Northern Ireland protection of heritage is not covered by specific regulations but is covered by the Planning (Northern Ireland) Order 1991, amendment 2003 and The Planning Strategy for Northern Ireland – Shaping our Future 2025, as well as Development Control Advice Notes and Planning Policy Statements

> • TREE PRESERVATION •

> • CONSERVATION AREAS •

> • LISTED BUILDINGS •

> • ANCIENT MONUMENTS AND ARCHAEOLOGICAL AREAS •

> • PARKS/GARDENS OF SPECIAL HISTORIC INTEREST •
> • LISTED LANDSCAPES •

Tree Preservation Orders (TPO)

The Town and Country Planning Act recognizes the importance of trees by requiring planning authorities to make appropriate provision for the planting and preservation of trees. In addition, Planning Policy Guidance states that planning authorities should seek to protect trees, groups of trees and areas of woodland where they have natural heritage value or contribute to the character or amenity of a particular locality. If a planning authority considers that, 'it is expedient in the interests of amenity', provision should be made for the preservation of any trees or woodland; a tree preservation order can then be made under:

- Town and Country Planning Acts (Current).
- The Town and Country Planning (Trees) Regulations 1999.
- The Planning and Compensation Act 1991.
- The Forestry Act 1967.

Types of tree preservation orders that exist under the regulations include Individual, Groups and Woodland.

Purpose and extent of a tree preservation order

- Prevents the felling, mutilation and harming to the health of a tree or woodland covered by an order.
- Protects selected single or groups of trees and woodlands if their removal would have significant impact on the environment and its enjoyment by the public.
- Prohibits the cutting down, uprooting, topping, lopping, wilful damage or wilful destruction of a tree/trees *unless consent* is obtained from the local authority.
- Secures the replanting of trees, the felling of which has been permitted by the local authority.

Exemptions to Orders

Hedges and shrubs, trees on Crown Land (without consent of the appropriate Government department) and forestry authority land (unless no dedication covenant in force and consent is obtained) are specifically exempt from orders being placed on them. There are exemptions to obtaining consent for carrying out work on protected trees:

- Dead, dying or dangerous trees.
- Preventing/abating a nuisance.
- Trees on airfields/defence installations.
- Ornamental fruit trees and orchards.

- Forestry authority plans of operation.
- Trees on/adjacent to ancient monuments or churchyards.
- Work by a statutory undertaker as defined, e.g. gas, water, sewerage, a relevant airport operator, NRA, electricity, post office and telecommunications (not utility companies except in certain situations, e.g. safety).
- Planning permission.

Procedure for making a tree preservation order

- A TPO must be in the form of the model order contained in the regulations and it must define the number, species and position of the trees, groups or woodlands to which it relates.
- Copy of the order, map and reasons for the order being made are served to the occupiers of the land and also deposited at a place in the locality where they can be inspected.
- Copy of the order is served to conservator of forests, district valuer or the keeper of the register in Scotland.
- The local authority is advised to inform affected neighbours and provide a site notice if the TPO will affect the interests of the neighbourhood.
- Objections may be made within 28 days to the local authority who makes a decision and stops, modifies or confirms the order.
- If no objections are made an order can be confirmed within 42 days but must be made within six months or the trees covered will cease to be protected. A TPO can be challenged only by application to the High Court within six weeks of confirmation of an order.

Penalties for Non Compliance with an Order

The maximum penalties associated with an offence against an order were substantially increased by the Planning and Compensation Act 1991. This major change takes account of the substantial profits, which may accrue, to an offender as a result of the illegal felling or destruction of protected trees.

Penalties

- On summary conviction, to a fine not exceeding £20 000.00 (Magistrates' Court)
- On conviction on indictment, to an unlimited fine (Crown court).

Replanting of Trees and Woodlands Covered by an Order

The local authority has powers to enforce the replacement of a tree with a Tree Replacement Notice, which must be served within four years of unauthorized work.

- Through a condition of a consent to fell.
- Where the tree is dead/dangerous. (Not applicable if by *force majeure*.)
- Where a tree is destroyed in contravention of an order, a notice is served to the owner of the land specifying a minimum period to plant an appropriate replacement tree. Appeals against a Replacement Notice can be made to the Secretary of State.
- Replacement trees are to be of an appropriate size and species and in the same place.
- Where the offender fails to carry out the prescribed replanting the council can serve an Enforcement Notice requiring them to do so.

Provisional Tree Preservation Orders

Provisional tree preservation orders have a duration of six months and are made when an urgent order needs to be placed. A normal tree preservation order takes effect when confirmed. In order to prevent tree felling before an order can come into effect the local authority can make a provisional tree preservation order that includes a provision for the order coming into effect on the date specified.

Effects of Planning Permission on Tree Preservation Orders

No application under the TPO regulations is required to be made to the planning authority for work to trees covered by a tree preservation order:

'*. . .immediately required for the purpose of carrying out development authorised by. . . . planning permission granted on an application.*'

This does not apply to outline planning consent or permitted development. However, through PPG1 and attached conditions to the consent the LPA may control what work occurs. The Act places a duty on LPAs to ensure they make adequate provision for the preservation and planting of trees when granting planning permission by imposing conditions and making TPOs.

The LPA will take into account the effect of any loss of amenity when assessing any development likely to have an adverse effect on trees, groups of trees and woodlands specified in a TPO. In assessing proposals affecting a TPO all the following criteria must be met before a development is looked on favourably:

- Development proposals must aim for a high quality landscape design that respects the existing trees and the local environment.
- Where proposals would result in the loss of any individual trees, groups of trees or woodlands, the applicant must provide for compensatory planting as part of the overall scheme or elsewhere within the vicinity. (This may involve the use of section 106/75 agreements).

- Proposals must include details of methods to be adopted, including legal agreements, to guarantee future maintenance arrangements.
- The size and position of the trees after development, including their future growth, must be considered. If a tree in the future interferes unreasonably with an occupier's enjoyment of a property or poses a danger, the LPA will find it difficult to object to a consent to lop or fell.

Statutory Undertakers' and Utility Companies' Powers in Relation to Trees

Under the 1999 order, statutory authorities, as defined in the order, do not need to obtain the LPA's consent before cutting down or carrying out work on a tree situated on the undertaker's operational land:

- In the interest of safety.
- When inspecting, repairing or renewing their apparatus.
- When carrying out their permitted development rights.

Protection for street trees from statutory authorities, under the New Roads Public Utilities and Street Works Act 1991, is under S82 which states that undertakers may be required to compensate street authorities for damage or loss suffered by them in their capacity, which could apply to street trees. All utility operators are committed to implementing the guidelines prepared by the National Joint Utilities Group in 1995 to take care to avoid damaging all trees.

British Waterways have powers to clear trees to keep waterways open and navigable.

Dangerous Trees and The Legal Framework

Apportionment of blame in relation to collapsing trees can either be through criminal or civil law under the following legislation:

- **OCCUPIERS' LIABILITY ACTS (OLA 1957 AND 1984)**
- **THE HEALTH AND SAFETY AT WORK ACT (HASAW 1974) AND ASSOCIATED REGULATIONS**
- **THE HIGHWAYS ACT 1980**

Occupiers Liability Act (1957 and 1984)

The overriding principle is that of a 'duty of care'. Everyone with control over land or property should take reasonable measures to prevent foreseeable harm befalling others (visitors or passers-by or trespassers), i.e. your trees must not fall on people while they are on your land.

You should also take reasonable precautions to prevent the 'escape' of your property onto the public highway. This principle applies equally to escaped animals, noxious chemicals, poisonous plants and trees falling onto the public highway/footway. This allows for an injured party, e.g. neighbour or visitor to your property, to take a civil action against you and the Crown to bring a criminal action against you. For tree owners to discharge their duty of care they must take 'reasonable' measures to establish the condition of their trees.

The courts differentiate between 'lay' members of the public and large corporations or local authorities responsible for managing land, who are expected to know what condition their trees are in through effective and frequent tree inspections and take necessary action. The new Trees in relation to Construction BS 5837:2005 requires surveys to be carried out by arboriculturalists. Additionally, the law differentiates between trees that collapse as a result of an identifiable defect and those that collapse unpredictably, e.g. an extraordinary event such as lightening.

The Health and Safety Act at Work (1974)

HASAW confers a duty of care on those at work towards bystanders. The HSE prosecuted Birmingham City Council for a breach of HASAW when an ash tree fell and killed 3 people. The tree had fallen due to an identifiable defect and it was a foreseeable danger; the council was prosecuted for negligence in its tree management.

The Highways Act (1980)

Section 130 of the Highways Act places a duty on highway authorities to prevent either the 'stopping up' or the 'obstruction' of the highways under their jurisdiction. This relates to trees or branches that might fall across the highway, but also it is inferred to include trees on land adjacent to the highway even though they may not be under their ownership.

Section 154 gives highway authorities powers to compel remediation by the owners of trees that are deemed to be a danger to the highway. The power also provides entry onto private land by highway authority contractors should the owner fail to put in hand the necessary measures. The authority can recover costs from the owners.

- Government Circular 90/73: 'An authority … responsible for the safety of a tree is under a duty to have it inspected by a competent person at reasonably frequent intervals so that any indication of disease … can be noted and acted upon'.
- Trunk Routes Maintenance Manual (TRMM 1999).
- All highway trees (defined as trees within falling distance of the highway) require an arboricultural inspection every five years, but this period may be reduced on the advice of the arboriculturalist.

Other guidance to authorities responsible for trees includes:

Overhanging Trees

The whole of a tree growing on a plot of land belongs to the owner of the land even if roots penetrate into the soil or the branches overhang the adjacent land. Natural growth of trees over adjoining land may constitute a trespass (in England and Wales) or a nuisance. A neighbour may abate the nuisance provided that they:

- Do not commit a breach of the peace.
- Do not interfere with rights of an innocent party or the public.
- Do not interfere with owner's property in excess.
- Choose the least damaging method of abatement.

In order to abate the nuisance, entry can be made onto the land provided notice requesting the removal of the nuisance is given. Lopped branches belong to the owner of the tree.

Conservation Areas

Designation of conservation areas

- Town and Country Planning Act 1990 and Planning (Listed Buildings and Conservation Areas) Act 1990.
- Town and Country Planning Act 1997 (Scotland) and Town and Country (Listed Buildings and Conservation Areas) Scotland Regulations 1997.
- Town and Country Amenities Act 1974.
- Planning (NI) Order 1993.

It is the duty of the local planning authority to determine which parts of their area should be treated as Conservation Areas, that is, areas of special architectural or historic interest, the character or appearance of which is desirable to preserve or enhance. Other features may contribute to the appearance of a conservation area such as trees or other buildings.

Once an area has been designated as a Conservation Area notice of the fact must be published in the press. Notice must also be entered in the local land charges register.

Effect of a Conservation Area status

Demolition

- Demolition is prohibited of any building without Conservation Area Consent.

Trees

- Trees already protected by a TPO are subject to normal controls.
- Trees not protected by a TPO have a special provision that anyone who wishes to cut down, top, lop, uproot, wilfully damage or wilfully destroy any tree in a conservation area must give six weeks' notice of their intention to the local planning authority.
- The authority then has six weeks to prepare a provisional tree preservation order. If a notice is not submitted then penalties are similar to those for contravening a tree preservation order.
- The LPA has powers to enforce the replacement of a tree with a Tree Replacement Notice, which must be served within four years of unauthorized work.
- Exemptions exist including: land owned by LPA and work carried out with LPA's consent; trees under 75 mm dia; and work in accordance with a Forestry Authority licence or covenant.

Advertising

- There are special regulations prescribing the classes of advertisements that may be permitted in Conservation Areas.

Listed Buildings – Buildings of Special Architectural or Historic Interest

Designation of Listed Buildings

- Town and Country Planning Act 1990 (England and Wales) and Planning (Listed Buildings and Conservation Areas) Act 1990.
- Town and Country Planning Act 1997 (Scotland) and the Town and Country (Listed Buildings and Conservation Areas) Scotland Regulations 1997.
- Planning (NI) Order 1991.

The Secretary of State is required to compile lists or give approval to lists compiled by other bodies (Historic Scotland, English Heritage, Historic Scotland, CADW (Welsh Historic Monuments) and the DOENI Built Heritage: Environment and Heritage Services) of buildings of special architectural or historic interest.

Buildings are listed with regard to the contribution that its exterior makes to the architectural or historic interest of a group of buildings and the desirability of preserving any feature fixed to the building or contained within its curtilage.

The local authority is required to give notice of a listing to the owner and occupier of the building, who has no right to object to the listing.

Effects of listed building designation

Demolition or alteration

- It is an offence to demolish, alter or extend in any manner which would affect the character as a building of special architectural or historic interest unless listed building consent has been obtained. Application for listed building consent is made to the local planning authority.

Landscape

- Special regard has to be paid not only to the building but also to its setting. The local authority must therefore be consulted before making any alteration to landscape within the curtilage of a listed building.

Building Preservation Notice

A local authority may serve a Building Preservation Notice in order to protect a building that has not yet been listed from demolition or where alteration is threatened. Compensation is payable if within six months the Secretary of State decides not to list the building, or if no decision is made. The local authority will be liable for compensation, which may include breach of contract payments.

Ancient Monuments and Archaeological Areas

Designation of ancient monuments and archaeological areas
- **Ancient Monuments and Archaeological Areas Act 1979** •
- **Historic Monuments and Archaeological Objects (NI) Order 1995** •

Ancient Monuments

Under the Act the Secretary of State is required to maintain a schedule of monuments of national importance including those in private ownership and those whose ownership is vested in the Secretary of State. The Secretary of State has the power to compulsory acquire a monument for the purpose of securing its preservation.

Effects of Designation

Demolition or alteration

- Offence to carry out, without consent, any works resulting in the demolition, destruction, damage, alterations or repair to the monument.
- Offence to carry out any flooding or tipping operations on the land.

Ancient Monuments (Class Consents) Order 1981

- Covers a range of work for which there is deemed consent.

Scheduled Monument Consent

- Other works that require specific consent from the Secretary of State who is required to hold a public inquiry before determining the application, which may be granted with or without conditions or refused. A consent will lapse after five years.

Archaeological Areas

The provisions of the Act are designed not to prevent development on archaeological sites but simply to enable archaeological records to be made. Once an area has been designated by the Secretary of State as being of archaeological importance, a developer is required to serve an 'operations notice' on the local authority six weeks prior to the carrying out of any designated operations.

Operations Notice

- Operations that disturb the ground.
- Flooding and tipping operations.

Once the notice has been served, the 'designated investigating authority' (appointed by the Secretary of State) has the right to enter the land to investigate archaeological excavation or to record material of archaeological or historical interest. A notice of intention to excavate must be served on the developer prior to the six-week period ending. The developer must bear the cost of this.

Parks and Gardens of Special Historic Interest – Gardens and Designed Landscapes

English Heritage, Historic Scotland, CADW (Welsh Historic Monuments) and the DOENI Built Heritage: Environment and Heritage Services maintain the inventory of historic gardens and designed landscapes. They are statutory consultees for any development affecting landscapes on the list.

The effects of a listing

- There will be a presumption against any development that is likely to have an adverse effect on the integrity, landscape setting or distinctive character of gardens and designed landscapes listed in the inventory.
- Proposals for the restoration of the original landscapes and removal of unsympathetic planting or structures will be viewed favourably.
- New structures and/or landscape works will generally only be acceptable where they will enhance the design and setting of the garden or designed landscape. All works must be well designed, carefully sited and constructed. Future maintenance arrangements must be put in place.

- Development proposals must be shown in the context of the garden or the designed landscape and demonstrate that they recognize their integrity and offer enhancement of the existing situation.
- The LPA will seek to encourage the sensitive management of gardens and designed landscapes.

The Garden History Society has produced guidance notes about how to deal with the value of these sites in the planning process. The planning conservation advice notes (PCANs) may be downloaded from www. gardenhistorysociety.org

Revisions to the English Listing System
(To keep up to date visit www.english-heritage.org.uk)

The Department of Culture, Media and Sport (DCMS) has put forward proposals to amend the current legislation that will result in the following changes to the English Heritage protection system:

- Single listing and consent process for all listed buildings, monuments, parks and gardens.
- English Heritage to have responsibility for designation.
- Applicants will apply directly to the agency, which will assess building against set criteria and recommend listing, delisting or grade amendment. Culture Secretary of State will make final decision.
- English Heritage will inform owners if application to list building is made by another party.
- English Heritage will consult owners and local authorities on applications. If owners are unhappy with the decision, they may write to the DCMS within 28 days requesting that it be reconsidered.
- English Heritage will introduce clearer information for owners of listed buildings, including a map showing the extent of the listing and a summary of the building's importance. Since April 2006 information packs with guidance about the implications of listing and with sources of expert advice are being sent to all owners of newly listed buildings.
- All consents for items on new list dealt with by local authorities.
- Transfer of some listed buildings onto local lists.

Planning Consent Procedure

Application for Permission

There are five kinds of planning application and consent. These are:
- Full
- Outline
- Approval of Reserved Matters

- Variation to Planning Consent
- Notice of Intention to Develop

Definition

Full planning permission refers to an application for full permission with complete details. All reserved matters are decided at this time. Conditions may be imposed.

However, before purchasing land or incurring the cost of preparing plans, a developer may wish to know whether or not their proposed development is likely to get development consent if they apply for it. Therefore they apply for outline planning permission.

Definition

Outline planning permission refers to application for consent in principle. Then the local planning authority can either:
- **Grant** outline planning consent subject to a condition of that authority of any 'reserved matters'.
- **Hold** the application for consideration of further particulars, i.e. the reserved matters may be relevant at the initial stage.
- **Decline** the application. Reasons must be given.

'**Reserved Matters**' include, for example, details relating to:
- siting.
- design.
- external appearance.
- means of access.
- landscape for the site.

Definition

Approval of reserved matters refers to resolution and agreement of reserved matters. Once this is approved, the application has full planning permission.

Definition

Variation to planning consent refers to approval agreement of insignificant changes to consent already given, e.g. change of house type in a housing scheme.

Definition

Notice of intention to develop (NID) refers to development proposals by local authorities. They cannot give themselves planning permission but, instead, publish a NID in a local newspaper describing the scheme and where and when details may be viewed before development takes place.

Application Requirements

Local planning authorities design their own application forms and the detail required in an application may vary between planning authorities. However, in 2004 the ODPM issued best practice guidelines for compulsory and additional information to be requested of applicants.

Compulsory requirements in applications for full planning permission:

- The completed application form.
- The correct fee (where one is necessary).
- Ownership certificates.
- Agricultural holdings certificates.
- Part 1 notice.
- Location plan.
- Site plan.
- Drawings (including floor plans if relevant).
- Elevations.
- Section drawings.
- Environmental statement.

Additional information:

Depending on the nature and type of the application and the character of the proposed location, the local planning authority may require further details about any of the following:

- Supporting planning statement.
- Design statement (for all applications where design is an issue).
- Access statement.
- Transport assessment.
- Draft travel plan.
- Planning obligations.
- Flood risk assessment/drainage strategy.
- Listed building appraisal and conservation area appraisal.
- Regeneration statements.
- Retail assessments.
- Affordable housing statement.
- Open space.
- Sustainability appraisal.
- Landscape details.
- Tree survey/arboriculture statement.
- Historic archaeological features and scheduled ancient monuments.
- Nature conservation, ecology or natural beauty.
- Noise impact assessment and sound insulation requirements.
- Air quality assessment.
- Assessment for the treatment of foul sewage.

- Utilities statement.
- Energy statement.
- Mineral working and restoration.
- Sunlight/daylight assessment.
- Ventilation/extraction and refuse disposal details.
- Structural survey.
- Details of lighting including light pollution statement.
- Photographs and photomontages.

The Application Form

A basic application form requires the following:
- Name, address and telephone number of the applicant, their agent and any person preparing the plans if different from the applicant or agent.
- Purpose for which permission is sought.
- Location of the proposed development.
- Intended start and completion dates for the development.
- Estimated cost of the works.
- Storage of hazardous materials.
- Details of lighting and other external design details.
- Certification of neighbour notification and a list of those notified.
- Certification that the land is not an agricultural holding or that notice has been given to the tenant of the agricultural land to which the application relates.
- Confirmation that the plans are available for viewing for 21 days.

Local planning authorities are responsible for publicizing planning applications. However, permitted development requiring prior notification to the local authority (e.g. some agricultural or forestry works) requires a site notice posted by the developer.

Under the Planning and Compensation Act 1991, neighbour notification comprises a form and location plan delivered to each neighbouring property, with copies addressed to each occupier, owner and lessee. A plan identifying the site must be included with each notification. Plans are available for view for 21 days. If interested parties have not been informed, the applicant should explain why not. In this case (and also if the local planning authority is seeking development consent) a notice of the proposal should be posted on the land concerned for 21 days during the 28-day period before the application is made.

Rules on publicity are set out in DoE Circular 15/92. In England and Wales, a newspaper advertisement *and* site notices are required in the following cases: for development applications accompanied by an environmental statement (i.e. EIA); departure from the development plan; development affecting the setting of a listed building; or the character or appearance of a conservation area. Minor developments require a site notice *or* neighbour notification.

Major developments require a newspaper advertisement *and* either site notices *or* neighbour notification. Major developments include: erection of 10 or more dwellings; developments of $1000\,m^2$ floor space or more; mineral workings; waste developments; developments causing nuisances, attracting crowds traffic or noise into a quiet area or in unsocial hours; tall buildings; loss of light or privacy beyond adjacent premises; proposals affecting the setting of ancient monument or archaeological site; or trees with TPOs.

There is a difference in notification rules and terminology between England and Wales on the one hand, and Scotland on the other. In Scotland there has been a formal system of neighbour notification of all planning applications since 1984. Interestingly, the Town and Country Planning (General Development Procedure) (Scotland) Order 1992 is used also in England and Wales to define 'neighbouring land'.

Building Regulations
In addition to the application for planning permission building standards regulations may have to be complied with.

Planning Applications Fees
Fees may vary according to acreage. Changes of use fees have a standard rate. Other developments' fees relate to the floor space. If development consists of more than one item, fees may be cumulative. The arithmetic of this is complicated and a practising landscape architect would be advised to check with the relevant planning office for each application. Since about 2005, some planning authorities in London have introduced fees for pre-application advice.

E-planning
In 2005, the Government published targets for more efficient public services, increasing public access and involvement in planning and raising the public's knowledge of the system. The use of the Internet is a key part of these aims and is intended to speed handling of applications and reduce the time planning officers spend on administration. Local councils will receive Government funding to assist putting pre-application planning information on line and enabling submission of planning applications, appeals, enforcement cases, consultation and associated services to be conducted electronically. The system is intended to enable applicants and consultees to track the progress of applications and receive automatic notification once a decision has been reached.

Local Planning Authority Actions
When a local planning authority receives an application, it must follow procedures that comply with rules set down in the Town and Country Planning Acts.

A local planning authority decision on planning application must:

- Comply with any Secretary of State directive.
- Have regard to views of other government department and other authorities.
- Consider representations and views of interested parties, e.g. neighbours and other consultees.
- Comply with provisions of the development plan (structure or local).
- Does not consider cost or need.

Local planning authority actions

On receipt of an application for development consent, a local planning authority:

- May call in further information.
- Undertakes consultations.
- Complies with guidelines.
- Considers views of consultees.
- Considers landscape design.
- May require Environmental Assessment.
- May require a bond.
- May require a Planning Obligation/Section 75 Agreement.

The notes that follow refer particularly to legislation and policy guidelines that are relevant to landscape design.

Legislation and Policy Guidelines Relevant to Landscape Design

Under the Town and Country Planning Acts the local planning authority has a duty to preserve trees and enhance the environment by planting them. The value of trees was restated in ODPM Circular 06/2005, but with a shift in emphasis towards biodiversity: it stated that veteran and other substantial trees or many types of wood, especially ancient and semi-natural woods, can be important for biodiversity conservation. Along with amenity, nature conservation value is a relevant consideration in considering whether trees or woods merit a TPO.

Planning Policy Guidance Note 1 (General Policy and Principles) 1997 included several paragraphs important to the landscape architects, indicating that the 'wider setting' around buildings should be respected, though not necessarily imitated. Particular weight should be given to the impact of development on existing buildings and the landscape in environmentally sensitive areas such as national parks, areas of outstanding natural beauty and conservation areas, where the scale of new development and the use of appropriate building materials would often be particularly important.

'The appearance and treatment of the spaces between and around buildings is also of great importance. Where these form part of an application site, the landscape design – whether hard or soft – will often be of comparable importance to the design of the buildings and should likewise be the subject of consideration, attention and expert advice. The aim should be for any development to result in a 'benefit' in environmental and landscape terms.'

For the first time, the process and application of landscape design was recognized and incorporated in government planning guidance. A landscape architect would apprise a client of this policy development and that the planning authority may require attention to this issue, for example by the planting of trees.

Circular 11/95 (which is still in force) raised the required standard of landscape associated with new development, including design details, earth moving guidelines, and enforcement of landscape requirements by planning authorities. Completion of a housing development may be prohibited until the previously agreed planting scheme is complete. Long-term maintenance and management, together with more effective tree protection during construction, are also discussed.

PPG1 was replaced by the Planning Policy Statement 1 (PPS1) in 2005. The PPS is less specific than PPG1, but it sets out key principles of sustainable development, spatial planning and community involvement. PPS1 states that sustainable development should be linked to the promotion of high quality and inclusive of design for all developments. Design that is inappropriate in its context or fails to take opportunities to improve the character and quality of an area should not be accepted. Authorities 'should take account of the range of effects on the environment as well as the effects of development in terms of economic benefits and social well-being'.

Planning Policy Statement 9 (PPS9) Biodiversity and Geological Conservation, published in 2005, introduced a specific principle promoting the introduction of biodiversity into development design. PPS9 is intended to give greater protection to ancient woodlands, priority habitats and species listed in the UK biodiversity action plan. Local authorities must take UK and local biodiversity action plan targets into consideration when assessing applications. PPS9 also recognizes the biodiversity value of previously developed sites and the need to retain this in the design of redevelopment schemes. It also advises planning officers to require up-to-date information and the prevention of harm.

This guidance is accompanied by Circular 06/2005 detailing legal duties on biodiversity and geological conservation applied through the planning process. This circular also specifies how the Countryside and Rights of Way Act 2000 amends the general duty of local authorities under the Wildlife and Countryside Act 1981. A good practice guide will accompany the Act and circular.

> **Other guidance papers include:**
> - 'Better places to live' (DTLGR 2001) which is a companion document to PPG3, and 'Sustainable Communities: Building for the Future' (ODPM 2003).
> - 'A policy statement for Scotland: Designing places' (2001). This set out the Scottish Executive's policy for architecture and has led to a cascade of new PANs and SPPs.
> - 'Rethinking Open Space' (2001) Scottish Executive Research Unit written by Kit Campbell Associates. This is a highly regarded review of open space planning.

Calling In Further Information

Even after plans have been submitted, a local authority may request the applicant to supply further information to enable it to determine the application. For landscape, this may include a tree survey, detailed proposals for tree protection and replanting.

Site visit

Planning officers and elected members have no statutory obligation to visit a site before deciding a planning application. However, they may be vulnerable to challenges on appeal and award of costs on grounds of unreasonable behaviour if they fail to take into account a material planning consideration that would have been evident if a site visit had been made.

Possible Consultations

Before granting consent, the local planning office consults relevant authorities, unless the planning office considers that the proposed development accords with advice issued by the relevant authority. (This rule has applied in England since 2003.) Under the Planning and Compulsory Purchase Act 2004, statutory consultees must respond within 21 days.

> **Consultation**
> - The district planning authority where relevant (England and Wales).
> - Regional planning bodies where a planning application may affect the regional spatial strategy.
> - The Secretary of State/Regional Roads Department for development affecting trunk roads or level crossings.
> - Highway authority for formation or alteration of access to highways.
> - The coal authority for erection of building in an area worked for coal.
> - Secretary of State for development within 3 km of Windsor Castle and parks or within 800 m of any other Royal Palace or park.

- Water authority for operations in or on the banks of a stream, for refining or storing of mineral oils, refuse or waste, mining, fish farm, sewers and cemetery.
- SNH, EN, CCW, ES (NI) for areas/sites of special scientific interest and a 'consultation area' around the SSSI designated by EN. Other possible consultees for SSSIs are the Environment Agency, County Wildlife Trusts, Herpetological Conservation Trust, Plantlife, and the Butterfly Conservation Society.
- Theatres Trust for theatre development.
- DEFRA for loss of more than 10 acres of agricultural land, or loss of less than 10 acres of such land if it will lead to losses greater than 10 acres.
- Secretary of State advised by English Heritage or Historic Scotland in Scotland for listed building consent (Category A buildings) or development in areas identified in the Inventory of Gardens and Designed Landscapes.
- The Twentieth Century Society for listed building consent involving partial or complete demolition of listed twentieth century buildings.
- Environment Agency/Scottish Environment Protection Agency (as waste disposal authority) about development within 250 m of land used, or used in the last 30 years, as a waste or refuse tip.
- Secretary of State about a scheduled monument.
- EPA and SEPA for industrial development.
- British Waterways Board for canals and reservoirs.
- Regional development agencies for development likely to affect the provision of infrastructure projects or frustrate implementation of neo-government agency strategies.
- Commission for Architecture and the Built Environment (CABE). This is a non-statutory consultee, referred to for significant developments in England (by size or precedent). The Scottish equivalent is Architecture and Design Scotland; and in Wales, the Design Commission for Wales.
- Regional development agencies for development likely to affect the provision of infrastructure projects or to frustrate the implementation of quango strategies.
- Twentieth Century Society for listed building consent involving partial or complete demolition of twentieth-century listed buildings.
- Regional planning bodies where a planning application may have an impact on the regional spatial strategy.

Character Maps and Tranquil Zones

Landscape character assessment is a tool for identifying features that give a locality its sense of place and distinctiveness. Landscape character has been defined as a 'distinct and recognizable pattern of elements that occurs consistently in a particular type of landscape. Particular combinations of geology, landform, soils, vegetation, land use, field patterns and human settlement create character'. The key guidance for landscape architects is

'Landscape character assessment: guidance for England and Scotland' prepared for the Countryside Agency and Scottish Natural Heritage by C. Swanwick, Department of Landscape, University of Sheffield and Land Use Consultants (2002). (See also www.countryside.gov.uk/cci/guidance)

Landscape character assessment may be used as a part of and as a guide in local plan development policies, studies of development potential and landscape capacity, environmental impact assessment and landscape management proposals. It is different from visual assessment, but may be closely linked to it, for instance when assessing landscape capacity.

There are six main stages in landscape character assessment:
- Define the scope and geographical scale of the study (this is critical to successful completion by the researcher and for the practical use of the study to the client).
- Desk study.
- Field survey.
- Classification and description.
- Making judgements – deciding on the approach.
- Making judgements – drawing conclusions.

'The Character of England (1995)' was produced by the Countryside Commission and English Nature in association with English Heritage. The map charts the character and wildlife character of the whole country, divided into 159 separate 'character areas' with a concise summary of a region's historic character, landscape and natural history. Twenty-two maritime areas have also been identified.

In November 2004 this was made accessible on the Internet by the Countryside Agency. The database also holds the results of local landscape character assessments including basic information about the owner, extent and context of landscape character assessment studies, the methodology employed and how it has been applied to inform policy and strategy. The database is accessible via www.ccnetwork.org.uk

The landscape character of Scotland and Wales has also been analysed and mapped, but the Welsh approach called LANDMAP uses a different methodology from that used in England and Scotland.

Tranquil zones: a technique developed by the Countryside Agency and the council for the protection of rural England (CPRE) to evaluate the degree of noise and visual disturbance in the countryside.

Environmental Impact Assessment/Statement (EIA)

EIA is a technique and process by which information about the anticipated environmental effects of a project are collected, both by a developer and from other sources, and taken into account by a planning authority in forming their judgement on whether or not a development should proceed.

For EIA purposes, projects are of two kinds:

- Annex I projects for which EIA is required in every case.
- Annex 2 projects for which EIA is required only if a particular project is judged likely to give rise to significant environmental effects.

(Further detail is given later in the chapter.)

Town and Country Planning (Mineral) Act 1981

This is an important Act because it brought open-cast mining under the control of local planning authorities. Before 1981, such mining was assessed at county level and decisions were made by the Secretary of State. Now, a mining company has to apply to the Secretary of State for a licence to work minerals and to the local planning authority for planning consent. Owners of any interest in a mineral in the land must also be notified of any application for mineral working. The licence is not valid unless planning consent has been granted. In Scotland the provisions of this Act are incorporated into the Town and Country Planning (Scotland) Act 1997.

The Environmental Protections Act 1990 and the Environment Act 1995 revised the requirements for acceptable environmental standards and restoration proposals.

Review of Sites

Under the 1981 Act, every planning authority has to review all sites 'at such interval as they consider fit'. This means that planning conditions on current workings may be updated. This review covers all permissions except where operations ceased more than five years previously; in other words, this Act has a retrospective element. With the 1991 Planning and Compensation Act, the Secretary of State became able to prescribe the period within which reviews must be carried out and their contents. Planning authorities may also make revocation, modification or suspension orders as they see fit. Under the Environment Act 1995 reviews should take place every 15 years.

Aftercare Conditions

Note also that aftercare conditions can be imposed as a part of the development consent. Mining will be permitted if restoration conditions require the site to be brought back to agricultural, forestry or amenity use. Conditions may also impose a time limit, up to five years, by which time restoration measures must be complete. Conditions may either specify actions to be taken or require steps to be taken in accordance with a scheme approved by the planning authority.

Prohibition and Suspension Orders

The Act also made provision for prohibition (if workings have ceased for more than two years and resumption is unlikely).

If development is temporarily suspended the planning authority may require that steps shall be taken for the protection of the environment. There must have been no working for at least 12 months and resumption of work is likely. Resumption of work is notifiable to the local planning authority. Suspension orders must be reviewed every five years.

Compensation may be available where prohibition or suspension orders have been served and, since 1987, for expenditure voluntarily incurred in alleviating damage to amenity, or for restoration. The coal authority is exempt. Town and Country Planning (Compensation for restrictions on mineral working and mineral waste depositing) Regulations 1997 (SI 1997:1111). (See also MPG 4.)

Old Workings

The Planning and Compensation Act 1991 included provision to address problems arising from consents for mining issued between 1992 and 1947. These consents (termed 'interim development orders'), if implemented prior to 1979, remain valid until 2042. However, planning authorities often had no record of the existence of these consents. They could be reactivated without warning and without the sort of conditions designed to safeguard the environment that would be expected by current standards. The 1991 Act therefore required these old interim development order permissions to be registered with the local planning authority by 24th July 1992 or they ceased to have effect.

Under the Environment Act 1995 operators of dormant sites must obtain approval for their proposed scheme of operating and restoration before work may resume. For both active and dormant sites covered by this legislation, which registered by July 1992, conditions for environmental or amenity amelioration works could be imposed, without compensation.

Under the Environment Act 1995 operators of dormant sites must obtain approval for their proposed scheme of operating and restoration before work may resume. Note also that in judgements arising from local plan inquiries, reporters have ruled that if a former extraction site has blended into the surrounding landscape or looks like set-aside land due to the growth of native vegetation, the land may not be held to be 'previously developed land' under the terms of PPG3. As a result, prospective developers would not be able to claim that a site was 'spoilt already'.

Mineral Planning Guidance Note 13: Guidelines for Peat Provision in England, Including the Place of Alternative Materials

This note has statutory force under the Environment Act 1995. It describes peat production, reserves, consumption and likely trends in the use of alternatives to peat. It advises that future extraction should be confined to areas already damaged by recent human activities and or of limited or no nature conservation value.

Planning policy statements since 2000 have implied that open-cast mining applications should be approved only if they have acceptable and beneficial effects on local communities and the environment which outweigh adverse impacts. Extension of existing sites is likely to be approved only if the adjoining reserves were identified in the original application.

Scottish Planning Policy 16

Published in 2005, this followed the tighter constraints on open-cast mining already introduced in England. SPP16 states that applications should be approved only if they are environmentally acceptable or provide local benefits including jobs or land improvements. Proposals are unlikely to be approved if they are: within 457 m of a community; would disturb the area for more then ten years; are close to landfill or mining sites; or would adversely affect natural or heritage sites.

Planning Obligations (Section 106 Agreements) (England and Wales)

The Government recognizes that local planning authorities will seek *improvements to development proposals where those improvements would be to the general public benefit,* rather than for the benefit of some specific piece of neighbouring land. Under the Town and Country Planning Act 1971 section 52, improvements could be achieved by the use of agreements (also called 'covenants'). This measure was retained in the Town and Country Planning Act 1990 section 106, but renamed 'planning obligation' and now called 'section 106 agreement'. This can be a controversial and complex procedure that may take many months to resolve. Circular 05/2005 includes a standard legal agreement intended to speed up negotiations.

The purposes for which planning obligations can be used were specified in Circular 05/2005. Obligations are intended to make acceptable development that would otherwise be unacceptable. A 106 agreement is made: 'For the purpose of restricting or regulating the development or use of land either permanently or during such period as may be prescribed by the agreement'.

Agreements may be positive or negative. Obligations may: restrict development or use of the land; require operations or activities to be carried out in, on, over or under land; require land to be used in a specific way; and require sums to be paid to the local authority as a single sum or periodically. Planning obligations can either require the person giving the undertaking, or successor, to do a specified thing or prevent the use or development of the land in a specified way.

A planning authority should include details in its local plan of its policy in regularly seeking planning obligations in connection with certain types of development. Circular 05/2005 sets out a number of tests, all of which must be satisfied for an obligation to be acceptable to the Government. These include: necessity, relevance to the planning application, directly related to the proposed development, fairly and reasonably related in scale and kind to the proposed development, and reasonable in all other aspects. For example, planning obligations may be used to secure planting of new boundaries or resurfacing of a public right of way.

Negotiation is a vital component in this process and the existence of policies does not preclude the negotiation of obligations on an ad hoc basis. However, Circular 05/2005 stipulates that councils should not permit unacceptable developments as a result of inducements offered by developers. Planning obligations must be governed by the principle that planning permission may not be bought or sold.

Planning obligations can be entered into between the local planning authority and the landowner or unilaterally by the landowner. The latter may be used where negotiations with the local planning authority are unnecessarily protracted or unreasonable.

Planning obligations run with the land and are therefore enforceable against successors in title. They are legally binding, but need not be agreed in detail before planning permission is granted. However, planning consent (a formal letter) is unlikely to be issued until all details of the obligation have been agreed. Unlike section 52 agreements, planning obligations can be modified or discharged by formal application to the local authority with right of appeal to the Secretary of State.

The Planning and Compulsory Purchase Act 2004 gave the Government power to regulate contributions in 106 agreements, but there is little sign that this will be implemented.

Scottish Section 75 Agreements

Scottish planning authorities are bound by section 75 of the 1997 Town and Country Planning (Scotland) Act. The principles described above apply.

Planning Authority Decision Options

On determining an application for planning permission, a local planning authority can:

- Grant unconditional permission. (Since 2003, in England, reasons have to be given. In Scotland reasons have to be given only if the decision is contrary to the local plan, but widespread good practice is that reasons are given for all decisions.)
- Grant permission with conditions.
- Refuse permission: reasons must be given. These must be precise, specific and relevant and refer to relevant policies and proposals in the development plan.

It is a statutory requirement that planning committee decisions pay attention to current national and regional policies, therefore clear and convincing reasons have to be given for any departure from such policy.

Planning permission decisions are normally taken by the town planning or equivalent committee of the local authority; increasingly decisions are taken by delegated action, that is by the chairman of the committee or chief planning officer to speed up the process.

A decision should be made within a period of 13 weeks unless the applicant agrees in writing to an extension of time. Lack of decision can be treated as a refusal. Grant of planning permission does not come into effect until written notice is given to the applicant.

If the planning authority imposes conditions, according to DoE Circular 11/95 these must:

- Be imposed freely, without preconceptions due to previous applications.
- Relate to the application and serve some useful planning purpose, e.g. amenity, social need, comfort and convenience of occupants, relate to existing rights.
- Be certain and unambiguous.
- Not be wholly 'unreasonable'.
- Not effect an alteration to general law.
- Be enforceable.

Reason for conditions must be given.

The 1990 Planning Act gave planning authorities the power to revoke or modify a consent, full or outline, provided that this order is confirmed by the Secretary of State.

Duration of Permissions

Since the 1971/1972 Acts all permissions have been of limited duration. Under section 51 of the Planning and Compulsory Purchase Act 2004, the period within which development must start was shortened from five to three years, unless the planning authority agrees or decides that there should be a different period. New Scottish planning law due in 2006 is likely to be similar in effect.

Duration of planning permission

- Full planning permission – three years.
- Outline planning permission three years with two years for details and reserved matters.

Development is deemed to have begun when any one of the following has taken place:

- Any work of construction.
- Trench for foundations has been dug or begun.
- Laying mains or pipes.
- Laying out/construction of a road.
- Any material change in land use.

If a trench is dug but no further work occurs, the local planning authority may serve a 'Completion Notice' to take effect within a specified period of not less than 12 months. (Notice confirmed by Secretary of State.)

The Planning and Compulsory Purchase Act 2004 dispensed with section 73 applications, which had been used to extend the lifetime of permissions already granted. The reason for this change is to prevent developers banking sites which then become derelict.

Refusal of Application and Appeals

If planning permission is refused, a landscape architect has three options:

- With the client's approval **accept the refusal.**
- **Recommend amendments** to the proposals to suit the local planning authority's conditions, and then resubmit within one year free of charge.
- In England and Wales only, **appeal** to the local planning authority's elected members.
- **Appeal** to the Secretary of State.

Although plans may be resubmitted within one year free of charge, note that under the Planning and Compensation Act 1991 authorities are able to decline to determine an application for planning permission if the Secretary of State (on appeal or call-in) has turned down a similar application in the last two years and there has been no significant change in the development plan or any other material consideration. The Planning and Compulsory Purchase Act 2004 reinforced this, giving authorities the power to decline to determine repeat and subsequent applications for proposals that are similar to ones they have rejected in the past two years, or if an application has been dismissed at appeal within the same period. However, ODPM guidance in Circular 08/2005 advises that if a genuine attempt has been made to address previous objections, the authority should determine the application.

Appeals

The relevant legislation includes section 78 of the Town and Country Planning Act 1990, the Highways Act 1980, the Highways (Assessment of Environmental Effects) Regulations 1988, the Transport and Works Act 1992, the Transport and Works (Assessment of Environmental Effects) Regulations 1995 and the Planning and Compulsory Purchase Act 2004. The process differs according to the covering legislation, but the process in general is similar and adversarial.

If aggrieved by the decision of the local planning authority the applicant can appeal within three calendar months to Secretary of State. (The time limit was changed from six months in 2003.) Appeals can be made against refusal of planning permission, conditions imposed or the non-determination of a planning application.

An appeal submission will initially include:

- A notice of appeal stating the grounds of appeal.
- A copy of the application and plans/drawings, etc.
- A copy of the decision notice.
- All other relevant correspondence.

The normal method of hearing an appeal is by public local inquiry but if parties agree it can be by either:

- An informal hearing. (Government 1999 target states 80 per cent of cases should be determined in 24 weeks.)
- Or written representation (evidence by both applicant and LPA). (Government 1999 target states 80 per cent of cases should be determined in 18 weeks.)

The only further challenge is by appeal to the High Court on a point of law, although judicial review and appeals to the House of Lords are permissible. Judicial review used to be rare, but is becoming more common. The judicial review process is intended to assess whether procedures have been followed correctly, rather than looking at the merits of a decision. The usual argument for a judicial review is that a decision is unreasonable and that either irrelevant considerations were taken into account or relevant considerations were not. Increasing awareness of the EIA regulations has led to an increase in the number of judicial reviews. Commercial rivals are also increasing their use of reviews.

Third party rights of appeal

There is no third party right of appeal that would enable objectors from the community to challenge the merits of planning decisions. The UK

Government in 2000 and the Scottish Executive in 2004 considered and consulted on this issue in the context of Human Rights law, but both rejected the idea following opposition from many businesses, developers, national and regional agencies and most local authorities. The Government concluded that third party rights of appeal 'would not be consistent with our democratically accountable system of planning and could add to the costs and uncertainties of planning'.

However, other law may ameliorate this situation for third parties. The Freedom of Information Act 2000 and the UN Aarhus Convention (which came into force in May 2005) gives the 'right of every person present and future generations to live in an environment adequate to his or her well-being'. The convention gives members of the public rights of access to environmental information, participation in environmental decision-making and justice in environmental matters.

Planning Inquiry Commissions

These are held where usual appeal type public inquiry is not best suited to development, for example, for the third London airport or Sizewell Nuclear Power Station. The minister sets up a commission, which works in two stages:

- Taking written and oral evidence and carrying out the necessary research at the Secretary of State's expense.
- The normal public inquiry with cross-examination.

A report is prepared to the minister who makes the decision.

Public Inquiries

Public inquiries are not courts of law. Inspectors are usually respected members of the planning profession.

Appellants, local planning authorities and other people making representations to the inquiry are bound by strict timetables before the inquiry sits. The local planning authority has two months in which to prepare a statement of case and must send copies of its evidence to appellants and other 'S27 parties' no less than 28 days before the inquiry sits. Four weeks before the inquiry, the appellant and the local planning authority prepare an agreed statement of common ground, which is sent to the Secretary of State and any statutory party.

'S.27 parties' refers to section 27 of the Town and Country Planning Act 1971, and any persons making representations to the Secretary of State through the inquiry process.

The local planning authority's statement of case deals with four matters:

- Statements of submissions they propose to put forward.
- A list of all plans and documents where these can be inspected and copied.
- Reference to relevant directions of Secretary of State.
- Views of other Government departments if they are to be used.

The statement of case cannot be departed from without leave of the inspector.

The inquiry process

1 The inspector opens the inquiry formally.
   The appellant's and local planning authority's advocates name the witnesses they will call. The inspector asks if any other parties wish to be heard.
2 Appellant's advocate summarizes their client's case. Like the local planning authority, the appellant's evidence should be submitted in advance of the inquiry.
3 Summary of proof now usually required and read out. The local planning authority's advocate cross-examines, S27, and third parties can cross-examine.
4 Appellant's advocate re-examines (often to correct or clarify any confusion that has arisen during cross-examination).
5 The local planning authority's advocate follows steps 2, 3 and 4 above.
6 S.27 and third parties state their case.
7 Appellant's advocate makes closing speech.
8 The local planning authority's advocate makes closing speech.
9 Inspector closes inquiry and makes accompanied site visit.

The decision

Having heard the case for and against, the Secretary of State/inspector may:
- Sustain or dismiss the appeal.
- Reverse or vary any part of the original decision – whether the appeal relates to that part of the decision or not.
- May deal with the application as if it had been made to him or her in the first instance.

Inspectors make 80 per cent of decisions, but where the minister is to make the decision the inspector reports findings of fact and their conclusions; then the minister makes a decision and notifies the parties. If the minister disagrees with the inspector he or she must inform all parties, allowing 21 days for representations, and ask for the inquiry to be reopened. A Government 1999 target stated that 80 per cent of appeals decided by inquiry should be determined in 36 weeks.

Technical and Expert Evidence

If you are involved in an inquiry, do not leave preparation until the last moment as the outcome may depend on the quality of evidence.

Evidence should include:

- Any fact that may be disputed by the other side – prove with reason and evidence.
- Any technical questions and answers that may assist the inspector.
- Any intentions the landowner/developer may have for the land in the future.

Landscape Architect

A landscape architect may have to prepare a written precognition stating the landscape case on behalf of their clients, and or illustrative material about visual or landscape matters and environmental impact assessment. After the appeal decision, landscape architects may advise on reasons for refusal or implementation of landscape conditions.

Ethics

As a landscape architect you may be appearing on behalf of either the local authority or the appellant. As a local authority employee you will be expected to defend the decision of your authority; if you are in private practice your client will have appointed you to represent their interests. Either may pose professional and ethical problems.

A professional witness is not meant to be an advocate but to put forward their 'bona fide professional opinions'. A professional expert is expected to give evidence in 'good faith', that is, be able to present, declare and distinguish between generally accepted ideas and individual theories. If testimony is not given in good faith, then there may be a 'failure of candour' – true reasons may be being withheld because it is thought they may not gain wider agreement or further the client's case. Finally, note that any witness (scientist, expert or professional) who gives evidence in a large number of cases will be under pressure (psychologically) to sustain and continue the original argument even if he or she is correct all the time.

Enforcement

Enforcement is based on Part V of the Town and Country Planning Act 1972 and was amended by Part II of the Planning and Compensation Act 1991. (For England only: Environment Circular 10/97; Enforcing Planning Control; legislative provisions and procedural requirements.)

Planning authorities are responsible for taking enforcement action in the public interest. Decisions and resulting action should be taken without undue delay. Failure to act promptly could constitute maladministration. Under the time limit rules in the UK's Town and Country Planning Acts, unauthorized developments automatically acquire lawful status after four years for buildings (or change of use to a single dwelling house) or ten years for uses or breaches of condition. Lawfulness is defined as being immune from enforcement action.

Enforcement action should be commensurate with the breach: it is usually inappropriate to take formal action against a trivial or technical breach that causes no harm to amenity.

A breach of planning consent can be:

- An unauthorized operation.
- An unauthorized material change of use.
- A breach of condition.

A breach is a civic offence with a maximum penalty of £20 000. The court may consider any financial benefit accruing in consequence of the offence. Breach of planning control does not normally constitute a criminal offence, however, once enforcement proceedings have been taken, non-compliance with the specific notice can lead to criminal prosecution. Breaches of special controls such as those relating to listed buildings can constitute a criminal offence in themselves (where damage is intentionally carried out to a listed building, it is a criminal offence).

A planning authority may serve:

- **Planning Contravention Notice** where it appears there may have been a breach of planning control.
- **Enforcement Notice** requiring the breach to be remedied. Failure to comply may lead to prosecution.
- **Breach of Condition Notice** where there has been a failure to comply with conditions or limitations attached to a permission.
- **Stop Notice:** this makes it an offence to continue with the alleged breach until the issue has been determined. This comes into effect not less than 3, and no more than 28, days after it is issued.
- More commonly, the LPA will seek an *injunction*.
- **Temporary Stop Notice.** This gives local authorities power to take early action at the beginning of an unauthorized development. This has immediate effect. It was introduced by the Planning and Compulsory Purchase Act 2004 and will be in the Town and Country Planning (Scotland) Act.

An Enforcement Notice is served on the owner, lessee and occupier of the land to which it relates or on any other person with a material interest in the land. The notice must specify:

- The matters alleged to constitute the breach of control.
- The steps required to restore the position or to bring the land to a condition satisfactory to the planning authority.
- The date on which the notice is to take effect.

- The period(s) within which any steps are to be carried out.
- The exact boundaries of the land to which the notice relates.
- The reason for serving the notice.
- An explanation of the rights of appeal.

Immunity from enforcement action

This applies to all breaches occurring before 1965. Notices must be served within specified periods of the breach (building, engineering, mining or other operations, or change of use of a building to a single dwelling – four years; any other breach – ten years).

In 2005, the UK courts ruled that Article 8 of the European Convention on Human Rights (the right to respect for the home) is not an 'absolute' right and does not exist in a vacuum. It operates in the context of the legal and democratic structures that protect the rights of all of us. Therefore, Enforcement Notices cannot be ignored.

Grounds for appeal to the Secretary of State:

- Permission should be granted or the condition discharged.
- The matters alleged do not constitute a breach.
- The alleged breach has not taken place.
- Immunity due to timing.
- Notice served incorrectly.
- Steps required are unreasonable or time allowed is inadequate.

There is a good practice guide/circular on enforcement available from the DCLG.

Environmental Impact Assessment

Key Legislation

The following comprises the key legislation that covers Environmental Assessment:

Source Legislation

- The EC Directive 'The Assessment of the Effects of Certain Public and Private Projects on the Environment' adopted 27 June 1985.

UK Legislation

Brought the EC Directive into force in the UK through the implementation of:
- Town and Country Planning (Assessment of Environmental Effects) Regulations 1988 (England and Wales) amended 1999 to:
- The Town and Country Planning (Environmental Impact Assessment) (England and Wales) Regulations 1999.

Scotland and Northern Ireland

Due to the different legal and administrative arrangements that apply in Scotland and Northern Ireland separate provision for EIA is made under:
- The Environmental Impact Assessment (Scotland) Regulations 1999.
- The Planning (Environmental Impact Assessment) Regulations (Northern Ireland) 1999.

The Need for Environmental Impact Assessment

Government guidelines to environmental assessment procedures stress that environmental assessment is a process:

Environmental Impact Assessment: a process

'by which information about the environmental effects of a project is collected, both by the developer and from other sources, and taken into account by the planning authority in forming its judgement on whether the development should go ahead'.

The regulations require that certain types of projects, which are likely to have significant environmental effects, should not proceed until these effects have been systematically assessed. The regulations apply to two separate lists of projects. (Refer to www.opsi.gov.uk Office of Public Sector Information – formerly HMSO, under the legislation section.)

• ANNEX/SCHEDULE 1 PROJECTS •
EIA is required in every case.

• ANNEX/SCHEDULE 2 PROJECTS •
EIA is required only if the particular project in question is judged likely to give rise to *significant* environmental effects.

Significance

Significance is a key issue in environmental impact assessment. How is it assessed?

Significance?
- Is the project one of more than local importance in terms of scale?
- Is the project in a sensitive or vulnerable location, e.g. a national park or SSSI?
- Is the project unusually complex with potentially adverse environmental effects?

To help developers and planning authorities judge when a development is likely to have a significant effect on the environment, the Government has issued indicative thresholds for some Schedule 2 projects. This is based on a three-tier system of thresholds:

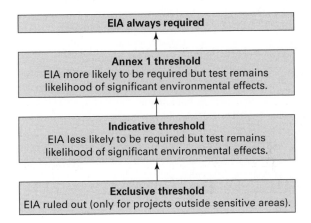

Screening

The regulations allow a procedure that enables a developer to apply to the planning authority for an opinion on whether an EIA is needed prior to applying for planning permission. For all Schedule 2 development (including that which would otherwise benefit from permitted development rights), the local planning authority (LPA) must adopt its own formal determination of whether or not EIA is required (screening opinion) before (regulation 5) or after (regulation 7) a planning application has been submitted and place it on the planning register. The local planning authority must provide a written statement as to its reasons for an EIA being required. Appeal on a decision is to the Secretary of State who must provide a written statement on their decision within three weeks.

The Environmental Statement

An environmental statement is submitted alongside the planning application for projects requiring an EIA. An environmental statement comprises a document detailing the likely impact on the environment of the proposed development in relation to the information specified in paragraph 2 (referred to as 'the specified information').

Schedule 3 of the Town and Country Planning (Assessment of Environmental Effects) Regulations 1988 specifies information that an environmental statement has to provide.

Environmental statement and the specified information

- A description of the development proposed, comprising information about the site and the design and size or scale of the development.
- The main alternatives studied and an indication of the main reasons for choosing the development proposed, taking into account the environmental effects (added by 1999 Regulations). This may now be considered at a strategic level with the new SEA Directive.
- The data necessary to identify and assess the main effects which that development is likely to have on the environment.
- A description of the likely significant effects, direct and indirect, on the environment of the development, explained by reference to its possible impact on human beings, flora, fauna, soil, water, air, climate, the landscape, the interaction between any of the foregoing, material assets, the cultural heritage.
- Where significant adverse effects are identified with respect to any of the foregoing, a description of the measures envisaged in order to avoid, reduce or remedy those effects.
- A summary in non-technical language.

An environmental statement should include, by way of explanation or amplification of any specified information, further information on any of the following matters:

- The physical characteristics of the proposed development, and the land-use requirements during the construction and operational phases.
- The main characteristics of the production processes proposed, including the nature and quality of the materials to be used.
- The estimated type and quantity of expected residues and emissions (including pollutants of water, air or soil, noise, vibration, light, heat and radiation) resulting from the proposed development when in operation.
- The likely significant direct and indirect effects on the environment of the development proposed which may result from:
  - the use of natural resources.
  - The emission of pollutants, the creation of nuisances, and the elimination of waste.
  - The forecasting methods used to assess any effects on the environment about which information is given including secondary, cumulative, short-, medium- and long-term, permanent, temporary, positive and negative effects.
  - Any difficulties, such as technical deficiencies or lack of know-how, encountered in compiling any specified information.

Scoping

Regulation 10 allows developers to obtain a formal (scoping) opinion from the relevant planning authority on what should be included in the environmental statement (ES). This ensures that the LPA (or the Secretary of State in the case of scoping directions) and the relevant consultees can consider the project and the likely impacts at an early stage and can focus the EIA process on those which are relevant. The 'specified information' (Schedule 3) covers all potential situations. It is unlikely that all the items will be relevant to any one project and this is why scoping is of particular importance.

Environmental Assessment Submission Procedure

The local planning authority receives a request from a developer for an opinion on the need for an EIA. If an EIA is necessary the developer is notified within three weeks and a reason is provided. For all Schedule 2 developments the local planning authority must determine whether or not an EIA is required and record the decision on the planning register.

EIA submission process

- The developer can request a formal scoping opinion from the local planning authority.
- Local planning authority informs statutory consultees listed in the regulations and they are required to provide any information to the developer as required.
  - principal council (if not the planning authority).
  - conservancy councils (English Nature, Scottish Natural Heritage, The Countryside Agency, Countryside Council for Wales, Environment and Heritage Service – Northern Ireland).
  - Environment Agency/SEPA/Northern Ireland environmental service for pollution (special waste or pollution).
  - Highways authority.
  - Secretary of State.
  - anybody that a planning authority would normally be required to consult as part of a planning application, e.g.: HSE – for hazardous operations; DEFRA/SDEFRA for loss of agricultural land; coal authority for mining
- Specialist team assembled and statutory and relevant consultees are consulted.
- Environmental statement is prepared and submitted alongside planning application.
- Applicant publishes notice in press, posts site notice and information on where environmental statement can be inspected for 21 days.

Environmental Assessment Decision Process

- ES placed on planning register and copies sent to Secretary of State.
- Local planning authority consults statutory consultees who have 14 days to comment.
- Local planning authority considers representations from third parties and statutory consultees and gives decision. It must not be made in less than 21 days but must be within 16 weeks.
- When determining an EIA application the LPA or Secretary of State must inform the public of their decision to grant or refuse the application and their main reasons for it. (Added by 1999 Regulations.)
- If the local planning authority is also the applicant then certain procedures do not apply, e.g. requesting opinion on the need for an EA, or the type of application (S1 or S2, etc.).
- Public notice is required to be given of any further information which the applicant or appellant is required to provide unless it is to be provided for the purpose of a local inquiry.

Implementation and Monitoring

The granting of development consent is not the end. The developer, advisors and determining authority all have a responsibility to ensure that all commitments made in the ES are honoured. Implementation is achieved through the enforcement of consent conditions and legal agreements. A financial bond is often used to ensure mitigation measures are completed.

Monitoring is the responsibility of the developer and determining authority. Enforcement action can be carried out to ensure that mitigation measures implemented are effective.

Projects that are not subject to planning control

All require an EIA under separate regulations if defined as schedule 1 and 2 projects, e.g. trunk roads and motorways, forestry, fish farming, railways, trams, inland navigation, tunnels, bridges, harbour works, electricity works, port works. EIAs are submitted to the governing agency or authority, e.g. the Forestry Authority, the Highways Agency.

Landscape Assessment

Landscape assessment forms part of the environmental impact assessment procedure. The Landscape Institute and the Institute of Environmental Management produced 'Guideline for Landscape and Visual Assessment' in 2002. (Due for revision in 2008.) The guidelines emphasize that 'landscape and visual impact assessment' forms part of the environmental impact assessment regulation requirements under Schedule 4. Methodology to carry out assessments should be agreed with the regulatory authority at the scoping stage and should be appropriate for the nature, location and scale of the project.

The guidelines set out an outline methodology that should be flexible to suit modifications required during early stages of the project.

Assessment Methodology

Baseline studies

Review existing landscape and visual resource through:

- Research and survey work.
- Classification of landscape into character types.
- Analysis of information.

Description of the proposed development

A general description of the siting, layout and characteristics of the proposed development.

Consideration of alternatives

Description of the main alternatives considered including environmental effects.

Stages in the project life cycle

A description of the development at each stage in the life cycle and the landscape and visual impacts at:

- Construction stage.
- Operational stage.
- Decommissioning and restoration stage.

Identification and assessment of landscape and visual effects

- Identify the sources of effects throughout the project life cycle.
- Identify the nature of the effects.
- Direct (as a result of the development).
- Indirect (as a result of an associated development secondary to main development)
- Cumulative.
- Identify the landscape effects in relation to:
  - the sensitivity of the landscape.
  - Scale and magnitude.
- Identify the visual effects in relation to:
  - Sensitivity of visual receptors.
  - Scale or magnitude.
- Identify the significance of landscape and visual effects.

Mitigation

Proposals to address likely negative effects on the environment arising from the development through:

- Avoidance.
- Reduction.
- Remediation.
- Compensation.
- Enhancement.

These should be considered for all stages in the project life cycle.

Consultation

Consultation with the local community and special interest groups is vital during this stage of the assessment and can be carried out through.

Strategic Environmental Impact Assessment (SEA)

Environmental Assessment of Plans and Programmes Regulations 2004 came into force in July 2004 from the EC Directive 'The assessment of the Effects of Certain Plans and Programmes on the Environment (Directive 2001/42)'; it covers England, Scotland, Wales and Northern Ireland. Detail was provided in The Environmental Assessment of Plans and Programmes Regulations 2005.

The objective of the regulations is 'to provide for a high level of protection of the environment and to contribute to the integration of environmental considerations into the preparation and adoption of plans and programmes with a view to promoting sustainable development'.

The regulations require environmental assessments to be carried out for a range of plans and programmes likely to have significant effects on the environment. It applies to plans and programmes whose formal preparation began after July 2004 and also to those already in preparation by that date. They will be adopted until July 2006.

The plans and programmes that fall within the scope of the regulations are those which:

- Are subject to preparation or adoption by an authority at national, regional or local levels; or
- Are prepared by an authority for adoption, through a legislative procedure by Parliament or Government; and, in either case,
- Are required by legislative, regulatory or administrative provisions.

This could include plans prepared for:

- Agriculture, forestry, fisheries, energy, industry, transport, waste management, water management, telecommunications, tourism, town and country planning or land use which set the framework for future development consent for projects listed in Annex I and II of the EIA Directive.
- Or those that have been determined to require an assessment under the Habitat's Directive.

A screening process is required to determine whether plans are likely to have significant environmental effects and whether an SEA is required. The regulations list criteria for determining the likely significance of effects. The SEA must be carried out during the preparation of the plan and before its adoption.

An environmental report is prepared by the authority producing the SEA and should cover:

Environmental report

- The environmental protection objectives of the plan.
- The existing state of the environment.
- The significant effects on the environment and the interrelationship between these factors.
- The mitigation measures.
- An outline of the reasons for selecting the alternatives dealt with.
- Monitoring measures and a non-technical summary.

The regulations require that the public, environmental bodies and authorities concerned by the environmental effects of implementing the plan are consulted as part of the process. Responses are taken into account and used to develop ways to mitigate the negative effects in the final preparation and adoption of the plans. Monitoring is required after adoption.

Building Acts and Regulations

The current building Acts and regulations control the construction and design of buildings. They originate from earlier Victorian and public health Acts and now they lay down the principles necessary to achieve reasonable requirements for public health and safety in and around buildings.

England and Wales

The basic framework of control is found in the Building Act 1984, and The Building Regulations 1991 (latest amendment in effect April 2006) contain the detailed rules and procedures governing building control by local authority. Each functional requirement is supported by an approved document.

Schedule 1 sets out the requirements to be met in respect of:

Part A – Structure.
Part B – Fire safety.
Part C – Site preparation and resistance to moisture.
Part D – Toxic substances.
Part E – Sound insulation
Part F – Ventilation.
Part G – Hygiene.
Part H – Drainage and waste disposal.
Part J – Combustion appliances and fuel storage systems.
Part K – Protection from falling, collision and impact (formerly Stairways, Ramps and Guards).
Part L – Conservation of fuel and power.
Part M – Disabled access to and use of all buildings.
Part N – Glazing.
Part P – Electrical safety.

The 1999 revision substitutes a new Regulation 7 which retains the obligation to carry out building works using appropriate materials and for those materials to be used in a workmanlike manner. In addition, it provides that materials used in building works must be adequately mixed or prepared to perform the functions for which they are designed.

There are two alternative means of control:

- By local authorities operating under the Building Regulations 1991 (latest amendment 2002).
- By a system of private certification which relies on 'approved inspectors' operating under the Building (Approved Inspectors) Regulations 1985 (latest amendment 2002).

Scotland

Building control in Scotland is based on a series of building Acts (Building (Scotland) Acts 1959, 1970 and most recently 2003) and bylaws. The basic purpose of building control is the protection of the public interest as regards health, safety and welfare where they are in and out of buildings, and also to further the conservation of fuels and power and further the achievement of sustainable development.

Building Standards (Scotland) Regulations 2005 were introduced in May 2006 and are based on a short statutory instrument written in functional requirement terms with statutory enforceable building technical standards, which are the relevant standards for compliance with the building standards. The standards must be considered and applied as a whole.

Northern Ireland

Under the Building Regulations (Northern Ireland) Order 1979 (amended 1990), the Northern Ireland Department of Finance and Personnel (DFPNI) is empowered to write building regulations. The current regulations are The Building Regulations (Northern Ireland) 2000; they set out technical requirements and reference particular provisions that are deemed to satisfy these requirements which take the form of technical booklets, British Standards and other specified requirements.

4 Environmental legislation

Introduction

Legislation is a revealing documentation of the state of our culture, scientific knowledge and attitude to resources at a particular time. The content of each Act of Parliament is usually the result of much lobbying and bargaining between different interest groups and the balance of political power when the law was debated in Parliament.

The previous chapter contained a summary of planning law, but landscape architects need to take cognisance of other aspects of legislation about the environment, including law covering countryside, protected environments and pollution control.

Environmental legislation now includes a great number of Acts of Parliament, statutes and regulations. The approach taken here is a selective one, giving an introduction to the law and the many conservation designations that cover different habitats and approaches to conservation in the UK. The emphasis is on themes that have been of interest to landscape architects in recent times.

The Development of Environmental Legislation

While the control of development and land use in urban areas has stemmed from concern for public health and safety, legislation for environmental matters has been based on an interest in managing scarce resources, public amenity and access to the countryside, and the conservation of certain natural habitats.

The Town and Country Planning (General Permitted Development) Order and the Environmental Assessment Regulations extended the interest of planning authorities into the countryside. For example, permitted development rights are not available for farm or forestry dwellings or livestock units sited near residential or similar buildings.

However, operations to do with the business of agriculture and forestry are still considered to be permitted development and thus are free from planning control. For example, temporary uses of land, agricultural buildings below a certain size, forestry buildings and forestry roads, caravan sites and related buildings in some circumstances do not require planning permission. In addition, much country activity, including wetland drainage, woodland clearance and afforestation is only marginally affected by conservation legislation. (See the section on environmental assessment in Chapter 3.)

In contrast, European Union legislation for the environment, society and economy has significant impact on European landscapes, for example, through the Common Agricultural Policy (CAP) and the law on biodiversity. In addition, environmental policy was strengthened by the Treaty of Amsterdam of October 1997, which established that sustainable development will be an explicit European objective and that environmental issues are to be integrated into all EU policies, e.g. transport, energy and agriculture.

Statutory control in the countryside is conveniently divided into five groups:

- Planning law.
- Management of scarce resources.
- Protection of areas for amenity, landscape quality and natural habitat.
- Access.
- Pollution control.

Planning Law

As described in Chapter 3, the Town and Country Planning Act provides a comprehensive definition of development and provision for its control throughout Britain.

Elements of planning law with particular relevance to the countryside include:

- Trees.
- Conservation areas.
- Buildings of historical or architectural interest.
- Open-cast mining sites.
- Designated or bad neighbour developments.
- Areas where permitted development rights have been withdrawn such as national parks.

In addition, this legislation provides specific control of development in the countryside through development plans, planning policy guidance and specific orders.

Development Plans

These afford protection to some agricultural land, particularly immediately around settlements. However, where development is likely on agricultural land which is not protected by such a plan, consultation must be carried out with the Ministry of Agriculture, which has a system of *grading* so that the most valuable land is readily identifiable and the loss of grades 1, 2 and 3a land is minimized.

Planning Policy Guidance

Some is particularly relevant to rural areas. For instance, PPS 7 on 'Sustainable Development in Rural Areas' gives guidance on farm diversification in keeping with a rural location. It ended the loophole that allowed construction of new houses in the countryside of exceptional architectural merit.

PPS 9 'Biodiversity and Geological Conservation' succeeds PPG 9, which dealt with habitat creation and management of landscape features important to wildlife, as well as the adaptation of derelict sites to provide extended habitats. PPS 9 makes the link between conserving biological and geological diversity and achieving planning's overall purpose of sustainable development. It also refers to ancient woodlands and veteran trees.

Guidance for farmers

DEFRA produced 'A farmer's guide to the planning system' www.defra. gov.uk/farm/planning-guide/index.htm In Scotland see 'A guide to farm diversification' at www.scotland.gov.uk/planning Wales will issue a guide in the near future.

Residential Property in Farming Areas

Planning departments normally restrict rehabilitation of derelict buildings in rural areas in order to discourage settlement that has little to do with the rural economy.

In addition, there is some control of agricultural development. For example, in 1992 a 400 m *'Cordon Sanitaire'* was introduced in agricultural permitted development in order to protect residential property fromobnoxious odours. Buildings used for intensive accommodation of livestock within 400 m of residential, hotel or office property require planning permission.

Environmental Impact Assessment (EIA)

Environmental assessment legislation becomes applicable in the countryside where Schedule 1 and Significant Schedule 2 projects are proposed.

For instance, EIA may be required for forestry particularly for conserved areas such as national nature reserves or SSSI, national parks, national scenic areas, AONB and environmentally sensitive areas. EIA may also be required in other locations where, due to the proposal's size, location or nature, there are likely to be significant effects on the environment.

Landscape character assessment

Planning authorities are beginning to use landscape character assessment as a method of identifying and describing variations in local landscape. Some, such as County Durham, have put their assessments on the Internet for public information. In addition, landscape character studies are being commissioned with the aim of assessing the impact of certain kinds of development on the countryside such as major urban expansion, reassessment of the greenbelt and the location of wind farms.

Local Designations

In addition to the national designations described above, many local authorities have undertaken landscape assessments, landscape character assessments, habitat surveys, access reviews and the like as a foundation for structure plans, local plans and inter-district habitat and amenity management strategies.

The more widely recognized local planning designations include green belts and areas of great landscape value. These are discussed below in the context of protection of areas for amenity.

When dealing with a particular area or site, a prudent landscape architect would check with the local authority, region or county for information on such designations as these may materially affect applications for development consent, provision of grants and interagency co-operation.

Management of Scarce Resources

Some natural resources in limited supply and strategic value are subject to special regulation, generally by government ministries or specialized statutory bodies. These include agricultural land, forests, water and minerals. EU policy has a significant impact on some strategic resources, particularly agriculture.

European Policy

Historically, the Common Agricultural Policy (CAP) was concerned with agriculture, especially the encouragement of food production to avoid the food shortages that followed the Second World War. These early CAP policies were effective, but also produced excesses of production and intensification of agriculture, with harmful impacts including destruction of hedgerows, walls, ditches, drainage of wetlands and increased soil erosion. Early CAP policies also encouraged people to leave farming because it was viewed as economically unviable. However it is now recognized that the varied agricultural landscapes of Europe, and the associated biodiversity stemming from centuries of agriculture, may be jeopardized if cultivation ceases. As a result of these negative impacts, a succession of European Acts, agreements and regulations has highlighted the need for an integrated approach to agriculture, the rural economy, society and the environment.

The Single European Act 1986 acknowledged the need to integrate the environment into agricultural practice. This was reinforced by the environmental undertakings in the Rio Summit in 1992. The Treaty of Amsterdam of October 1997 established that sustainable development will be an explicit European objective and that environmental issues will be integrated into all EU policies, e.g. transport, energy and agriculture. CAP reform also sought to address the distortion of world trade it was thought to have caused and the enlargement of the EU from 15 to 25 countries.

The CAP has been reformed several times, but radical change has followed the European Agenda 2000, which was agreed in 2003. A core feature was the decoupling of support from production (financial assistance no longer depends on the amount produced), which means that it is possible to limit the environmental damage caused by over-cropping and pollution from farming. Production subsidies have nearly ceased, being replaced by direct payments to farmers based on compliance with environmental, food safety, animal and plant health and animal welfare standards, keeping farmland in good condition for farming and preserving the countryside.

Funding in rural areas is intended to go beyond application of good agricultural practice and compliance with environmental law. Minimum environmental standards are now an integral and compulsory part of agri-support programmes and member states may attach specific environmental conditions to grants. These rules make it possible to reduce payments to farmers who do not make the effort to comply with European environmental legislation.

The CAP has been implemented through the Rural Development Policy (RDP). The 1999 Regulation recognized that the role of agriculture goes beyond production and includes good agricultural practice, water, chemicals, land use, genetically modified organisms (GMO), climate change, air quality, landscape biodiversity, animal welfare and forests. RDP Regulation 1257/1999 set up a transition period from 2000–2006.

The Common Agricultural Policy from 2006 will:
* Make agriculture more competitive through restructuring and means such as investment aid for young farmers, more information, etc.

- Improve the environment and countryside through support of land management by including rural development in Natura 2000 sites, agri-environment and forestry.
- Improve the quality of life in the countryside and diversify economic activity, e.g. by focussing on food quality.

The Single Farm Payment Scheme is intended to balance producers' income more effectively. Farmers can decide what to produce while still receiving income aid. Decoupling is being phased in between January 2005 and 2007.

EU financial support comes from the European Agriculture Guarantee and Guidance Fund set up in 1962 and divided into two strands in 1964. The Guarantee Fund supports agricultural incomes, e.g. by guaranteed prices. The Guidance Fund (Structural Funding) is paid to defined Objective areas.

Some schemes that were previously given in direct support of agricultural production have been assigned to fund the revised Rural Development Regulation (RDR), which comes fully into force on 1 January 2007. Each member state will have a Rural Development Plan (RDP) that specifies how the RDR will be applied. There are separate RDPs for England, Wales and Scotland. In the UK the RDR is being channelled into agri-environment schemes such as Environmental Stewardship and the Forestry Commission's revised Woodland Grant Schemes.

The RDR specifies geographical areas to which structural funds may be directed. Member states may designate up to 10 per cent of their territory as areas subject to specific handicaps in which farmers should receive support to protect the environment or retain the rural population.

Not all of the UK is in Objective areas. Objectives are mutually exclusive: an area may receive Objective 1 funding, but not Objective 2. Objective area status is time limited and defined geographically. Objective 1 funding provides high levels of funding to raise wealth creation capacity. It usually applies to areas where wealth creation per head is less than 75 per cent of the European average, e.g. the Highlands, Merseyside, South Yorkshire, Cornwall and West Wales. Objective 2 areas have been hit by industrial decline and funding aims to create a new economic base. These areas have high unemployment or unusually high employment in industrial jobs, e.g. parts of North Wales, or the Lomond area in Argyll. Some extra funds from RDR are also available for forestry and agriculture.

National strategic resources

National strategic resources

These resources are managed centrally by the government and its agencies:
- Agriculture.

- Forestry.
- Water.
- Minerals.

Agricultural Land

Agricultural land is a strategic economic resource fundamental to the UK's food supply that should be conserved and protected from urban development and other forms of permanent change.

The productive value and output of farmland is managed through several instruments including:
- EU Common Agricultural Policy.
- Agri-environment schemes.
- Set-aside regulations.
- Planning policy guidance.
- Grading of agricultural land.
- Ministerial powers to protect agricultural land.
- Weed Act 1959.

The Department of Environment, Food and Rural Affairs has various powers to protect the productive value of farmland. These powers include authority under the Agriculture Act 1947 to acquire land in order to restore it to agriculture. DEFRA also retains the power to make directions for the use of land for up to a year, in the interest of the national supply of food or agricultural products.

The fertile layer itself is also protected. Under the Agricultural Land (Removal of Surface Soil) Act 1953, unauthorized removal of agricultural topsoil for sale is a form of development treated as a crime. DEFRA has produced a draft soil strategy (2003). The EA, SEPA, SNH and the NI Environment and Heritage Service have commissioned research to consider how to conserve and enhance soils (and to consider how the planning process could help this) and to provide planning guidance.

The productive value of land is protected by controlling 'notifiable' weeds. The Weed Act 1959 contains powers to prevent the spread of spear or field thistles, curled or broad-leaved docks and Ragwort.

Extraction of minerals on farms is not in general considered to be development if the mineral is retained on the land, e.g. as fertilizer or hard core.

Agri-environment schemes

Legislation also controls production through agri-environment schemes. These are now defined by each of the nations of the UK. For instance, in England there is the over-arching 'Strategy for Sustainable Farming and

Food' which includes the England Rural Development Programme (ERDP) administered by DEFRA. Its first round was a seven-year programme from 2000–6 and included 10 schemes intended to:

- Provide opportunities for farmers and others to protect and improve the countryside.
- Develop sustainable enterprises.
- Help rural communities to thrive.

The first round ERDP schemes with conservation elements were the:
- Environmentally Sensitive Areas Scheme.
- Countryside Stewardship Scheme.
- Organic Farming Scheme.
- Farm Woodland Premium Scheme (see Forestry section below).
- Rural Enterprise.
- Vocational Training.
- The Hill Farm Allowance is an additional scheme, which is a compensatory allowance for beef and sheep farmers in English less favoured areas in recognition of the difficulties they face and the role they play in maintaining the landscape and rural communities of the uplands.

The Government published '*A new strategy for sustainable farming and food*' in 2002. This aims to set up a broadly-based agri-environment scheme that rewards management practice that goes beyond what regulation and the market demand. It is referred to as a 'whole-farm approach'. The new scheme complies with the EU Rural Development Regulation 1999. The new phase of agri-environment schemes are expected to run from 2007 to 2013. Schemes are of two types: land based and project based.

Land-based schemes provide financial incentives for land managers (particularly farmers and foresters) to adopt environmentally beneficial land management practices. These include:

- Environmental Stewardship.
- Countryside Stewardship. (The scheme closed to new applications in 2004.)
- Energy Crop Scheme.
- Environmentally Sensitive Areas Scheme. (Closed to new applications in 2004.)
- Farm Woodland Premium Scheme.
- Hill Farm Allowance.
- Organic Farming Scheme.
- Woodland Grant Scheme. (Closed to new applications in June 2004. Replaced by the new England Woodland Grant Scheme in 2005.)

Project-based schemes aim to promote imaginative and varied schemes within rural areas. They include:

- Rural Enterprise Scheme.
- Processing and Marketing Grant.
- VocationalTraining Scheme.
- Energy Crops Producer Scheme. (Closed to new applications in June 2006. Replaced by new scheme to run from 2007–13.)

The Set-aside Scheme continues as part of the revised RDP. The set-aside regulations were introduced from the EU with the initial purpose of reducing food production and eliminating surpluses. Subsequent additions have added further aims and values, namely conservation of buildings, structures, water courses and semi-natural habitats in the countryside, and the restoration of habitat diversity. Set-aside is available only for land that could grow cereals, oilseeds, proteins (beans, peas and sweet lupins), linseed, flax and hemp for fibre. Permanent pasture, permanent crops (e.g. top fruit) woodland and non-agricultural uses were not eligible for set-aside.

Environmentally Sensitive Areas Scheme (ESA) 1987–2004

ESA was introduced by the Agriculture Act 1986. The Act applied in principle throughout the United Kingdom. The ESA Scheme was unusual and interesting because of its comprehensive approach to managing rural activity while simultaneously attending to the appearance and conservation of the environment.

In England, ESA was replaced in 2005 with a new scheme intended to combine the best aspects of ESAs and the Countryside Premium Scheme. In Scotland, ESA closed to new applicants in January 2001 and the ESA Scheme was replaced by 'Rural Stewardship'. Existing ESA agreements should continue till contractual completion.

ESAs were farm areas of outstanding ecological or landscape importance that were under threat from actual or potential changes in farming practice. Designation encouraged the maintenance or adoption of agricultural methods that facilitated British agricultural policy and achieved a balance between four sets of interests, which could conflict. Namely:
- The provision and maintenance of a stable agricultural industry.
- The economic and social interest of rural areas.
- The conservation and enhancement of the natural beauty and amenity of the countryside (including its flora and fauna, geological and physiographical features) and any features of archaeological, architectural and historic interest.
- Provision for enjoyment by the public.

The designation is made by the Secretary of State for Scotland (DEFRA in England and Wales), after first consulting the conservancies and after agreement was made with those with an interest in the land.

The consequences of ESA designation were:
- A management agreement between the Secretary of State and those with interest in the land in return for payment.

The designation order might specify:
- Agricultural practices/operations to be used, usually traditional methods.
- A minimum period of an agreement.
- Provision for breach of agreement.
- Rate of payment.
- Further provisions could be added by the Secretary of State.

ESA agreements were vulnerable and sometimes abandoned when farmers learnt that they might realize greater profit by using the land for crops heavily supported by CAP than by accepting ESA payment.

The Welsh equivalent of this scheme was the Tir Gofal Scheme, which was influenced by Landscape Character Assessment through the LANDMAP system.

Countryside Stewardship (CS) 1991–2004
(Countryside Stewardship Regulations 1996–9)

CS closed to new applications and was replaced by the Environmental Stewardship Scheme in 2005, although existing agreements should complete their term. CS aimed to make conservation a fundamental part of farming practice by offering farmers, landowners, voluntary bodies and local authorities management agreements to enhance and conserve landscapes in England and Wales.

The scheme gave payments for changes in management practice that would conserve the landscape and its wildlife, improve access to the countryside and increase people's enjoyment of it.

The Countryside Stewardship Scheme sought to:
- Sustain the beauty and diversity of the countryside.
- Improve and extend existing habitats for plants and animals.
- Conserve archaeological sites and historic features.
- Create new opportunities for enjoying the countryside.
- Restore neglected land or special landscape features.
- Create new wildlife habitats and landscapes.

Priority was given to land already with landscape, wildlife or historical interest and where conservation and recreation could be combined. The priority landscapes were: chalk and limestone grassland, waterside land, historic landscapes, lowland heath, uplands, hedgerow restoration, the coast, old orchards, old meadows and pasture in the Culm grassland and Hereford and Worcester, community forests, local target areas and traditional boundaries (e.g. banks, ditches).

The CS agreement incorporated:
- Management measures (e.g. managing hay meadows or grazed pastures; recreating heath).
- Capital items (e.g. hedge-laying, pond creation, bracken control).
- Special additional works (e.g. controlling docks and thistles).
- Public and educational access.

The scheme was open to anyone who managed suitable land and who was able to enter a 10-year agreement.

Public access was not essential but was an important way for people to enjoy the benefits created by the scheme. Land near towns and villages, or with existing access, may have had priority. There were payments for creating new footpaths, rides or opening up an area, and for improving opportunities for disabled people to enjoy the countryside or for schools to visit.

CS was not normally available in Environmentally Sensitive Areas, Nitrate Sensitive Areas, set-aside land or land covered by the Premium Grass Scheme agreement unless over and above that required by DEFRA.

Initially the scheme was run by the Countryside Commission (now the Countryside Agency), working with English Nature, English Heritage and the Ministry of Agriculture. It transferred to MAFF, now DEFRA, on 1st April 1996.

Rural Stewardship Scheme (RSS) (2005 to date)

In Scotland, the ESA Scheme and the Countryside Premium Scheme were replaced by the Rural Stewardship Scheme (RSS). This makes little mention of landscape character issues. RSS is designed to encourage farmers, crofters and Common Grazings Committees to adopt environmentally friendly practices and to maintain and enhance particular habitats and landscape features. Aid such as the RSS is mandatory under the EU's Rural Development Regulation.

The Rural Stewardship Scheme is expected to:
- Deliver demonstrable benefits to the environment and biodiversity.
- Contribute to farm income.

- Provide employment opportunities for contractors.
- Support the retention or development of rural skills such as dyking or hedge management.

Participants must agree to manage specified areas of land and undertake capital works in accordance with the requirements of agreed options and follow certain General Environmental Conditions and the Standard of Good Farming Practice over all the land.

Scotland also has the Organic Aid Scheme (from 1 May 2004) designed to help conversion to organic farming. Part of the scheme includes grants for building or restoring dry stone dykes or walls and support to hedges.

Environmental Stewardship Scheme 2005 to date

This came into force in England in March 2005. Farmers may receive subsidies for management of the countryside, such as maintaining hedgerows, conserving historic farm buildings and caring for medieval settlements. It is supported by English Heritage, but has been criticized for being a way of continuing to pay farmers in a way that is acceptable to the public and to the World Trade Organization.

Primary objectives of Environmental Stewardship are:

- Conserve wildlife (biodiversity).
- Maintain and enhance landscape quality and character.
- Protect the historic environment and natural resources.
- Promote public access and understanding of the countryside.

Secondary objectives:

- Genetic conservation.
- Flood management.

Three elements of Environmental Stewardship:

- Entry Level Stewardship (ELS) is a 'whole farm' scheme available to all farmers and land managers in England who farm their land conventionally. It is aimed at delivering simple environmental management (i.e. prevent diffuse pollution, loss of biodiversity, damage to the historic environment and loss of landscape character. The last aspect is closely tied to Landscape Character Assessment carried out by the Countryside Agency).
- Organic Entry Level Stewardship is a 'whole farm' scheme open to farmers who are not receiving aid under the Organic Aid Scheme or Organic Farming Scheme.

- Higher Level Stewardship 'aims to deliver significant environmental benefits in high priority situations and areas'. It is intended to bring together the best elements of the current Environmentally Sensitive Areas and Countryside Stewardship Schemes (i.e. wildlife conservation, protection of the historic environment, maintenance and enhancement of landscape character and quality, improving public access, and resource protection; with flood management and genetic conservation as secondary objectives).

Forestry

The Forestry Acts 1919, 1967, 1979, 1986, 1991.

The Forestry Commission and its duties

The Forestry Commission was founded under the Forestry Act 1919 as the Government's authority on forestry. Since the 1991 Forestry Act it has carried out most of its activity through the Forestry Authority and Forestry Enterprise. The Commission owns large tracts of forest itself, but also operates extensively through agreements with private landowners.

The Forestry Commission is required by the Forestry Act 1919 to:
- Promote the interests of forestry.
- Develop afforestation.
- Oversee production and supply of timber and other forest products in England, Scotland and Wales.
- Promote, establish and maintain adequate reserves of growing trees.
- Control timber pests and diseases.
- The Wildlife and Countryside (Amendment) Act 1985 required the Forestry Commission to endeavour to achieve a reasonable balance between (a) the development of afforestation, the management of forests and the production and supply of timber and, (b) the conservation and enhancement of natural beauty and the conservation of flora, fauna and geological or geophysiographical features of special interest.

It is difficult to measure forest cover accurately, but it is estimated that tree cover in Britain has increased from 5 per cent in 1919 to 11.3 per cent in 2000 and about 12 per cent in 2003.

Forest production is managed through controls on felling, allocation of grants, forest plans, Indicative Forest Strategies and Community Forests.

The UK Forestry Standard

Published in 1998, this sets out the Government's framework for the practice of sustainable forestry management. Compliance with the standard is necessary for receipt of grant aid, environmental impact assessment and felling licences.

The Forestry Standard includes six standards:

- General forestry practice.
- Creating new woodland.
- Creating new native woodland.
- Felling and restocking planted woodland.
- Managing semi-natural woodland.
- Planting and managing small woods.

The standard also builds on the Helsinki Guidelines (1993) and Pan-European Criteria (PEC) (1994) on environment, sustainability, biodiversity, productivity and socio-economic functions and conditions.

Implementation of the UK Forestry Standard

The standard is implemented through several mechanisms including:

- Woodland Grant Scheme.
- Forest design plans.
- Forest plans
- Felling licences.
- Environmental impact assessment.

Woodland Grant Scheme (WGS)

The WGS was introduced in April 1988 as a successor to the Forestry Grant Scheme and the Broad-leaved Woodland Grant Scheme. This has been replaced by individual grant schemes in England, Wales and Scotland. Applications to the WGS closed in Scotland in 2003 and opened for the Scottish Forestry Grant Scheme (SFGS) on 16 June 2003. A new grant system for Wales was published in 2005.

Generally, Woodland Grant Schemes aim to:

- Encourage the creation of new forests and woodlands, to increase the production of wood, enhance the landscape, provide new wildlife habitats and offer opportunities for sport and recreation.
- Encourage appropriate management.
- Provide jobs and increase the economic potential of rural areas.
- Provide a use for land as an alternative agriculture.

Since 1998, owners have been encouraged to produce 20-year plans for management, harvesting, replanting and public access, in return for greater flexibility and faster approval of applications.

English Woodland Grant Scheme (2005 to date)

This scheme includes six different grants, which may be applied differently according to regional targets:

- Woodland Planning Grant: to prepare plans to help with managing woodland and to meet the UK Woodland Assurance Scheme.
- Woodland Assessment Grant: gathering information to improve management options.
- Woodland Regeneration Grant: changing the composition of woodland through natural regeneration and restocking after felling.
- Woodland Improvement Grant: to create, enhance and sustain public benefits under three headings: Woodland Biodiversity Action Plan; Woodland SSSI condition improvement; Access. There are also grants for East of England Forest Schools and in the West Midlands to encourage people to use woodlands to improve their health.
- Woodland Management Grant: assisting with the additional costs of providing and sustaining higher quality public benefits.
- Woodland Creation Grant: to encourage creation of new woodlands where they deliver greatest public benefit. Farm Woodland payments from DEFRA are also available to compensate for agricultural income foregone.
- Woodland Harvesting Processing and Marketing: to help improve the competitiveness of forestry businesses. This is being piloted in South-East England, Yorkshire and the Humber and North-East England.

Scottish Forestry Grant Scheme (2003 to date, to be revised in 2007)

Grants are available for:

- Expansion: for creating new woodlands. Farm premium annual payments are available from SEERAD for planting trees on land that has been in agricultural use during the past three years.
- Restocking: for replacing woodlands.
- Stewardship grants for activities to improve the value of existing woodlands.
- Location premium: encouraging woodland planting in Central Scotland, Ayrshire, Grampian and the Northern Isles.
- Challenge funds: available by bidding for money for certain forestry operations.
- Short rotation coppice: to establish willow or poplar.

Grant rates are 90 per cent for all native woodlands and for improving woodland biodiversity (with effect from February 2005). See www.forestry.gov.uk/scotland for further details.

Wales: 'Better Woodland for Wales'

A WGS for Wales is expected to be introduced during 2006. However, the Farmland Premium Scheme continues through the Department for Environmental Planning and Countryside (DEPC) in Wales.

The aim of the new scheme will be to emphasize good woodland management. Management is emphasized because the timber industry is increasingly looking to buy timber from woods that have been certified as being sustainably managed. In order to secure certification, owners and their plans must comply with the minimum standards of the UK Woodland Assurance Scheme (see the section after Environmental Impact Assessment, below).

'Better Woodland for Wales'

Applicants are given access to professional help from woodland managers and must meet the following conditions:

- They must comply with legal requirements such as health and safety, maintaining public rights of way and action against fly-tipping and dumping.
- They must produce a management plan for the next five years with a view to the next 20.
- Woodland design must adhere to the UK Forestry Standard including restructuring even-aged woods to diversify age and species, low impact management systems, protecting important habitats.
- Operations should minimize environmental impact and protect special ecological or archaeological features.
- Include strategies for protection and maintenance – including from natural pests and disasters and browsing animals including deer.
- Must conserve and enhance biodiversity including retaining and enhancing any ancient woodland.
- Identify and consult stakeholders in the community, if necessary.
- Maintain existing public access.

Forest Design Plans (FDP)

A mechanism used by Forest Enterprise, a Forest Design Plan (FDP) is a long-term outline design plan covering at least 20 years. The first few years of planting, felling, regeneration and environmental management plans are set out in detail.

Forest Plans

Forest plans have been required since 2000 to enable owners to obtain Forestry Commission approval for felling and replanting grants for a 10-year period on private estates in England, Scotland and Wales. The Forestry Commission will not pay grants in the absence of an approved plan and any felling would be subject to the licensing procedure.

Felling licences

Since the 1967 Forestry Act, a licence from the Forestry Commission has been required to fell growing trees, but there are many exemptions for tree maintenance, small-scale cropping, health, safety, nuisance and work to trees in gardens and urban areas.

When the Forestry Commission officers assess an application for a felling licence, they will inspect the trees and also consult with the local authority and any other relevant statutory authority such as English Nature/Natural England, Scottish Natural Heritage, Red Deer Commission, Civil Aviation Authority, Historic Scotland and the Countryside Agency. In addition, special permission from the local planning authority is required for felling in conservation areas and of trees covered by a TPO. Permission is required from the nature conservancies (SNH, EN, CCW and ES (NI)) in Sites of Special Scientific Interest.

In the interests of good forestry or the amenities of the district, the Forestry Commission may impose replanting conditions on the issue of a licence.

There are penalties for felling without a licence and replanting may be required.

Felling licences are not required in Northern Ireland, but the environmental impact assessment regulations are applicable.

Environmental Impact Assessment

Control of forestry is also exerted by the Environmental Assessment (Afforestation) Regulations 1988. Any new planting proposals which are likely to have significant effects on the environment and which may lead to adverse ecological change due to their size, nature and location will require an environmental assessment by the Forestry Commission.

Proposals definitely requiring an environmental assessment include:

- Any new planting in a national nature reserve or SSSI where such an operation will be listed as damaging.
- Other nationally important areas, i.e. national parks, national scenic areas and AONBs.
- Areas over 100 hectares.
- Other locations where, due to the proposal's size, location or nature there are likely to be significant effects on the environment.

UK Woodland Assurance Scheme

This scheme was published in 2000 and is supported by the Forestry Commission, Forest Stewardship Council, Timber Growers Association and World Wildlife Fund for Nature. It is designed to demonstrate the high quality and managed impact of forestry management. Certification means that woods are well managed and provide benefits for the present generation while protecting the environment and maintaining benefits for future generations. A management plan with detailed maps is essential for certification. Woodland managers have to be able to demonstrate sound management of chemicals, health and safety, access and active monitoring in order to be able to report on status in relation to objectives.

Ancient and veteran trees

The conservation agencies maintain registers of ancient and semi-natural woodlands. Ancient woodland is woodland that has been in continuous existence since 1600 in England and Wales and since 1750 in Scotland.

There is no automatic statutory protection for ancient woodland, but development affecting semi-natural woodlands should be notified to the Forestry Commission. The PPG9 on nature conservation supports the retention of ancient woodland, which is protected by the need for a licence from the Forestry Commission to fell more than two trees.

Trees on land listed in the registers of designed and historic landscapes may have greater protection as listing on the registers is a 'material consideration' in planning applications. Trees may also be protected indirectly if they are the habitat for protected species.

Veteran trees – individual trees of great age and value – have no statutory protection unless they are the subject of a TPO, but they are now mentioned in the new PPS9.

Dedication Schemes

Dedication schemes were closed to new application in 1981. Owners of existing dedicated estates may continue to put forward plans of operations for Forestry Commission approval.

National Schemes
Scottish Forestry Strategy

This includes priorities to create opportunities for public enjoyment and community benefit from woodlands and trees. This is supported by the Woodland In and Around Towns (WIAT) Scheme with £3.5 m in 2004–8 for urban fringe woodland and £4 m in 2004–8 for forestry grants for new woods in the central Scotland forest area between Glasgow and Edinburgh. The strategy has been revised and a new scheme is expected to be implemented in 2006.

The Scottish Forestry Strategy aims to:

- Maximize the value to the economy of the wood resource through the next 20 years.
- Create a divers resource of high quality for the twenty-first century and beyond.

- Ensure trees and woodland make a positive contribution to the environment.
- Create opportunities for enjoyment.
- Help communities to benefit from woods.

Indicative Forestry Strategies (IFS) (Scotland)

Regional councils in Scotland are encouraged to prepare indicative forestry strategies, which should be incorporated into structure plans. An IFS is intended to represent a broad assessment at regional level and an outline basis of the opportunities for new planting, taking account of environmental and other factors. The basic aim of IFS is to encourage the expansion of forestry (33 000 hectares of new planting a year required by the Government) in an environmentally acceptable way. The Highland regional council produced an IFS in 1993.

These indicative forestry strategies should identify:

- *Preferred areas* for new planting.
- *Potential areas* where planting may be acceptable subject to resolution of particular issues.
- *Sensitive areas* where there is a concentration of sensitive issues. A successful strategy will ease the pressure on sensitive areas.

National Forest (England)

Conceived as part of a Government strategy to develop a 'multi-purpose countryside' and initiated in 1990 by the Countryside Agency, the National Forest has been run by a private company (the Forestry Company) since 1995. The National Forest is located between Burton-upon-Trent, Tamworth and Leicester and is about 40 km east to west and 10 km north to south. All bids for funding have to comply with the Forestry Authority's Woodland Grant Scheme. Take up by farmers has been low, but all together, by 1995, 230 ha. had been planted. Participation by landowners is voluntary.

Community Forests (England 1988)

The Forestry Commission and the Countryside Agency have provided funding and guidance for the creation of 12 community forests on the outskirts of major cities in England. The aim is to include woodland, farmland, heathland, meadows and lakes with facilities for nature study and outdoor leisure and recreation.

Some of the other Woodland and Tree Organizations

Tree Council

The Tree Council is a registered charity formed in 1974 to help counter-act the problem of diminishing tree cover in the UK. It promotes the improvement of the environment by the planting and conservation of trees and woods in town and country and provides grants for tree planting.

> **The aims of the Tree Council are:**
> - To make trees matter to everyone.
> - More trees of the right type in the right place.
> - Better care for all trees of all ages.
> - Inspiring effective action for trees.

The Tree Council's main campaign is National Tree Week held annually in late November and early December, but it also organizes 'A walk in the woods' in Spring, seed gathering in late September/early October, and TLC for young trees, i.e. tending, loosening tree ties and clearing grass and weeds. The Tree Council runs the Tree Warden Scheme and gives grants to schools and communities. (See www.treecouncil.org.uk)

Countryside Around Town (CAT) (Scotland)
The board of directors includes SNH, local authorities and Scottish Enterprise. CAT undertakes planting in countryside areas.

International Tree Foundation (ITF) (Formerly Men of the Trees)
A charity founded in 1924 by Dr Richard St Barbe Baker. The organization campaigns to maintain tree cover around the world and prevent the formation of dust bowls and desertification. The ITF plants trees, educates children and campaigns to protect ancient, significant and vulnerable trees and forests throughout the world. (See www.international treefoundation.org)

The Arboricultural Association
The main aim of the Arboricultural Association is to advance the science of arboriculture for public benefit. It organizes conferences and seminars and produces publications including an annual directory of approved contractors and registered consultants. (See www.trees.org.uk)

The Woodland Trust
A conservation charity dedicated to preserving native woodlands. It campaigns to protect ancient woodlands, improve woodland biodiversity, increase native woodland cover, and increase understanding and enjoyment of woodlands. (See www.woodland-trust.org.uk)

Water

Responsibility for Water Resources
Overall responsibility for water policy, regulatory systems, conservation, quality and supply of water, sewage, inland navigation, reservoir safety and amenity rests with the Department for Environment, Food and Rural Affairs (DEFRA) in England and Wales and the Scottish Executive in

Scotland. DEFRA is also responsible for drainage, fisheries and marine waters. It works closely with the Environment Agency, which manages water resources and enforces water quality standards, and the Office of Water Services, which is responsible for the economic regulation of the water industry.

Three main aims of controlling water:

- Fair distribution of limited resources, i.e. supply.
- Preservation of water purity.
- Flood prevention or other harm from accumulation or poor drainage.

Water management is also concerned with:

- Control of pollution.
- Conservation and recreation.

In England and Wales the Environment Agency (EA) has independent jurisdiction over all water companies in England and Wales. It has responsibilities for pollution prevention, water quality, flood defences, licences to abstract water and discharge effluent, fishing regulation, conservation of aquatic wildlife, water recreation, navigation channels, information about rivers, coastal waters and groundwaters.

The Scottish Environmental Protection Agency (SEPA) has some of the same functions, but with a remit concentrating on pollution control rather than overall water resources management. SEPA has taken over the role of the former River Purification Boards.

In Northern Ireland, the Water Executive is responsible for public water supply and sewerage. From 1st April 1997 it became a non-statutory authority.

The organizations above must execute their functions in such a way that furthers conservation and enhancement of natural beauty and the conservation of flora, fauna and geological or physiographical features of interest.

The 1973 Water Act created nine regional water authorities in England, the National Water Development Authority in Wales, and water and sewerage services as a regional function in Scotland. In the 1980s the English Water Authorities became private companies. On the 1 April 1996 the regional water services in Scotland were reorganized into three 'public' boards with limited public accountability. The boards were recombined in April 2002 into Scottish Water, which is answerable to the Scottish Executive but operates as a private company.

Water companies have an express duty to take steps to secure the use of water and land associated with water for recreation (Water Act 1973). They also have legal duties under the Water Resources Act 1991 for conservation, access and recreation together with a code of practice for conservation, measurement of environmental impact and consultation on wildlife.

English Nature, SNH and the Countryside Council for Wales have a duty to notify a water authority where it is of the opinion that the authority's operation may harm any features of special interest.

Abstraction of more than 1000 gallons in any one or a series of operations is restricted by the Water Resources Act 1963 to those with a licence and certain other users. Land drainage and risk of flooding is addressed by the Land Drainage Act 1976. Water company drainage authorities have the power to maintain existing water courses and drainage channels.

EU Water Framework Directive 2000 (WFD)
This is designed to tackle both qualitative and quantitative aspects of water management in order to protect the aquatic environment and bring it to good ecological status by 2015. If this is not possible or desirable, then modified status may be agreed. No deterioration in water quality in any water body should occur. The WFD covers all groundwaters and surface waters, defined as rivers, canals, lakes, reservoirs, estuaries and coastal waters up to one mile from the shore of the community.

Integrated water management plans will be required for each river basin, which would incorporate assessment of current status, monitoring, assessments of water needs and costs, setting objectives and public participation. These River Basin Management Plans (first round) have to be published by 2009. The new Directive supplements and relates to earlier water Directives on surface water and sampling methods, fish, shellfish and groundwater.

Strategic planning guidance for the River Thames
Regional Planning Policy Guidance (RPPG) 3B/9B
This extends from Windsor to the sea. Implementation has involved landscape architects in extensive public consultation and identification of land use options.

The sea
The sea is a strategic resource for the UK for food, employment, recreation, extraction of materials such as sand and gravel, for trade and defence. Using the sea in these different ways has direct and indirect impact on the use of the coast and the occurrence of buildings and other structures.

Use of the sea also has an impact on the maritime habitat and the flora and fauna that depend on it. The Marine Health Check 2005 undertaken by the WWF – UK indicated that serious harm has taken place to UK seas in the five years since the last check. The deterioration has been blamed on inadequate planning and poor management by authorities.

DEFRA has proposed a Marine Bill which will recommend designation of a network of nationally important marine sites to ensure careful planning of marine resources. A pilot project for spatial planning of the Irish

Sea is being carried out. (See www.PlanningResource.co.uk for further details.)

Minerals

Gold, silver, petroleum and natural gas are all Crown property. They may be abstracted under licence.

Other minerals run with land ownership rights and may be extracted with planning permission.

Landscape architects should be aware of the land restoration provisions in various Acts of Parliament.

- Generally: Town and Country Planning (Minerals) Act 1981 and amendments.
- Planning and Compensation Act 1991.
- Coal: Coal Mining Subsidence Act 1957.
- Salt extraction: the Brine Pumping (Compensation for Subsidence) Act 1981.
- Ironstone operators in Northamptonshire and neighbouring counties: the Mineral Working Act 1951 and 1971.

Guidance for landscape and restoration is given in Mineral Planning Guidelines. A new guide on 'Reducing the effects of surface mineral workings on the water environment' has been published by DETR.

Protection of Areas for Amenity, Landscape Quality and Natural Habitat

From 1938 a series of Acts have enabled the identification and protection of certain sites for amenity, landscape quality and natural habitat. Increasingly, human cultural landscape history has also been recognized as worth conserving.

The source legislation and the main features of over 20 designations are described briefly below. See the summary table.

Designations for amenity and landscape

These are characterized by stronger planning controls and some support for site enhancement.

- Green belts.
- Areas of great landscape value (AGLV).
- Country parks.
- Urban parks and green spaces.

- National parks.
- Areas of outstanding natural beauty (AONB).
- National scenic areas (NSA).
- Hedgerows.

Designations for species and special habitats

These have been established mainly to prevent destruction of species and habitats rather than for active management.
- UK protection of species.
- Badgers and their setts.
- Bats and their roosts.
- Limestone pavements.

Designations about active management for conservation

These have been established to achieve a range, usually a combination, of aims.
- UK Biodiversity Action Plan (UKBAP).
- Sites of Special Scientific Interest (SSSI). (ASSI in Northern Ireland).
- Nature reserves.
- Marine reserves.
- The Habitats Directive 'Natura 2000' (and Special Areas of Conservation (SAC) and Special Protection Areas (SPA).
- Ramsar sites – wetlands.
- World Heritage sites.

Designations for amenity and landscape

Green belt

Green Belt (London and Home Counties) Act 1938; Town and Country Planning Acts (for places throughout the UK outside London).

Green belts are designated areas immediately around urban areas, created to:
- Protect the amenity of towns.
- Check the unrestricted sprawl of built-up areas and safeguard the surrounding countryside against further encroachment.
- Prevent towns merging into one another.
- Preserve the special character of towns.

The first green belt was established to protect the amenity of London, to check the unrestricted sprawl of built-up areas and to safeguard the surrounding countryside against further encroachment. The 1938 Act was used as the prototype to encourage establishment of other green belts as described in Circular 42/55. All other green belts are designated under the Town and Country Planning legislation, supported by planning policy guidance.

Green belts are intended to prevent towns merging into one another or to preserve the special character of towns. It is recommended that green belts should be several miles wide and sacrosanct from new buildings and alterations of buildings unless for sport, agriculture, cemeteries or institutions standing in extensive grounds.

Development within green belts should:

- Safeguard the countryside.
- Assist urban regeneration.
- Maintain the essential characteristics of green belts.
- Constitute a special circumstance.
- Lend itself to a rural environment.
- Maintain the visual amenity of the area.

In England, PPG2 Greenbelts (1995) is still in force. In Scotland, new government guidance on green belts was published in 2005 in the draft SPP 21. It sets out the main objectives of greenbelt policy as:

- To direct planned growth to the most appropriate locations and support regeneration.
- To protect and enhance the character, landscape setting and identity of towns and cities.
- To protect and give access to open space within and around towns and cities as part of the wider structure of green space.

Areas of Great Landscape Value

Town and Country Planning Act 1947 and subsequent consolidating Town and Country Planning Acts for England, Wales and Scotland.

An area of great landscape value (AGLV) is designated as land of particularly high landscape quality, therefore any development that is permitted should be designed to such a standard that it would not be detrimental to the landscape quality of that area.

AGLV status may afford slightly more protection to countryside areas than green belt designation, but local planning officers have a good deal of discretion about how that protection may be defined in the local plan. In a green belt it is permissible to build a house on agricultural land. In AGLVs permitted development and reserved matters may be more strictly controlled. The AGLV 'rules' should comply with planning policy guidance on housing in the countryside.

Country Parks

The concept of country parks was established in the Countryside Act 1968 (England and Wales) and extended to Scotland in the Countryside (Scotland) Act 1981.

Country parks were created by local authorities on their own or private land as pleasure grounds especially near conurbations. Councils may acquire land compulsory for this purpose and provide public amenities on these and common lands. The authorities have special powers to encourage water recreation.

The country parks website at www.countryparks.org.uk is funded by the Countryside Agency and managed by the Civic Trust's Country Park Network (CPN) which aims to help develop, promote and manage country parks. Country parks have few resources for maintenance or development, but in England and Wales the CPN provides guidance on good practice.

Urban parks and green spaces

Private parks have existed in Britain in some form since the eleventh century, but public parks, i.e. parks that are fully and freely open to the public, date from 1833 with the foundation by Preston Council of Moor Park. Formation of several famous parks followed including Derby Arboretum (1840), Victoria Park, London (1845) and Birkenhead (1847). However, the number of public parks increased rapidly after the Public Health Act 1875, which was the first major Act that enabled local authorities to acquire and maintain land for recreation and raise government loans to do so.

The population of England and Wales doubled between 1851 and 1911 (18 to 36 million) and the proportion of town dwellers shifted from 50 to 80 per cent in the same period. As towns were expanding rapidly, it became clear that there was a need to acquire land for parks on their outskirts. The Town Planning Act 1909 provided a formal mechanism for planning for open space in new housing areas. The need to preserve the open countryside was also recognized, leading to the foundation of the National Trust for Historic Sites and Natural Scenery in 1895. Formation of parks continued into the 1920s but after the Second World War, priority shifted to slum clearance, urban renewal and zoning. However, the new towns of the 1950s and 1960s also featured open spaces for recreation, parks and green ways.

Public parks started to decline after the Bains Report 1972, which recommended merging parks and leisure departments. Parks departments lost their identity and had to compete for resources. Also, the Government made no allowance for the upkeep of parks in allocations to local authorities. In 1968, legislation allowing designation of country parks took attention away from existing parks and in 1988, the Local Government

Act introduced compulsory competitive tendering, which led to acute pressure on budgets, the disappearance of park keepers and on-site horticultural expertise. As a result of these factors, many parks have had insufficient maintenance and repair, and activities and features have been removed.

In recent years, attention has started to be given to public parks and green spaces, partly as a result of their evident decline in many areas of the UK and the social problems associated with some of them. Research by the Urban Task Force set up in the 1990s and feedback from public performance reporting indicated that the public was concerned at the poor condition of parks in urban areas. This has led to recommendations for a systematic planned approach to the provision of parks and green spaces in each area.

Ideas and principles have been published recently in PPG17 and its companion guide, PAN65 in Scotland and Planning Policy Statement 8 in Northern Ireland. These guides recommend that local authorities carry out open space assessments as a base for strategies that link planning with management. Open space should be shown to be surplus to all possible uses not just its current use before it may be sold. Planning obligations may be used to enhance open spaces. Commercial and industrial developments may include open spaces for visitors, enabling investment in tourist areas.

At an Urban Summit in October 2002 the Government announced the creation of the Commission for Architecture and the Built Environment (CABE). CABE works with the Institute of Leisure and Amenity Management (ILAM) and GreenSpace (until 2003 called the Urban Parks Forum (UPF)) to develop skills training, disseminate good practice and advise local authorities in England about the improvement and upkeep of parks and green spaces. (See www.cabe.org.uk)

In 2003 the UPF was relaunched as 'GreenSpace' in order to extend its remit to all open spaces in urban areas. GreenSpace works with Groundwork UK to administer the Living Spaces Scheme (£30 m) aimed at encouraging people to become involved in practical projects to improve their local environment. CABE Space was also set up in 2003 as a unit of CABE to help local authorities develop green space strategies, carry out research, promote training and raise the profile of green spaces. Its steering group includes representatives from Groundwork, GreenSpace, the Landscape Institute, the Institute of Leisure and Amenity Management and the Development Agency.

The National Playing Fields Association (established in 1925) 'aims to ensure that everyone has access to quality recreation space close to where they live' and also campaigns against development of open space that would harm outdoor physical sport and recreation. Together with Sport England, it has produced a guide to community groups and local authorities about how they may use charity law to protect land (www.npfa.co.uk). Guidance on long-term recreational land protection is available at www.sportengland.org.uk.

National Parks

National Parks and Access to the Countryside Act 1949, the Environment Act 1995 and the National Parks (Scotland) Act 2000 (www.nationalparks. gov.uk).

From 1949 to 2000 national parks' legislation applied only to England and Wales. Ten parks were designated; all remain largely in many private hands. The Cairngorms and the Loch Lomond area are the first two national parks in Scotland.

National parks are extensive tracts of country designated for their natural beauty and the opportunities they afford for open-air recreation in regard both to their character and their position in relation to centres of population.

In 1949 the aims of management were to:
- Preserve and enhance the natural beauty of the parks.
- Encourage the provision and improvement of facilities within the parks.

In 1995 these aims were significantly extended to include:
- Conservation and enhancement of the natural beauty, wildlife and cultural heritage of the Parks.
- Promotion of opportunities for the understanding and enjoyment of the special qualities of those areas by the public.

In 2006, the national parks website stated that conservation has priority if these aims conflict.

What's in a name?

The governing organization for National Parks in England has had several names:

1949-1968	National Parks Commission.
1968-1990	Countryside Commission.
1990-2007	The Countryside Agency.
2007 to date	Natural England.

Powers of the Countryside Agency/Natural England in National Parks

- Action on any proposals for enhancement, preservation or promotion.
- Encouragement of the provision and improvement of facilities for accommodation, refreshments, camping sites and parking places.
- It may erect buildings and carry out such work as may appear to be necessary and expedient (only where existing facilities are inadequate or unsatisfactory).

In addition, there are:
- Strict planning controls on development
- Access arrangements
- A management plan
- By-laws
- Special protection of moor and heath e.g. from ploughing.
- Grants and loans.

In Scotland, the National Parks have four aims, listed below, the first two of which are similar to the aims in the 1949/1995 legislation. The third and fourth aims however, are new. It is accepted that the four aims may conflict from time to time, but in that case the 'Sandford Principle' would apply, that is the aim of conservation would prevail.

Aims of the national parks in Scotland:

- To conserve and enhance the natural and cultural heritage of the area.
- To promote understanding and enjoyment (including enjoyment in the form of recreation) of the special qualities of the area by the public.
- To promote sustainable use of the natural resources of the area.
- To promote sustainable economic and social development of the area's communities.

The Scottish national parks (Loch Lomond and the Trossachs designated in 2002, and the Cairngorms designated in 2003) are also governed by national parks authorities. The Loch Lomond and the Trossachs authority has full planning powers, but in the Cairngorms these powers are split between the national park authority and four local councils.

Areas of Outstanding Natural Beauty (AONB)
The concept was established in the National Parks and Access to the Countryside Act 1949 and applies to England and Wales.

AONB refers to any area in England and Wales which is not a national park, but which appears to the Countryside Agency to be of such outstanding natural beauty that it is desirable that the provisions of the Act should also apply. AONBs have valuable and distinct landscapes, but unlike national parks, extensive outdoor recreation may not be appropriate.

These areas are protected:

- Like national parks by restrictions on development that would normally be permitted under the General Development Order.

- By the requirement that the County council (or equivalent) must be consulted in the formation of development plans.
- Management agreements are encouraged to control farming methods.
- The local authority may make by-laws for its own land in an AONB and appoint wardens.

AONBs are not managed by completely independent organizations like national parks authorities, but usually have a Joint Action Committee (JAC) or similar. The composition of a JAC depends on the organizations relevant to the area, but will include local authorities with land in the AONB, one of which will provide the core administration. JACs tend also to include some of the following organizations depending on circumstances: Countryside Agency, Cadw, the Rural Development Service of DEFRA, the Forestry Commission, parish councils, the Country Land and Business Association, English Nature, English Heritage, the National Farmers Union, local water companies and the Ramblers Association.

Unlike in a national park, a JAC is not a planning authority, but may advise the local planning authorities with jurisdiction in the AONB. In turn the local planning authorities are heavily involved in achieving the purposes of AONB designation. They deal with planning issues and all local authority functions including public rights of way, countryside services, tourism, and public services. This responsibility was reinforced in section 8.4 of the CROW Act 2000 by which they are empowered to 'take all such action as appears to them expedient for the accomplishment of the purpose of conserving and enhancing the natural beauty of the AONB'.

The CROW Act 2000 made it a statutory requirement that AONBs have a management plan by 2004 to be reviewed every five years. These documents vary a good deal in their approach, partly because they reflect the different AONB histories and complex relationships of organizations within the JACs. For instance the Wye valley AONB management plan involved four local authorities, the Countryside Agency, the Countryside Council for Wales and English Nature. The plan runs from 2004–9 and has received national recognition for four aspects, namely: its comprehensive public consultation process inclusion of a State of the AONB Report; a listing of the special qualities of the area; and robust policies and targets. The State of AONB Report recorded the condition of the AONB in 2004 and was intended to provide a baseline against which changes in the condition of the AONB may be measured in the future. In contrast, the Howardian Hills AONB plan and the Mendip Hills plan involved 11 and 14 organizations respectively. Their plans seem to reflect, differently, the complexity of the discussions, values and priorities that must lie behind the finished plans.

The main aim of AONB designation is conservation of natural beauty, but management plans tend to add the need to integrate this with sustainability and socio-economic goals.

There are 35 AONBs in England, four in Wales and one straddles the England – Wales border; there are nine in Northern Ireland with a possible two further AONBs being considered. AONBs are funded by their local authorities and by grants from the Countryside Agency Natural England and the Countryside Council for Wales. They may have a small permanent staff.

AONBs have websites, which vary in content, style and quality, but some are very interesting and informative. See for example: www. mendiphillsaonb.org.uk, www.howardianhills.org.uk, www.wyeval-leyaonb.org.uk, and www.actions.aonb.org.uk

National Scenic Areas (NSA) (formerly National Heritage Areas)

NSAs (and AGLVs) became formally recognized by a circular from the Scottish Development Department (SDD) in 1980 as recommended in the report Scotland's Scenic Heritage 1979; National Heritage (Scotland) Act 1992.

A **National Scenic Area** is an area recommended by Scottish Natural Heritage (SNH) as being of 'outstanding natural heritage of Scotland and that special protection measures are appropriate for it'. The natural heritage of Scotland includes flora, fauna, geological and physiographical features and the natural beauty and amenity of Scotland.

The legal consequences of this designation are minor, amounting to an obligation on planning authorities to maintain a list of such designations in their area and to pay special attention to the character of the area in the exercise of their functions. Permitted development rights may be strictly controlled. In this, NSAs are similar to AONBs.

It is intended that SNH will co-operate with relevant public authorities and private interests to produce a management statement setting out a basis for sustainable land use in the area, which would be carried into effect through development plans, grants and management agreements. Policy development appears to lag a long way behind AONBs, but Dumfries and Galloway NSA has led the way in coherent analysis and planning.

The 40 sites identified in 1978 in *Scotland's Scenic Heritage* have international recognition, being listed as Category V (Protected Landscapes) in the International Union for the Conservation of Nature (IUCN) World List of Protected Sites.

Hedgerows

The Environment Act 1995 (Part V) Hedgerow Regulations 1997 (SI 1997 no 1160). This law applies in England and Wales only. Scotland has only 7 per cent of Britain's hedgerows and this legislation was deemed to be unnecessary in Scotland.

> *'Important'* hedgerows are those of significant historic, wildlife or land-
> scape value.

This was linked to Countryside Stewardship where grants were available
to landowners for maintaining hedgerows. Generally, hedgerows should
be at least 30 years old, in the countryside and over 20 m in length.
Garden hedges are not covered by these regulations.

Designations are identified by local planning authorities and confirmed by the Secretary of State for the Environment and DEFRA in
England and by the Secretary of State for Wales. A land manager must
notify the local planning authority if he or she wishes to remove a protected hedge. The local planning authority has 42 days in which to give
or refuse consent. The local planning authority has to consider the reasons given for wanting to remove the hedge.

Note that this legislation did not consider landscape visual character as
a criterion, nor did the rules include conservation measures or prevent
loss through neglect. However, research indicates that the regulations
successfully stemmed the loss of hedgerows, but failed to protect locally
distinctive, ancient or species-rich hedgerows. DEFRA issued proposed
amendments for consultation in 2003, which included measures for holly,
elm and willow and hedges that form habitat for protected species. Local
authorities would also have longer to consider removal notices (eight
weeks instead of six).

Conservation of hedges appears to have been strengthened by ODPM
Circular 06/2005. The circular referred to Article 8 of the Habitats Directive
which requires member states to encourage management of linear landscape features with a continuous structure, or function, of major importance for wild flora or fauna as stepping stones essential for migration,
dispersal or genetic exchange, e.g. rivers and their banks, traditional field
boundary systems, ponds and small woods. Planning conditions and obligations may be used to promote their management.

Designations for Species and Special Habitats

These were established mainly to prevent destruction of species and habitats rather than for active management. The SSSI designation used to be in
this category, but the Countryside and Rights of Way Act 2000 and the
Nature Conservation (Scotland) Act 2004 have transformed SSSI status
into a powerful and positive measure for active conservation.

UK Protection of Species

Wildlife and Countryside Act 1981, amended in 1985 replaced the
Protection of Birds Acts 1954–67 and the Conservation of Wild Creatures

and Wild Plants Act 1975. The scope of the Wildlife and Countryside Act is reviewed every five years, most recently in 2003. The revision of schedules is contained in Statutory Orders 1989–95. For Northern Ireland, see the Wildlife (NI) Order 1985 and Nature Conservation and Amenity Lands (NI) Order 1985.

Other statutes dealing with protection of species are the SOED Circular 13/1991. Wild Mammals (Protection) Act 1996, Countryside and Rights of Way Act 2000. Protection of Wild Mammals (Scotland) Act and the 2002 Nature Conservation (Scotland) Act 2004. Also the Convention on International Trade in Endangered Species of Wild Fauna and Flora (CITES) and European Wildlife Trade Regulations (EC 338/97).

The purpose of this legislation is protection of wildlife, habitats and species.

Plants

It is an offence intentionally or recklessly to pick, uproot or destroy, sell, deal in, transport or advertise Schedule 8 plants. This applies to *everyone* including the landowner. All other plants growing wild and native may not be intentionally uprooted. The landowner or those authorized by them are excepted. It is an offence to plant or cause to grow Giant Hogweed, Giant Kelp, Japanese Knotweed and Japanese Seaweed.

The Nature Conservation (Scotland) Act 2004 made it illegal to intentionally or recklessly uproot any wild plant without the permission of the landowner. For rare plants listed in Schedule 8 of the Act, it is an offence to advertise or sell, intentionally or recklessly pick, uproot or destroy such a plant or any seed or spore attached to it.

Birds

It is an offence intentionally or recklessly:
- To kill, take or injure any wild bird.
- To take, damage or destroy the nest of any wild bird while that nest is in use or being built.
- To take or destroy an egg of any wild bird.
- For anyone to have in their possession or control any live or dead wild bird or any part of one, or anything derived from such a bird, or an egg or part of an egg of a wild bird (a strict liability).

Schedule I birds (rare birds) are further protected: their dependent young must not be disturbed.

Exceptions include game birds during season, damage which is the incidental result of some lawful operation for animal health, e.g. against rabies, anthrax, disabled birds, public health and safety, under licence.

Other provisions stipulate that certain methods of killing are prohibited, e.g. electrical devices or poison, and rules about the sale of birds and laws concerning captive birds are also stipulated.

Sanctuary Order

An Order made by the Secretary of State to protect wild birds or specified birds, nests, eggs, or dependent young at any time or for a specified period. An Order can make it an offence for any unauthorized person to enter such an area of special protection. Owners and occupiers are consulted before the Order is imposed.

The Nature Conservation (Scotland) Act 2004

This Act made it illegal to intentionally or recklessly kill, injure or take any wild bird, or for any person to intentionally or recklessly damage or destroy the nest of any wild bird while it is being built or used, or prevent a wild bird from using its nest. It is also an offence to take or destroy an egg of any wild bird, or to cause or permit any of these acts. It is an offence to possess or control any live or dead bird or any part thereof, or any egg or part of an egg of any wild bird. It is an offence to disturb a Schedule 1 bird on a lek (capercaillie) or its young or harass a Schedule 1A bird (white-tailed eagle). It is an offence if people bring into Scotland any bird or egg, if the killing, taking or selling of that bird or egg would have been illegal if it had taken place in Scotland.

Animals

It is an offence intentionally or recklessly to kill, injure or take possession or control of animals listed in Schedule 5 (e.g. adder, bats, dolphin). It is an offence to damage, destroy or obstruct an access to any structure or place which a Schedule 5 animal uses for shelter or protection, or to disturb such an animal. Some Schedule 5 animals are excepted from some of the above. Selling, processing, dealing, transporting or advertising any Schedule 5 animal is an offence.

Exceptions and defence include if a wild animal was killed or injured or harm was accidental to a lawful activity such as crop spraying and pest control.

There are special provisions for bats, ground game, dogs (it is an offence to allow a dog to be at large in a field with sheep, except working dogs), deer, seals and badgers.

The Wild Animals Protection Act 1996

This Act makes it an offence to mutilate, kick, beat, nail or otherwise impale, stab, burn, stone, crush, drown, drag or asphyxiate any wild animal with intent to inflict unnecessary suffering. There is no offence if this occurs in the course of lawful shooting, hunting, coursing or pest control (including lawful use of snares, traps, dogs, poisons or falconry), or if the action occurs during the attempted killing of any animal seriously injured (other than by that person's prior illegal act) and there was no chance of the animal recovering.

The Protection of Animals (Scotland) Act 1912
This deals with cruelty to domestic and wild animals.

The Protection of Wild Mammals (Scotland) Act 2002
Offences under this Act include: deliberately hunting a wild mammal with a dog or dogs; for an owner or occupier knowingly to permit such hunting on their land; for a dog owner or someone having responsibility for a dog to permit the dog to be used to deliberately hunt a wild animal. This excludes rabbits and rodents.

This Act ended the use of dogs for fox hunting, but stalking and flushing wild animals for subsequent immediate shooting or falconry is permitted; this includes fox, mink, hare and (by use of a single dog) orphaned cubs below ground.

The Nature Conservation (Scotland) Act 2004: animals, lepidoptera, amphibians
It is an offence to intentionally or recklessly kill, injure or take any wild animal fully protected under Schedule 5 of the Wildlife and Countryside Act 1981, or to possess or control any live or dead animal in that Schedule.

Butterflies and moths, and their lava and pupa, dead or alive may not be intentionally or recklessly killed, injured, taken, possessed, controlled, sold or advertised for sale in any stage of their life cycle. It is an offence to knowingly cause or permit these offences. Fully protected (i.e. rare) butterflies and moths also have legal protection of their habitat while occupied for shelter or protection. Penalties are up to £5000 per offence and or six months' imprisonment.

All native amphibians are protected from sale under the Wildlife and Countryside Act 1981 and the Nature Conservation (Scotland) Act 2004. It is not illegal to collect the spawn of the common frog, common newt and palmate newt for your pond as long as you have the landowner's permission. Freshwater mussels, natterjack toad and great crested newt have full protection under UK and EU law.

Recent changes and implications for developers and landowners (1998)
Water voles and common or hazel dormice are now on the endangered species list. English planning authorities are advised to require environmental assessments for any development close to river banks, or to carry out a vole survey and state mitigating action if necessary. For hazel

dormice, developers will have to use nesting boxes to ascertain whether or not dormice are present. This may delay development!

Convention on International Trade in Endangered Species (CITES)

CITES has been strengthened by new European wildlife legislation that came into effect from 1 June 1997, which will control or ban the trade of over 25 000 species of animals, birds and plants. (European Wildlife Trade Regulations EC 338/97).

Penalties

The penalties for offences under the Wildlife and Countryside Act 1981 were increased under the CROW Act 2000 to make certain offences 'arrestable', leading to stronger search and seizure powers for the police and inspectors enabling them to enter premises to check species sales controls and require tissue samples for DNA analysis. The Act created a new offence of reckless disturbance and enabled courts to give heavier fines up to a maximum of £5000 and/or a custodial sentence up to six months.

PAWS

A multi-agency body has been set up to concentrate efforts and pool resources to combat wildlife crime. The main objective of the Partnership for Action Against Wildlife Crime (PAWS) is promotion and enforcement of wildlife conservation legislation.

Wildlife legislation in Scotland

The Criminal Justice (Scotland) Act 2003 made wildlife crime in Scotland liable to prosecution. The Nature Conservation (Scotland) Act 2004 allowed bigger fines and longer sentences. The Protection of Wild Mammals (Scotland) Act 2002 was intended to protect wild animals from being hunted with dogs. Use of dogs to stalk and flush game from cover for permitted purposes is still lawful. Use of dogs in falconry and shooting is also legal.

Application of the Habitats Directive and the Conservation (Natural Habitats, &c) Regulations 1994 (SI 1994/2716)

In addition to special regulations applying to SACs and SPAs (described later in the section on active management for conservation), the Habitats

Directive has general application to European protected species *wherever they occur* through the 1994 regulations. It is an offence to:

- Deliberately capture or kill a wild animal of a European protected species.
- Deliberately disturb such an animal.
- Deliberately take or destroy the egg of such an animal.
- Damage or destroy a breeding site or resting place of such an animal. This is an offence of strict liability, i.e. the destructive act does not have to be intentional or deliberate for an offence to have been committed.
- Keep, transport, sell or exchange, or offer for sale or exchange any live or dead wild animal or plant of an EU protected species, or any part of anything derived from such an animal. This applies to all stages of an animal or plant's life cycle.
- Deliberately pick, collect, cut, uproot or destroy any wild specimen of a European protected species of plant

Under this regulation, anyone proposing to develop land where European protected species live has to obtain a separate licence (from DEFRA or the Scottish Executive) after obtaining planning permission and before work commences. It was proposed that this process should be streamlined so that wildlife issues should be considered from the outset of the planning permission process. Guidance about the relationship between licences and planning permission was published as "European Protected Species, Development sites and the planning system" (SEERAD 2001). In this, local authorities were given the chief role in collecting the evidence relevant to issuing a licence as part of their evaluation of an application for planning permission.

Licences

Licences may be authorized for conservation reasons, for the prevention of serious damage to agriculture, for scientific research, public health or safety, imperative reasons of public interest including social and economic considerations, and 'beneficial consequences of primary importance for the environment'. Licences may be granted only if there is no satisfactory alternative, and that the action will not be detrimental to the maintenance of the population of the European protected species concerned at a favourable status in their natural range. Badgers and bats are examples of European protected species.

Badgers and their setts

Wildlife and Countryside (Amendment) Act 1985. Wildlife and Countryside Act 1981. Badger Act 1973. Protection of Badgers Act 1992. Conservation (Natural Habitats, &c.) Regulations 1994. This law applies throughout the United Kingdom. Nature Conservation (Scotland) Act 2004.

Badgers

The killing or taking of badgers is prohibited by the Wildlife and Countryside Act 1981. Landowners were excepted but must now have a DEFRA/SEERAD licence. With the 1985 Act, badger setts also became protected. For either killing and injuring badgers or disturbing setts the normal onus of proof is reversed: an accused must prove their innocence (strict liability).

Nature Conservation (Scotland) Act 2004 made it an offence to:

- wilfully take, injure or kill a badger.
- possess a badger, live or dead, or any part of a badger, if obtained in contravention of the Act.
- cruelly illtreat or dig for badger, or use badger tongs.
- intentionally or recklessly interfere with a badger sett by damaging, destroying or obstructing it, cause a dog to enter it, or disturb a badger occupying it.
- cause or permit, or attempt to commit any of these offences.
- be in possession of anything capable of being used to commit an offence against badgers.

Crimes are punishable by up to three years imprisonment and/or unlimited fines. The police have the power *without warrant* to enter and search property other than dwellings or lock-fast premises in pursuit of enforcement of this Act.

Licences are issued by conservancies or agricultural ministers for:

- scientific or education purposes
- conservation of badgers
- zoological gardens
- marking badgers
- works following granting of planning permission
- preservation of ancient monuments and archaeological investigations therein
- investigations into any offence
- controlling foxes in order to protect livestock, game or wildlife
- to prevent spread of disease or serious damage to land, crops, poultry or other property
- agricultural, forestry or drainage operation.

(For further guidance see English Nature's *'Badgers – guidance for developers'*.)

Bats and their roosts

Wildlife and Countryside Act 1981. The Conservation (Natural Habitats, &c.) Regulations 1994 (1995 in Northern Ireland). This law applies throughout the United Kingdom. Nature Conservation (Scotland) Act 2004.

Bats and their roosts

The purpose of the law is the protection of bats and their roosts. It is an offence to kill, take or disturb bats in the non-living area of a dwelling house or any other place without first notifying the conservancies. The statutory nature conservation organizations must be given reasonable time to advise.

The regulations implement the 'Habitats Directive' for bats and they became a protected species under European law. The Directive prohibits disturbance of bats *at any location,* not just at roosts as in the Wildlife and Countryside Act. Damage or destruction of a bat roost does not require the offence to be intentional or deliberate and is an offence of strict liability; if a breeding or resting site is damaged or destroyed the offence is complete.

The Nature Conservation (Scotland) Act 2004 made it an offence to:

- intentionally or recklessly disturb, kill, injure or take any wild bat or to be in possession or control of any wild or dead bat, or anything derived from a wild bat.
- intentionally or recklessly damage or destroy bat roosts or shelters whether bats are present or not.
- sell or advertise for sale live or dead bats in whole or in part.
- to set or use any articles that could be used to catch, injure or kill a bat.

Limestone Pavements and Limestone Orders
Countryside and Wildlife Act 1981. This law applies throughout the United Kingdom. Countryside and Rights of Way Act 2000 (England and Wales only).

Limestone pavement refers to 'an area of limestone which lies wholly or partly exposed on the surface of the ground and has been fissured by natural erosion and is of particular interest by reason of its flora, fauna, or geological or physiographical features'.

Limestone pavements are identified and designated by the nature conservancies. They notify the local planning authority of the existence of limestone pavements. The Secretary of State for the Environment, Food and Rural Affairs can then make an Order for the protection of these sites. The making of an Order allows for an inquiry into any objections.

It is an offence to remove limestone without reasonable excuse. Fines are possible up to £20 000. However, granting of planning permission is deemed a reasonable excuse for removal. Limestone pavements are protected in perpetuity and without compensation. There are no exclusions for the benefit of agriculture.

Designations about active management for conservation

These have been established to achieve a range, usually a combination, of aims. The emphasis is on nature conservation, but as most sites are owned privately or by land-owning organisations such as the Ministry of Defence, the National Trusts and the Forestry Commission, military, social and economic aims may also have to be incorporated into specific site management agreements. Consider also the agri-environment schemes in the Agriculture section of this chapter.

UK Biodiversity Action Plan (UKBAP)

Following the 1992 UN Convention on Biodiversity, the UK Biodiversity Action Plan (UKBAP) was published in 1994 and endorsed by the Government in May 1996. (See www.ukbap.org.uk)

> The UKBAP was created 'to conserve and enhance biological diversity within the UK and to contribute to the conservation of global diversity through all appropriate mechanisms'.
>
> It helps to co-ordinate and drive conservation at all scales from national to local by identifying priorities for action and biological targets for the recovery of habitats and species.

Under the Countryside and Rights of Way Act 2000 and the Nature Conservation (Scotland) Act 2004, Ministers of the Crown, any Government department, the National Assembly for Wales (NAW) the Scottish Executive and any public agency must have regard to the conservation of biological diversity. The Secretary of State and NAW must publish lists of species and habitats that are of principle importance for biodiversity and where possible, further their conservation.

The UKBAP includes Species Action Plans (SAPs) for 391 species and Habitat Action Plans (HAPs) for 45 habitats. SAPs and HAPs include a summary of objectives, targets and actions required to maintain or enhance populations and habitats. The UKBAP covers Britain's most rapidly declining and endangered species and habitats. It includes ambitious targets for recovery.

Since 1995, 436 UK action plans and about 150 local BAPs have been published. However, as real progress has been made, species and habitat priorities and targets were reviewed in 2005–6. This was co-ordinated by the Biodiversity Reporting and Information Group (BRIG) on behalf of the UK Biodiversity Partnership. The review included a 'reporting round' integrating national and local information, revision of targets for UK priority species and habitats, and updating of the UK priority lists. The revised UKBAP should be completed by summer 2006.

Several agencies have redirected money towards the UKBAP including the Forestry Authority (Woodland Improvement Grants), Environment Agency (river biodiversity action plans), Nature Conservancies, local wildlife trusts and the Ministry of Defence. So far schemes have had most take up on marginal agricultural land, rather than prime agro-industry areas.

The EU Biodiversity Action Plan

The EU adopted the EU Biodiversity Strategy in February 1998. The aims of the EU strategy are 'to anticipate, prevent and attack the causes of significant reduction or loss of biological diversity at source'.

Objectives are approached through 'sectoral action plans', e.g. for agriculture, fisheries and regional policies. The Habitats Regulations 1994 require local planning authorities to review existing incomplete planning permissions that are likely to have significant impact on an EU/Natura site and then affirm, modify or revoke permissions.

Sites of Special Scientific Interest (SSSI) (ASSI in N Ireland)

National Parks and Access to the Countryside Act 1949. Wildlife and Countryside Act 1981 (main emphasis). Wildlife and Countryside (Amendment) Act 1985. Nature Conservation SOED Circular 13/1991 Countryside (Scotland) Act 1981. Countryside and Rights of Way Act 2000. (CROW 2000) ODPM Circular 06/2005. In Northern Ireland: 'Nature Conservation and Amenity Lands (NI) Order 1985, succeeded by the Environment (NI) Order 2002. SSSIs/ASSIs exist throughout the United Kingdom. Nature Conservation (Scotland) Act 2004. (NC(s) 2004)

The Nature Conservation (Scotland) Act 2004 and the CROW 2000 Act and its supporting guidance clearly indicate that the Government has significantly strengthened the status of SSSIs in the UK.

An SSSI is defined as 'an area of special interest by reason of its flora, fauna, geological or physiographical interest. The purpose of SSSIs is protection of valuable species and habitats.

Guidance accompanying the CROW Act 2000 states that the purpose of the SSSI *series* is 'to safeguard, for present and future generations, the diversity and geographic range of habitats, species, geological and geomorphological features, including the full range of natural and semi-natural ecosystems and important geological and physiographical phenomena ...' DEFRA 1 September 2000.

SSSIs are regarded as collectively comprising the full range of natural and semi-natural ecosystems and the most important geological and physiographical sites, selected using well-established and publicly-available scientific criteria only. This guidance formally connects SSSIs to the UKBAP. Notification, effective management and conservation of SSSIs are core elements of achieving UKBAP targets.

Notification of SSSI status is no longer the end of the protection process. It is now expected that sites will be actively managed by owners and occupiers in partnership with the conservancies. The conservancies have a duty to further the conservation and enhancement of the features that make an SSSI of interest.

The Government believes that SSSI management should reflect the general principles of sustainable development set out in its strategy '*A better quality of life*' published in 1999. Accordingly, for example, English Nature is expected to assess how delivery of nature conservation object-ives may be integrated with its duty under the Countryside Act 1968 to have due regard to the needs of agriculture, forestry and the socio-economic interests of rural areas.

SSSI designation procedure

A conservancy such as English Nature or Scottish Natural Heritage selects SSSIs following published criteria: '*Guidelines for the Selection of SSSIs*' published by the Joint Nature Conservation Committee.

The conservancy issues a preliminary notice of intent to the local planning authority, owners, occupiers, anyone with a special interest, the Environment Agency and the Secretary of State. This notification takes effect immediately. The conservancies should also inform DEFRA or SEERAD, the forestry authority or water authority where relevant.

The notice must:
- Describe the location of the site.
- Make reference to a map.
- State the features that make the site of interest.
- Specify 'potentially damaging operations' (or in Scotland Operations Requiring Consent) likely to harm the special features.
- Specify a period (at least three months) and arrangements for making representations.
- The conservancy is also now required to advertise the notification in a local newspaper, so that people have an opportunity to inspect the proposals and comment on them. The advertisement must make it clear that notification is purely on scientific grounds and carries no additional public rights such as access.
- The conservancy is also now required to include a statement about how the land needs to be managed in order to retain its interest.
- Where SSSIs have been notified under the 1981 Act, English Nature and Scottish Natural Heritage are now formally required to issue a

statement of views about the management of every SSSI. This should have been completed by 2005 in England and by 2007 in Scotland.

The conservancy must consider any views expressed by the consultees including the Secretary of State for the Environment, Transport and the Regions (in England).

Owners and occupiers have three months in which to comment and then the conservancies may revise or issue the statement and confirm notification within nine months (1985 Amendment) or the notification will lapse. (Six months in Scotland).

Formal notification can include modification of the original list of potentially damaging operations, i.e. the list can be reduced by agreement with the owner/occupier.

In England and Wales, the SSSI is registered as a land charge. This constitutes notice to any purchaser of the land. In Scotland the land is registered with the Land Register of Scotland or in the General Register of Sasines. The conservancies and local authorities also have to keep a register of SSSIs. Owners and occupiers who dispose of their interest in an SSSI must give details of new ownership or occupancy to the conservancies, so that a new relationship may be set up with the owner.

Consequences of SSSI notification

It becomes an offence for an owner or occupier to carry out any potentially damaging operation (PDO) unless:

- Written notice has been given to the conservancies and the nature conservancy gives written consent. In Scotland, PDOs are now called Operations Requiring Consent (ORC) under the Nature Conservation (Scotland) Act 2004.
- The operation is by agreement under other Acts (1985 Amendment).
- Four months have elapsed from the owner or occupier giving notice (1985 Amendment). Under the CROW 2000 Act, English Nature may now renegotiate any agreement or withdraw or modify consent, whether it was given in writing or was tacit (absence of response). Reasons must be given. There is scope for appeal in the usual way and for payments if withdrawal or modification of consent leads to additional costs.
- The operation is in accordance with a management agreement.
- The operation has been authorized by another approved agency (CROW 2000 Section 28G and NC(S) 2004. 'Other agencies' are also expected to have full regard to their duty to further conservation and enhancement of the SSSI and to consult the conservancies before issuing any permission, authorization or consent which may affect the SSSI.

Under the CROW Act 2000 and NC(S) Act 2004, conservancies have the *right to refuse consent* for PDOs/ORCs and encourage positive management. Previously, they could only postpone them. If proposed operations are refused by English Nature, reasons must be given. Applicants may appeal to the Secretary of State for the Environment, Food and Rural Affairs. (ODPM 06/2005). The Secretary of State has the power to award costs if any party has acted unreasonably. In Scotland under the NC(S) Act 2004 appeal may be made to the Scottish Land Court.

Planning and SSSIs

Local planning authorities are expected to include proposals for protecting SSSIs in their local plans and to take account of them in mineral plans. SSSIs cannot be included in simplified planning zones.

The local planning authority has to consult the conservancies before giving planning permission for any development affecting SSSIs. A local planning authority must also tell the conservancy if it decides to grant consent against their advice to allow the conservancies to ask the Secretary of State/Scottish Executive to call in the application. If planning permission is granted, local planning authorities are expected to ensure any attached conditions are met in full and maximize the use of legally binding agreements.

Under SOED Circular 13/1991 and the Countryside and Rights of Way Act 2000, local planning authorities are asked to be aware that any development close to a protected site may have an effect within it. They are to consult the conservancies where this may occur or where there is doubt about the precise boundaries of the site. The CROW 2000 Act also set new duties for public bodies to further enhance the conservation of SSSIs. Under the Crow 2000 Act an explanation has to be provided to English Nature if its advice is not taken into account in the planning process.

Where the exercise of permitted development rights on an SSSI would constitute a PDO, the owner or occupier must apply to English Nature for consent in the usual way. If English Nature refuses consent, the applicant may appeal to the local planning authority or the Secretary of State.

Emergency Operations

It is a reasonable excuse to carry out a potentially damaging operation that is an emergency, e.g. felling a dangerous tree. The conservancies must be notified as soon as possible.

No public right of access

The public is confined to public footpaths unless an access agreement is in force.

Managing SSSIs

The Government now requires SSSIs to be appropriately and positively managed in order to achieve 'favourable condition', recognizing that lack of management is the commonest cause of deterioration of the special interest. Positive management is most likely to be secured through the active co-operation of land managers using voluntary agreements.

Management scheme

If necessary a 'management scheme' will be appropriate (drawn up by the conservancy in consultation with the owners or occupiers) that sets out measures for conserving or restoring a site. Owners or occupiers have three months to make representations and then the conservancy must either confirm or withdraw the existing or lesser requirements of the scheme.

Management Agreement

The nature conservancies or the owner may seek a management agreement (MA). This provision originally applied only in England and Wales but the 1981 Countryside (Scotland) Act extended it to Scotland. Management agreements may be used where conservation work requires payment to the owner or occupier.

Now management agreements may also be entered into on land not included in an SSSI, but where this would help sustain the special interest. This is in the spirit of the 'whole farm' approach being adopted in government support to farming and forestry; conservancy officers are now expected to be able to advise on agri-environment schemes relevant to the management of SSSIs.

A court judgement in 2004 ruled that English Nature's practice of seeking positive management of SSSIs under the Countryside and Wildlife Act 1981 was acceptable and compatible with the European Convention on Human Rights. The case indicates that a successful balance has been found between nature conservation and landowners' interests.

Management notice

If a management scheme is not being implemented, leading to the deterioration of the special features, *and* where a management agreement (including relevant payment) cannot be reached on reasonable grounds, under the CROW 2000 Act and NC(S) Act 2004, English Nature or Scottish Natural Heritage may issue a management notice requiring certain operations to be carried out by the owner or occupier. These operations must be those identified in the management scheme. Owners and occupiers may appeal against the management notice to the Secretary of State.

Failure to keep to a management notice is an offence and may lead to enforcement action. The conservancy may enter the land and carry out the work, charging the costs to the owner or occupier.

Compulsory purchase

The CROW 2000 Act gave English Nature enhanced powers to acquire land compulsorily if it cannot reach a satisfactory agreement about managing an SSSI within a reasonable period, or where the terms of an agreement have been broken and the special features are unlikely to be in favourable condition.

Statutory duty of public bodies

Under the CROW 2000 Act it is now a statutory duty for public bodies to adopt the highest standards to further the conservation and enhancement of SSSIs in all stages of their activities. This includes ministries, government departments, local authorities and statutory undertakers (public sector and private utilities) and other Crown officers.

If these agencies propose PDOs, they must consult English Nature who must respond within 28 days with advice about impact and mitigating actions. If agencies proceed with PDOs they must be able to demonstrate how they have weighed the balance between differing interests. Judicial review is available in exceptional cases.

Land owned by the Government, its departments, agencies and non-departmental public bodies will have an agreed biodiversity checklist. This encourages them to make statements of commitment and develop positive management regimes. A good example is the MOD, which has adopted a positive and systematic approach to maximizing biodiversity on the Defence Estate commensurate with its military remit.

Change of owner or occupier

Under the CROW 2000 Act and NC(S) Act 2004, the conservancies must be informed within 28 days if someone disposes of their interest in an SSSI or becomes aware of a new or additional owner or occupier of land within an SSSI.

By-laws

Note that there is no provision for by-laws. If by-laws are needed, designating the site as a nature reserve may be more appropriate.

Penalties

Penalties for damage to SSSIs by owners, occupiers and other parties were increased under the CROW 2000 Act and NC(S) Act 2004. Fines may not exceed £20 000 in the Magistrates' Court but can be unlimited in the Crown Court. Under the CROW 2000 Act and NC(S) Act 2004, new offences have been created which may lead to enforcement action if carried out without reasonable excuse.

SSSI owners and occupiers:

- Carrying out, causing or allowing operations likely to damage an SSSI without consent.
- Failing to keep to a management notice.
- Failing to let the conservancies know about a change in occupation or ownership of land in a SSSI.

Public bodies:

- Carrying out operations likely to damage an SSSI without meeting the requirements to notify the conservancies.
- Failing to minimize any damage to an SSSI and, if there is any damage, failing to restore it to its former state as far as is reasonably practical and possible.

Any person:

- Intentionally or recklessly damaging, destroying or disturbing any of the habitats or features of an SSSI.
- Preventing a conservancy officer from lawfully taking access to an SSSI.

Funding

Funding may be available from English Nature through the 'Wildlife and Reserves Enhancement Scheme', DEFRA agri-environment schemes or, in Scotland, through a SNH 'Natural Care' scheme, SEERAD Rural Stewardship Scheme or Forestry Commission Scottish Forestry Grant Scheme.

The condition of SSSI/ASSIs

Through the umbrella organization, the Joint Nature Conservation Committee, statutory bodies use the following categories to describe the condition of SSSI/ASSIs:

- **Favourable**: A feature of interest is recorded as favourable when its condition objectives have been met.
- **Unfavourable recovering**: A feature of interest can be recorded as recovering after damage or neglect if it has begun to show, or is continuing to show a trend towards favourable condition and all measures are in place to bring about favourable condition.
- **Unfavourable no change**: An interest may be retained in a more or less steady state by repeated or continuing damage or neglect.
- **Unfavourable declining**: Decline is another possible consequence of a damaging activity. In this case recovery is possible and may occur if suitable management input is made.
- **Partially destroyed or destroyed**: Self-explanatory.

Amendment to SSSI notification

The National Heritage (Scotland) Act 1991 provided for the scientific justification for designations of SSSIs to be reconsidered. This power is now UK-wide and nature conservancies have the power to amend the list of special features, the area of land covered, the list of damaging operations or its management statement, but they must follow the same consultation procedure including advertisement now required for initial notification of SSSIs. SSSI notification may also be cancelled following consultation with owners and occupiers, but this is expected to occur only in exceptional circumstances.

Critique of SSSIs

The CROW 2000 Act and NC(S) Act 2004 have addressed several criticisms that had been levelled at the SSSI designation:

- The SSSI system used not guarantee protection of sites as PDOs could only be delayed for a short time, but now the conservancies have the right to refuse consent.
- Protection can still be overridden by planning permissions, but under the CROW 2000 Act local planning authorities have a duty to further and enhance conservation of SSSIs.
- Designation of an SSSI used to intend merely preventing damage, not positive management: sheer neglect could cause deterioration in value. Positive management is now encouraged through management schemes and plans and/or local biodiversity action plans.
- Landowners and occupiers in the UK unhappy at designation on scientific grounds now have a right of appeal.
- SSSI rules used to apply only to owners or occupiers, but following the Crow 2000 and NC(S) Acts, public bodies and any other person may also have enforcement action taken against them.

Nature reserves

National Parks and Access to the Countryside Act 1949, reinforced by the Wildlife and Countryside Act 1981; this law applies to England, Wales and Scotland.

Nature reserve

Land managed for the study, research or preservation of flora, fauna geology or physiographical features. Opportunities for education are required for designation to be approved.

Nature reserve status provides significant protection for land and habitats through by-laws and other rules. For example, Orders may be made restricting or prohibiting vehicles on roads in a reserve in England or Wales. Also, the conservancies must be consulted before road building or improvement in or near a reserve is initiated. Reserve land cannot be included in Farm Woodland Premium Schemes. Works proposed under the Animal Health Act 1981 require prior notice to conservancies and effort to minimize damage done.

Nature reserves may be set up and managed by the nature conservancies or by local authorities or the two jointly. They enter an agreement with the occupier, lessee or an owner to establish a nature reserve. Costs are born by the conservancy, the owners or jointly.

By-laws
The conservancies have the important power of being able to make by-laws for protection of the site as long as they do not interfere with owners' rights or with a public right of way, statutory undertakers, drainage authorities, salmon fishery, and district boards or telecommunications bodies. By-laws may be used to restrict entry or movement, and to prohibit fires, littering and the killing or taking of living creatures, eggs, and plants. By-laws may also provide permits for things otherwise forbidden.

Dedication, covenant or management agreement
These run with the land and identify any special management requirements for the site. Management agreements may stipulate works to be done, payment for works and compensation for the loss of parties' rights.

Compulsory Acquisition
The conservancies may acquire a site compulsorily if they believe the site would be managed as a nature reserve, say by the RSPB, or if the management agreement has not been reached on reasonable terms or has been broken and notice sent to the owner.

National Nature Reserves
If it is of sufficient importance, the nature conservancy may designate a site as a 'national nature reserve' and manage it itself or by an approved body such as the RSPB. Such a site would normally be made an SSSI, but also have by-laws for greater statutory protection.

Local sites
DEFRA issued "Local Sites. Guidance on their Identification, Selection and Management" in 2006. The guide describes the legislative and policy context, site selection process management and resourcing of non-statutory sites of wildlife or geological interest. The guide may be downloaded from www.defra.gov.uk.

Marine nature reserves
Wildlife and Countryside Act 1981. Applies throughout the UK.

Purpose

To conserve marine flora or fauna or geological or physiographical features of special interest, or for suitable conditions for the study and research of those interested in any area of sea or tidal water and the land so covered. The reserve may extend from the seaward limit of territorial water to the high water mark and include tidal parts of rivers and estuaries.

Designation of marine nature reserves

The Secretary of State designates the sites on the advice of a nature conservancy. The conservancies manage the sites and may make by-laws to restrict entry of persons or vessels and prohibit acts damaging to animals, plants and fish and the deposit of rubbish.

However, by-laws cannot restrict non-pleasure boats, or even exclude such boats at all times of year. Pleasure boats are not defined. Actions to safeguard a vessel or life cannot be rendered unlawful by by-laws, nor discharge from a vessel, nor activity more than 30 m below seabed. By-laws cannot restrict activity of local authorities, the Environment Agency, water or sewerage authorities, SEPA, navigation, harbour, pilotage and lighthouse authorities, salmon fishery district boards and local fishery committees. In short, protection of these reserves is weak.

There are three MNRs in the UK: Lundy, Skomer and Strangford Lough.

Integrated Coastal Zone Management (ICZM)

The limited approach to coastal conservation of MNRs contrasts with the EU demonstration programme for ICZM initiated in 1997 to run for three years. In 2002 the EU Commission aimed to review the environmental status of the seas and move towards an ecosystem-based approach. This was intended to investigate: existing pressures on the environment in coastal areas; current action for environmental management; development and planning and causes of current problems. ICZM is now connected to the Water Framework Directive River Basin Planning by the Environment Agency.

The Habitats Directive "Natura 2000"

Conservation of natural habitats and wild flora and fauna – Directive 92/43 (OJL206, 22.7.92). This is an extension to the Birds Directive 79/409 which created the SPA designation and like the Birds Directive is a consequence of the Bern Convention of European Wildlife and Natural Habitats 1979.

The Directive is implemented in the UK under the Conservation (Natural Habitats &c) Regulations 1994 (1995 in N Ireland) and enabled by the European Communities Act 1972. The Habitats Directive created the SAC designation.

Natura 2000 refers to a network of important sites for birds, plants and mammals. The bird sites are designated as **Special Protection Areas (SPAs)**. Sites for plants and animals are designated as **Special Areas of Conservation**

> **(SAC).** SACs are terrestrial or marine areas that support rare endangered or vulnerable natural habitats and species of plants or animals (other than birds). They will require protection and positive management in the interests of the habitats or species for which they are established.

This is an important conservation measure, intended to maintain biodiversity in the Community and to maintain or restore "favourable conservation status" for habitats and wild species of flora and fauna identified as being of Community interest. The Directive will result in a "coherent European ecological **network**" of important sites including both SPAs (bird sites) and Special Areas of Conservation (SAC) under the title Natura 2000.

SACs are areas that support rare endangered or vulnerable natural habitats and species of plants or animals (other than birds). SACs are terrestrial and marine. They will require protection and positive management in the interests of the habitats or species for which they are established. Selection criteria are set out in Annex III of the Habitats Directive.

> **The Habitats Regulations 1994** requires government departments, local authorities and other public bodies to:
> * Establish necessary conservation measures including, if necessary development and management plans, and appropriate administrative and contractual measures.
> * Take appropriate steps to avoid deterioration of habitats or significant disturbance to species.
> * Subject any projects and plans, including Regional Spatial Strategies, Development Plan Documents and Supplementary Planning Documents or other land use plans, likely to have significant impact on the site to Appropriate Assessment to ensure that site integrity is not adversely affected. Therefore systematic assessment of the environment is a key part of the Directive.[CW1]
> * Projects may go ahead only if they do not damage the integrity of the site. Authorities should not agree to plans that have adverse impact unless: there is no alternative; there are over-riding socio-economic reasons of public interest; and the necessary compensatory measures have been taken to ensure that the overall coherence of the Natura 2000 network is protected.
> * Where a site hosts a priority species or habitat, the only considerations permissible are those relating to human health or public safety, to beneficial consequences of primary importance for the environment, or, further to an opinion from the EU Commission, to other imperative reasons of over-riding public interest. If over-riding public interest is claimed, the EU must give permission for the development.

UK Government policy is that all Natura 2000 sites must first be designated SSSIs (or Areas of Special Scientific Interest – ASSIs in N Ireland). The schedule of Potentially Damaging Operations associated with SSSIs can be reviewed and amended with immediate effect if proposed operations are incompatible with the conservation objectives of the Natura 2000 site.

If the site also hosts a **priority** species or habitat, development may take place only for human health and safety or if it has beneficial consequences of primary importance to the environment. However, if "overriding public interest is claimed", the EU must give permission for the development.

There was concern in the UK that Government plans for this Directive did not include a review of existing planning permissions which would affect any future conservation areas, but under Regulation 50 competent authorities became required to review, affirm, modify or revoke permissions once a site gains EU status. This enabled the Environment Agency or SEPA to tackle problems of pollution or low water levels. It also allowed for by-laws, statutory management schemes on marine sites and powers to impose Special Nature Conservation Orders if a site or species came under threat.

There were also fears that UK legislation would also lack mechanisms to prevent damage to conservation sites through neglect or poor management, or measures to restore previously damaged habitats e.g. English lowland heath. The watering down of the Directive reflected Government concern that implementation of this European law would prevent road construction, building development and quarrying.

However the Countryside and Rights of Way Act 2000 and the Nature Conservation (Scotland) Act 2004 have reinforced the commitment of the UK government and its agencies to the principles of the Natura 2000 network and EU biodiversity objectives; for example, through active SSSI management. Moreover European Court decisions relating to definitions of SPAs and SACs are binding on all member states.

By 2005 there were over 600 candidate SACs and 252 SPAs covering about 6.5 per cent of the land area.

Special Protection Areas for Birds (SPA)

This designation was required by the EC Birds Directive 79/409 and amendments. It provides Community-wide protection for all wild birds and their habitats. SPAs form part of the Natura 2000 network .SPAs are selected on the basis that the site and its habitat support either:

- 20,000 waterfowl or seabirds
- 1% of the UK population of birds listed in Annex I of the Birds Directive
- 1% of the biogeographical population of a migratory species.

Once designated, member states must take "appropriate steps to avoid pollution or deterioration of habitats or any disturbances affecting the birds".

Designation of SPAs is carried out by member state governments in consultation with conservancies and must be notified to the Commission of European Communities. In the UK, SSSIs, Nature Reserves and Nature Conservation Order sites have become SPAs. The European Court of Justice has ruled that SPAs afford a greater degree of protection than that of SSSIs etc. in that planning permission should not be given at all in SPAs.

Appropriate Assessment (AA)

AA has a narrow and detailed focus on a few sites in order to assess the impact of a plan or project on SAC/SPA ecology. This is in contrast to Strategic Environmental Assessment (SEA) which assesses impact on the whole environment at a wider scale, and Sustainability Appraisal (SA) which looks at a broad range of social, economic and environmental issues.

AA Stage 1: Screening:

This identifies the likely impact on a Natura 2000 site (SPA or SAC) of a project or plan, either alone or in combination with other projects and plans, and considers whether these impacts are likely to be significant. This stage may include impacts well outside an authority's boundaries. For example, many areas obtain their water supplies from reservoirs in other authorities' territory. The importance of 'in combination' effects on the final decision distinguishes AA from SEA where cumulative effects do not necessarily influence the final decision.

AA Stage 2: Appropriate assessment

AA considers the impacts of a project or plan, alone or in combination with other projects or plans, on the structure, function and conservation objectives of a SPA or SAC. Where adverse effects occur, potential mitigation is also assessed. This stage is likely to involve the nature conservancies and other nature conservation expertise.

AA Stage 3: Assessment of alternative solutions

This stage involves assessing options for avoiding adverse impacts. The relationship of AA and SA is relevant to this. If AA is done after SA, AA is likely to emphasise mitigation rather than avoidance. If AA is done before SA, the emphasis on avoidance may eliminate otherwise sustainable development options. Iteration of concurrent SA and AA processes should produce a balanced conclusion, but requires good judgement to avoid bias and manage complex data.

AA Stage 4: Assessment where there are no alternative solutions exist and where adverse impacts remain.

This stage (which should be avoided if possible) examines compensatory measures where, due to over-riding public interest, it is deemed that the plan or project should go ahead. The local planning authority is responsible for testing whether their plan may pass the rigorous IROPI (imperative reasons of over-riding public interest) test or the more stringent test for priority habitats and species. European Court of Justice rulings suggest that these tests are difficult to pass.

Comments:

AA is demanding on data collection, time, ecological skills, the culture of land use planning and possible inter-authority co-operation. The stringent nature of the AA requirements and processes may lead to authorities avoiding development anywhere near a Natura 2000 site. This may help preservation, but also lead to isolation of SPA/SAC sites amidst even more intense development. Increasing the size, connectedness, diversity and resilience of SPAs and SACs may be more important for long term sustainability than preservation in pristine condition.

Convention on Wetlands of International Importance (Ramsar Sites)

Ramsar sites are now covered by legislation in the Countryside and Rights of Way Act 2000 (England and Wales only), but as a matter of policy the Government chose to apply the same consideration to the protection of Ramsar sites as is given to SPAs. ODPM Circular 06/2005 Annex D reproduces the convention, reason and articles. The list is maintained by the International Union for the Conservation of Nature (IUCN), which must be apprised of any changes in site.

This agreement is known as the Ramsar Convention after the town in Iran where the convention was signed in 1971. The Ramsar Convention makes provisions for the protection of wetlands throughout the world, (not just the EU) which are disappearing as a result of drainage, land reclamation and pollution.

Ramsar sites are internationally significant for ecology, botany, zoology, limnology or hydrology. Specifically, designated Ramsar sites are wetlands that are representative, rare or unique natural or near-natural wetland in its bio geographic region, which may be habited by species or ecological communities, plants, or animals at critical stages in their life cycles. Sites regularly supporting 10 000 ducks or geese or 1 per cent of the breeding pair population of a species should be designated, as should sites important for fish or for food for fish.

Each nation selects a list of wetlands of international importance that they undertake to protect. Once designated, the nation must positively plan and promote conservation of the site, for example by establishing a nature reserve with a warden. Sites may be de-listed due to 'urgent national interest' but should be replaced by an alternative site. Ramsar sites are not immune from planning permissions but planning authorities should promote their conservation and avoid their loss.

World Heritage Sites

A designation based on the Convention for the Protection of the World Cultural and Natural Heritage 1972.

> **World Heritage sites** are the natural and man-made treasures of the world. Sites have 'outstanding universal value' for science, aesthetics or nature conservation.

The World Heritage Committee of UNESCO identifies sites according to strict criteria. States are expected to take active and utmost steps to conserve these sites and educate the public to appreciate them. International assistance may be available to promote their recognition and protection.

Examples in Britain include St Kilda, Stonehenge, Ironbridge and Edinburgh New Town. Examples abroad include the Grand Canyon and the Taj Mahal.

Specific Sites and Species

Several of the designations outlined above include the possibility of using management agreements as a means of securing conservation aims and benefit to landowners. For specific sites or species in particular danger, Nature Conservation Orders or Special Nature Conservation Orders may be issued.

> **Means of protection or management**
> * Management agreements.
> * Nature Conservation Order.
> * Special Nature Conservation Order.
> * Sanctuary Order.

Management Agreements

National Parks and Access to the Countryside Act 1949. Countryside Act 1968. Wildlife and Countryside Act 1981. Countryside (Scotland) Act 1981.

> A **management agreement is** an agreement for the conservation or enhancement of the natural beauty or amenity of land in the countryside or the promotion of public enjoyment of such land.

A management agreement is a deed binding both parties. It contains undertakings by both parties, which are called covenants. Breach of covenant by one party enables the other to bring an action for damages and/or for an injunction to restrain that breach. The agreement is made between a local planning authority or conservancy and any person with an interest in land, for example the owner or tenant. The agreement runs with the land entered into by owner or tenant for life.

> **Management agreements** may contain:
> - Restrictions on certain methods of cultivation or change of use.
> - Restrictions on the exercise of rights over land, e.g. no shooting.
> - Obligation on the owner/occupier to carry out certain works.
> - Permission for the local planning authority to carry out works to fulfil their functions under the National Parks, etc. Act 1949 or the Countryside Act 1968, e.g. picnic sites.
> - Financial payments.

Management agreements may be used in National Parks, SSSIs, National Nature Reserves, Nature Conservation Orders, ESAs, Countryside Stewardship and the Natura 2000 SAC network.

Sanctuary Order

> **Sanctuary Order** refers to an Order made by the Secretary of State to protect wild birds or specified bird, nests, eggs, or dependent young at any time or for a specified period. The order can make it an offence for any unauthorized person to enter such an area of special protection.

Nature Conservation Order (NCO)

Wildlife and Countryside Act 1981. This law applies in Scotland, England and Wales.

> A **Nature Conservation Order** refers to an instruction that land is of special interest for its flora, fauna, geological or physiographical interest and shall be designated by NCO:
> - To ensure the survival in Great Britain of any kind of animal or plant.
> - To comply with an international obligation.
> - Where land is of national importance, to ensure its natural features of interest.

> **Characteristics of NCO**
> - NCOs come into effect immediately, therefore they are used for urgent protection, usually used in conjunction with SSSIs.
> - Potentially damaging operations have to be specified. It is an offence for the owner, occupier or any other person to carry out the specified operation unless written notice is given to the conservancies and:
> - The conservancies give consent.

- The work is in accordance with a management agreement.
- Three months have elapsed from the notice of intention. This period can be extended.
- No offence is committed if work is carried out in an emergency or with planning permission.
- If a prohibited operation is carried out unlawfully, the offender can be prosecuted and obliged to restore the land to its previous condition.
- Compensation may be available to an owner or tenant affected by an NCO.
- NCOs are made on the recommendation of the conservancies. The owner or lessee is informed of the designation and may make representation to the Secretary of State if she or he objects or wishes modifications. The case would be decided by a local public inquiry.

Special Nature Conservation Orders

The Wildlife and Countryside Act 1981 and the Conservation (Natural Habitats &c) Regulations 1994. This law applies throughout the United Kingdom.

Special Nature Conservation Order refers to a designation authorized by a Secretary of State to protect Natura 2000 sites. It is the most stringent protection possible.

No time limits are specified after which an owner or occupier can carry out a potentially damaging operation. A PDO can be carried out only with written consent of a conservancy or in accordance with a management agreement.

Access to the Countryside

Public rights of access in Great Britain are restricted to specific locations: the Queen's Highway, the foreshore and to specific routes described below.

- **The Queen's Highway:** The Crown has always given the ordinary citizen the freedom to travel the Queen's Highway. This includes all scales from motorway to footpath. Public rights here are confined to passing to and from and to reasonably incidental purposes such as pausing to tie a shoelace.
- **The foreshore:** The public has the right to use water covering the foreshore for fishing and navigation.
- **Village greens:** Available for public recreation.
- **Common land:** Land over which a number of people share rights, e.g. for grazing. Often greens were also used for recreational purposes. The

Commons Registration Act 1965 required all commons to be registered and failure to do so meant all rights over it were extinguished. Until the CROW 2000 Act there was no general right of public access to common land. Under the Law of Property Act 1925, the general public was granted rights to air and exercise over any London Metropolitan common or manorial waste, and large areas of the Lake District and South Wales.

- **Water courses:** Public access is also permitted on most towpaths on canals and rivers.
- **Other accesses:** Some woodlands (e.g. most Woodland Trust and Forestry Commission sites); open country and coastline owned by the National Trust; the National Cycle Network; National Parks; AONBs; and Heritage Coasts.

See www.countryside.gov.uk/living landscapes/finest countryside for more about access to the English countryside.

Public Rights of Way in England and Wales

National Park and Access to Countryside Act 1949, Countryside Act 1968, Wildlife and Countryside Act 1981, Highways Act 1980 (S.25–6). Rights of Way Act 1990 Countryside and Rights of Way Act 2000.

Categories

Under the National Park and Access to Countryside Act 1949, county councils had to survey and keep up-to-date records of public footpaths, bridleways and roads used as public footpaths and bridleways. The Wildlife and Countryside Act 1981 defined three types of route: footpath, bridleway and Byway Open to All Traffic (BOAT) (the latter where there are vehicular rights over a route).

The Countryside and Rights of Way Act 2000 created a new category of highway called 'restricted byway', which replaces 'Roads Used As Public Paths'. Restricted byways will be open only to pedestrians, horse riders, cyclists and horse-drawn vehicles.

Definitive maps

Initially required under the National Park and Access to Countryside Act 1949 and reinforced by the Wildlife and Countryside Act 1981 and the CROW 2000 Act, county councils have to survey and record public footpaths, bridleways and roads used as public paths. These routes are recorded on 'definitive maps' with a 'statement' describing the route. These maps and statements are legally valid records and have to be kept up to date. The distinction between the different types of access (paths, bridleways, etc.) is not determined by their widths and the definitive maps and statements should be consulted to determine the type of route.

Legal consequences of definitive maps
- If the map indicates a public footpath or bridleway or byway, that designation is conclusive evidence that right exists (but does not preclude the possibility that a greater public right may exist).
- The written statement is conclusive as to the position and width of the appropriate right of way.

Under the Countryside and Rights of Way Act 2000 highway authorities have until January 2026 to record historic rights of way. Routes not recorded by that date would be extinguished, though there may be exceptions.

Changes to routes

Before new paths are created or existing ones are stopped up or diverted there must be publicity; objections and representations may be made and affected owners and occupiers informed. Copies of maps and statements must be available for public viewing. If there are no objections the county confirms the Order. If objections are not withdrawn, there will be a public local inquiry, private hearing or inquiry through written representations. The Order and objections will be submitted to the Secretary of State and DEFRA who will appoint an inspector.

Diversion of routes: Diversion Orders

Diversion Orders (DO) are made under the Highways Act 1980 S119. A Diversion Order can be made either 'in the interest of the owner/occupier – provided that the new route is not substantially less convenient to the public' or 'in the interests of the public'.

Before a **Diversion Order** is confirmed, the county council (or district or borough council) must also be satisfied with:
- The effect which the diversion would have on public enjoyment of the way as a whole.
- The effect which the Order would have on other land served by the public right of way.
- The effect of the Order on the land over which the new right is granted and any land held with it.

The council officers may consider:
- Physical features including distance and direction of travel, path widths and gradients, level and condition, convenience and future maintenance of surfaces and structures.
- Assessment of the public's enjoyment of the path, which requires subjective judgements to be made about views, amenity value and quality of experience offered to users of the path.

- The possible impact of any new path on other properties, for example, it would be unreasonable to divert a path in order to improve the applicant's privacy or security if the new route would have an adverse impact on the property of neighbours.
- The proposed route would have to compare reasonably favourably with the length of path to be stopped up by the DO in distance, other physical characteristics and amenity value.
- The needs of disabled people will also be taken into account, especially in view of the Disability Discrimination Act 1995. Separate application by the landowner would be required under the Highways Act 1980 S66 or S147 if a gate, stile or barrier is required by the DO applicant, rather than open access.

Other issues for **Diversion Orders**:
- Applicants need to make it clear if any other landowner will be affected by the proposed diversion.
- A site visit may be required. The council may stipulate route widths.
- District and parish councils, the police and any amenity groups concerned with pubic rights of way will be consulted about the proposal.
- The applicant will be required to submit details of the works required for the new route.
- The council rights of way committee or other designated committee will make the decision to approve or refuse the application.
- A decision to approve the Order will be published in the local press, giving the public 28 days in which to make an objection. If there are no objections, the Order is capable of being confirmed. The applicant is responsible for all costs involved in closing the old route and making the new route useable, including the provision of signs and the council's advertisement and administration costs. This is authorized through the Local Authorities (Recovery of costs for Public Path Orders) Regulations 1993 and the Local Authorities (Charges for Overseas assistance and Public Path Orders) Regulations 1996.
- If there are objections, which are not withdrawn after discussion, the Order is sent to the Secretary of State who may appoint an inspector to hold a public local inquiry before reaching a decision.
- If an Order is not confirmed by either the council or the Secretary of State, the applicant will normally and nevertheless have to pay all costs associated with the application, unless the council has been at fault in dealing with the process of the application.

Temporary diversion orders

Temporary diversion for necessary work is not open to objection. Paths are often closed for work to take place. A Temporary Closure Order will be required from the council.

New routes

New routes can be created in several ways:
- The public can request that a route be added to the map and statement if they are able to prove that a defined route (i.e. not wandering at large) has been used by right for 20 years of uninterrupted use. If the county council refuses, there is appeal to the Secretary of State (Highways Act 1980 S31 and Wildlife and Countryside Act 1981 S53).
- Public path creation agreement – an agreement between the local authority and the landowner.
- Public Path Order – compulsory powers used by a local authority.

Before a new path is created, owners and occupiers must be informed; there must be publicity and scope for objections and representations to be made. If there are no objections, the county council will confirm the route. If there are objections, there will be a public local inquiry or private hearing.

Extinguishment of routes

In law, an Extinguishment Order to stop up a public path or part of its width may only be made if the path (or part) 'is not required for public use'; applicants are required to supply detailed reasons to the county council explaining the extinguishment request. The considerations and process described above about Diversion Orders will apply to Extinguishment Orders also, including the right of appeal to the Secretary of State through local public inquiry.

Bulls

It is a criminal offence to keep a bull at large in a field or enclosure crossed by a public right of way. This law used to apply only in Scotland and certain counties, but from 1981 applies nation-wide. It is not an offence if the bull is not a recognized dairy breed run at large with cows or heifers.

Ploughing

Occupiers are obliged to restore a footpath or bridleway that crosses a field as soon as possible after ploughing it and in any case within two weeks. It is an offence to plough footpaths, byways or bridleways along the side or headland of a field. Local authorities are empowered to restore unlawfully ploughed routes.

Wardens

Local authorities may appoint wardens to advise and assist the public in their use of public routes.

Sign-posting

Local authorities are required to erect signs at every point where a public footpath, bridleway or byway leaves a metalled road (unless agreed to be unnecessary). Signs may also be erected within the width of the public right of way without the consent of the landowner or occupier, but they are normally informed as a matter of courtesy.

Improvement plans
Under the Countryside and Rights of Way Act 2000, highway authorities had to publish a rights of way 'improvement plan' by 2005. The plan would reflect: an assessment of whether or not existing routes meet the current and future needs of the public; opportunities for open-air recreation; and access for blind and partially-sighted people or others with mobility difficulties.

Cycle tracks
Cyclists may use bridleways. However, cycle paths are not recorded on definitive maps and statements. An Order may be made to turn a public footpath into a cycle track. The Order is open to public objection and tends to be contentious; consultation is necessary. Carriageway rights cannot be acquired on footpaths or bridleways through the use of bicycles. (Planning Inspectorate Rights of Way Note 17.)

New access rights: The Countryside and Rights of Way Act 2000

The Countryside and Rights of Way Act 2000 applies only to England and Wales except in reference to off-the-road use of vehicles and in making clear the relevant legislation for SSSIs in Scotland. The Act has not meant repeal of existing Access Orders but no new Access Agreements may be made to open country or registered common land. The new right of access was introduced in England in regional stages between September 2004 and December 2005.

The Act allows any person to enter and remain on any 'access land' (mainly mountain, moor, heath and down) for the purposes of open-air recreation such as walking, climbing and bird-watching, provided that this does not lead to damaged walls, fences, hedges, stiles or gates or contravene restrictions and actions deemed to be inappropriate and unlawful. Fishing and camping are not included in the Act. Restrictions are listed in Schedule 2 and some examples are given below.

The Countryside and Rights of Way Act 2000 makes it clear that driving any motor vehicle (including motor bikes, quad bikes and scrambler bikes) on footpaths, bridleways, restricted byways (formerly called 'Roads Used as Public Paths') or off-road is an offence, unless the driver has lawful authority.

Under this Act, landowners may not obstruct access, but neither have they been invested with more onerous responsibilities in relation to occupier's liability or risk in general. The Countryside Agency and the Countryside Council for Wales were required to produce maps showing all access land and common land. Local authorities put the draft maps on deposit for public inspection and to allow for consultation and appeal against designation. Maps must be reviewed within ten years of confirmation. Access land will be shown on Ordnance Survey maps. Bylaws, wardens and notices indicating boundaries may be established.

Access land includes:

- Open country (mountain, moor, heath or down).
- Registered common land.
- Land 600 m above sea level.
- Especially dedicated land.
- Coastal land may be included by Order.

Excepted land includes:

- Land ploughed or drilled in the last 12 months for planting or sowing crops or trees.
- Land covered by buildings including the curtilage.
- Land within 20 m of a dwelling.
- Parks and gardens.
- Quarries, surface working of minerals, and active mineral workings.
- Railways and tramways, airports or aerodromes.
- Golf course or race course.
- Utility structures such as electricity substations and telecommunications masts.
- Land being developed in accordance with the Town and Country Planning Acts.
- Land within 20 m of a permanent building or temporary pens holding livestock.
- Land regularly used for training race horses (gallops).
- Military land where by-laws apply.

Restrictions on access include:

- Vehicles other than invalid carriages.
- Bathing or using a vessel or sailboard on non-tidal river or lake.
- Access with animals other than dogs. Dogs must be on a short lead between 1 March and 31 July and at all times when near livestock.
- Criminal acts or intimidation of persons engaged in lawful activity.
- Lighting fires.
- Taking or disturbing flora, fauna or fish, eggs or nests, stones or fallen wood.
- Hunting, shooting or fishing or carrying the apparatus thereof.
- Metal detecting.
- Interference of drains or watercourses.
- Organized games, camping, hang-gliding or paragliding.
- Commercial activity.
- Advertising.

Restricted access

Landowners may exclude or restrict access, for example, for land management, nature conservation, shooting, agricultural works, fire risk, national security or other emergency, but generally for a maximum of 28 days in a year. Excluded days must not include Bank Holidays, Good Friday, Christmas Day, more than four days which are either a Saturday or Sunday, or any Saturday between 1 June and 11 August, or any Sunday between 1 June and 30 September.

Public rights of way in Scotland

Duties of local authorities

In Scotland, under the Countryside (Scotland) Act 1967, local authorities have a duty to keep public rights of way open. They may facilitate access by installing gates, stiles and signs. They do *not* have a duty to maintain routes, that is the responsibility of the landowner.

Identification of public rights of way

The system of definitive maps and statements used in England and Wales to establish legal authority to public rights of way does not exist in Scotland. To have such legal certainty in Scotland, each route has to be surveyed and tested individually in court.

Public rights of way in Scotland

Four criteria may be used to identify likely public rights of way:
- Routes must connect two public places to which the public resort for some definite or intelligible purpose.
- Routes must be reasonably well defined and capable of being followed from end to end.
- The route must have been used by the general public 'openly, peaceably and without judicial interruption' for a continuous period of not less than 20 years if the use is for a period ending after 25th July 1976.
- Use of public right of way must be as a matter of right and not merely a matter of tolerance or licence on the part of the proprietor of the land over which the right of way runs.

Land Reform (Scotland) Act 2003 (LR(S)A)

This Act deals with access, a community right to buy, and crofters' right to buy. These notes deal with access. Scotland has never had a trespass law, but the Land Reform Act clarifies where people have a right to be on land and water for recreation and education purposes, and for crossing over land and water. Access rights are intended to help people enjoy and appreciate the outdoors more, thus providing health benefits and economic gain for rural communities. The LR(S)A is further reaching than the CROW 2000 Act. It allows for most forms of recreation on, over and under land and inland water. Although motorized activity is not allowed, horse riding, caving, canoeing, parascending, camping and lighting fires are.

Scottish Natural Heritage has emphasized responsible behaviour by the public and land managers through the Scottish Outdoor Access Code (SOAC).

> The **Scottish Outdoor Access Code** is based on three principles:
> * Respecting the interests of other people.
> * Caring for the environment.
> * Taking responsibility for your own actions.
> It has been devised to guide the public and land managers to make informed decisions.
> See www.outdooraccess-scotland.com for details.

Public rights of way will continue to exist. The statutory right to access commenced on 9 February 2005.

Access Agreement and Order

National Parks and Access to the Countryside Act 1949, Countryside (Scotland) Act 1967, the Countryside Act 1968. This applies throughout the United Kingdom.

> **Access Agreements and Orders** are created to enable the public to have access for open-air recreation to open country, consisting wholly or predominantly of mountain, moor, heath, down, cliff or foreshore including banks, barriers, dune, beach, flat or other land adjacent to the foreshore. Also included are rivers and canals and expanses of water through which these run and adjacent land sufficient for access on foot, using boats and picnicking.

Local authorities were able to provide access by acquiring land themselves, by access agreements with landowners or by compulsory access orders. As a result of the CROW 2000 Act, no new Access Agreements will be made though existing ones remain valid.

> **Consequences**
> * A landowner is not responsible to the public using such rights of access to the same extent as he would be to other authorized visitors.
> * The public become trespassers if they abuse these rights, e.g. by damaging property, lighting fires, harming wildlife or stock, depositing rubbish, holding political meetings or generally annoy other people.
> * Local authorities (in England and Wales) are required to keep maps showing land in their area open for public access. In Scotland local authorities must map areas covered by Access Agreements.

- Access Agreements may include payment incurred in implementing an agreement.
- By-laws can be made and wardens appointed by the local planning authority.

Excepted land

- Agricultural land other than livestock grazing.
- Land covered by buildings or curtilage of such.
- Land plus curtilage for surface mineral extraction, golf courses, sports grounds, race courses, airfields.
- Land undergoing development for any of the above.

Access Orders

These are made on the authority of local planning authorities and must be confirmed by the Secretary of State. They can be recommended by the conservancies or required by the Secretary of State. The Order must include a map defining the land concerned. An Order may specify work or other things to be done on the land to facilitate recreational use.

Public Path Orders and Agreements

Countryside (Scotland) Act 1967, Highways Act 1980, Wildlife and Countryside Act 1981. This law applies in England, Wales and Scotland. Countryside and Rights of Way Act 2000.

A **public path** is created for the benefit to a substantial section of the public or to the convenience of persons living in the area, bearing in mind the effect on the landowner or occupier.

The local planning authority may create a path compulsorily or by agreement with a landowner or tenant. It may be created with or without special conditions. Payment may be involved. There is no set format for the document. Disagreement may be taken to the Secretary of State and compensation may be made. Under the Countryside and Rights of Way Act 2000, public paths may be designated only after an improvement plan has been published.

Other access provisions

- **Public Path Extinguishment Orders**
  Paths may be closed without compensation as long as closure does not adversely affect land adjoining the path.
- **Public Path Diversion Order**
  An owner or tenant or occupier can apply for diversion if he or she can demonstrate that there is a more convenient or direct route or prove that such a diversion will result in more efficient use of land.

Maintenance of public paths

Local planning authorities are responsible for maintenance of all paths created by Order or agreement. They can appeal to the Secretary of State/ Scottish Executive if they consider the maintenance requirements are unreasonable.

Long Distance Paths

National Parks and Access to the Countryside Act 1949 and the Countryside (Scotland) Act 1981. These laws apply in Scotland, England and Wales.

> **Long distance paths** refer to routes recommended by the conservancies along which the public should be allowed to make extensive journeys on foot, pedal cycles or horseback. For the whole or greater part of its length, a route should not be placed along roads used mainly by vehicles.

Detailed proposals are drawn up which have to be approved.

Disability Discrimination Act 1995 (DDA 95)

> The **Disability Discrimination Act 1995** makes it unlawful to discriminate against disabled people in normal day-to-day activities. 'Disabled' includes physical and mental disability and facial disfigurement.

Under DDA 95, by the end of 1999 service providers should have amended policies, procedures and practices that prevent service uptake, and also provide additional help (e.g. audiotape for interpretation) for disabled people. By 2000, where reasonable, physical boundaries that prevent access should have been removed or physical access provided in another way.

There are exemptions, including where:

- there is risk to health and safety.
- there is only one way to provide services to everyone else.
- a less favourable service is permissible only if it is otherwise impossible to serve disabled people at all.
- there is a legal duty under other legislation, e.g. listed buildings, national security.

In countryside provision, total *access* to all may be very expensive to provide. The next best option is total *information* so that all may make informed choices about, for example, steepness, steps, route length, transport possibilities, etc. as well as physical provision of route options.

Pollution Control

Public Health (Scotland) Act 1987. Alkali Act 1960. Clean Air Acts 1956–93. Rivers (Prevention of Pollution) Acts 1951 and 1965. Control of Pollution Act 1974. Water Act 1989. Environmental Protection Act 1990. Environment Act 1995. Noise and Statutory Nuisance Act 1993. Pollution Prevention and Control Act 1999.

Introduction

> **Pollution** issues may offer employment opportunities for landscape architects through Entrust (trusts associated with LandfillTax) projects or through environmental audit.
>
> Pollution control may impose obligations on clients and affect the management of construction sites. It may also imply a requirement to design surfaces that may be maintained mechanically.

As with planning legislation, statutes about pollution control have arisen from a concern for public health and safety. Early Acts dealt with particular forms of pollution, e.g. water, air, litter and ascribed control to separate agencies, but subsequent legislation has consolidated the different statutes and adopted the principle of integrated pollution control (IPC) under fewer but more powerful agencies.

> **Organizations to protect and enhance environmental quality**
>
> Department for Environment, Food and Rural Affairs DEFRA
> - DEFRA assumed control of waste disposal and management from DETR in 2001.
> - Waste planning is still the responsibility of the Department for Communities and Local Government (DCLG]
>
> Environmental Agency for England and Wales
> - Created on 1 April 1996 through the Environment Act 1995.
> - Combined the National Rivers Authority, Her Majesty's Inspectorate of Pollution (HMIP) and Waste Regulatory Authorities.
>
> Scottish Environmental Protection Agency
> - Created on 1 April 1996 through the Environment Act 1995.
> - Combined HMIPI, the River Purification Boards and the Waste Regulations Authorities and Local Authority Air Pollution Control functions under Part I of the 1990 Environmental Protect Act, although they remain with local authorities in England and Wales.

- The new independent Water and Sewerage Consumers Council moni-
  tors the three water authorities in the North, East and West of Scotland.
- SEPA, unlike EA, cannot undertake its own legal prosecutions.

Environmental Service in Northern Ireland ES(NI)
- Responsible for conservation and pollution control.

European Environment Agency
- Established on 30 October 1993.
- Based in Copenhagen.
- Ten tasks concerned with the provision of 'objective, reliable and comparable information at European level' as a basis for environmental protection measures, to assess the results of those measures and to ensure the
  public is properly informed about the state of the environment.

Integrated Pollution Control

Integrated pollution control is a response to the cross-media movement of
pollution and to the case for a unified inspectorate 'to ensure an integrated
approach to difficult industrial problems at source, whether these affect air,
water or land.' Royal Commission on Environmental Pollution (1976) "Fifth
report Air Pollution Control: an integrated approach." London, HMSO. IPC
recognises that reductor of a release (of pollution) to one medium could
well have implications for another.

The principle of IPC was established in statute in the Environmental
Protection Act 1990 and fully in force by 1996.

EC Directive on Integrated Pollution Prevention and Control (IPPC) 96/91

This Directive was adopted in autumn 1997 and was fully implemented
in the UK by October 1999. It is based on the UK IPC principles. It should
lead to harmonization throughout the member states of emission standards and other pollution controls.

IPPC ranges more widely than the UK legislation and covers installations for some intensive agriculture and food production facilities as well
as heavy industries. It is, like IPC, a formal legal system of regulatory
control, applying to a defined range of processes and activities. It should
have a major impact on *land reclamation*, as owners of industrial processes
will have to make a final environmental audit and produce a closure and
remediation plan agreed with the EA, SEPA or ES(NI).

IPPC Operators will have to:
- Take all appropriate preventative measures against pollution.
- Avoid waste production at source.
- Recover waste where practicable or deposit it in ways to minimize its environmental impact.
- Use energy efficiently.

Pollution Standards

Before IPC was developed, the degree of pollution in the UK was controlled by measurement against various standards. These standards still apply and include: specification standards that govern equipment, for instance to arrest grit and dust; emission standards that forbid more than a certain level of emission from a works; and receptor standards which restrict activities when they result in a certain level of harm.

Waste

The Environmental Protection Act 1990 created three new agencies: waste regulation, waste collection and waste disposal authorities.

Waste management licences are required from the regulation authority for the disposal, treatment and keeping of waste.
- Before a licence is granted, consultation is required with the local planning authority (where relevant), the Health and Safety Executive, EA or SEPA, and the relevant nature conservancy if an SSSI is involved.
- The terms of a licence require control of emission of liquids and gases from landfill sites, both during the filling process and for a number of years following closure.

There is a duty on all those producing, treating or disposing of waste to take all reasonable measures to ensure that there is no unauthorized handling or disposal of their waste.

Waste regulation authorities are under a duty to inspect their area for pollution risks caused by past disposal of waste. They should take steps to prevent any pollution or risk to human health, recovering the cost from the occupier of the land unless the authority has accepted the surrender of the relevant licence.

Litter

Environmental Protection Act 1990.

The leaving of litter is a criminal offence and islands and district councils have the power to serve fixed penalty notices on offenders.

Local authorities, educational institutions and statutory undertakers have a duty to ensure that their land is as far as practicable kept clear of litter, and this duty may be enforced by any person aggrieved by the defacement of land by litter seeking an Order from the courts.

Landfill Tax

This tax was introduced by the Finance Act 1996 and was further framed by the Landfill Tax Regulations 1996. It applies throughout the United Kingdom.

The tax is levied on material designated as waste deposited on a landfill site on or after 1 October 1996. The tax is paid by the landfill site operator. It is intended to reflect the environmental impact of landfill and to promote more sustainable waste management practices.

What is landfill?

Disposal is considered to be landfill if:

- It is deposited on the surface of the land, on a structure set into the surface or deposited beneath the surface.
- Disposal of material is not taxable if it is obtained by dredging, by dredging for navigational purposes or obtained during the course of sand or gravel extraction from the seabed.
- Deposits are not taxable if they result from commercial mining operations, reclamation of contaminated land (or deposits of dead domestic pets!)

Landfill Tax

Initially (from 1 April 1999) the tax was levied at £2 a tonne for inert waste and at £10 a tonne for everything else, but there have been planned increases in tax of £1 in most years. In 2006 the rate was set at £18 to rise by at least £3 a tonne yearly to at least £35 in 2010.

Landfill sites are licensed under the terms of the Environmental Protection Act 1990 and the Pollution Control and Local Government (Northern Ireland) Order 1978.

Environmental Body Tax Credit Scheme and Environmental Trusts

A tax rebate of up to 90 per cent will be deducted from the liability of landfill site operators if they are party to an Environmental Trust for a site. The trusts are to be managed by the local community and registered with the Commissioners for Customs and Excise. Approval and regulation of environmental projects is the responsibility of 'Entrust', an organization established for this purpose.

Environmental Trusts will be formed for purposes that may include:
- Research and development of sustainable waste management practices.
- Collection and dissemination of information about sustainable waste management.
- Remediation and restoration of sites unable to support economic or social activity, harmed previously by waste management or other industrial activities.
- Creation of habitats, wildlife and conservation areas within landfill sites.
- School-based education programmes to raise awareness of waste and its management.

Contaminated Land

Environmental Protection Act 1990 and Part IIA of the Environment Act 1995.

Contaminated land is defined as 'Any land which appears to the local authority in whose area it is situated to be in such a condition, by reason of substances in, or under the land that:
a) significant harm is being caused, or there is a significant possibility of such harm being caused; or
b pollution of controlled waters is being or is likely to be caused.

Contaminated land refers to a 'pollution linkage' comprising a source of contamination, a pathway and a receptor. If the pollution linkage is 'significant' the land is classified as statutory contaminated land.

With effect from July 1999, local authorities became required to inspect land within their boundaries for contamination in the form of pollution linkages. The local authority should determine remediation for each pollution linkage.

Landscapes, parks and gardens are not considered to be receptors in the definition of pollution linkages. Therefore, damage to vegetation on such sites could not cause land to be classified as contaminated unless humans, animals (livestock, other owned animals, or wild animals subject to shooting or fishing rights) or crops or certain habitats including SSSIs or buildings were also affected.

Planning Policy Statement (PPS23)

PPS 23 on planning and pollution control imposes requirements on developers to prove that their proposals will not create or allow continuation of unacceptable risks from the condition of the land or adjoining land. In other words the PPS enforces compliance with the Environmental Protection Act 1990 Part IIA. After treatment, the land should no longer be determined as contaminated as determined by the Environmental Protection Act 1990 Part IIA.

Remediation of contaminated land

Remediation is paid for by the people/organizations that caused the contamination, or by people/organizations that have acquired the land contaminated by others who are untraceable or unreachable for some reason. There is no State help, but local authorities may become involved particularly to aid regeneration. However, businesses can claim relief from corporation tax if they clean up contaminated land. They can also claim up to 150 per cent of the qualifying clean up cost provided that:

- The contamination was not caused by the company or a connected person or company.
- That the land was already contaminated when it was acquired.
- That the site is being used for legitimate business purposes.
  (See www.businesslink.org.uk)

In January 2005, the ODPM published the "Town and Country Planning Act 1990 section 215 Best Practice Guidance." This aims to help local authorities make better use of their powers to clear up derelict or unsightly land and buildings. The nature of the work required is determined by the local Environmental Health department.

The part IIA legislation is complicated, but despite the difficulty of enforcing it, owners of contaminated land have undertaken clean ups even if they did not cause the contamination in order to be able to use a site as they wish.

The Environmental Information Regulations 2004

These regulations work alongside the Freedom of Information Act 2000: the right of access to environmental information may be exercised against any public authority. It may, for instance, enable a developer to read records of why decisions were made about contaminated land.

Abandoned Mines

Following the Environment Act 1995, mine operators now have to give the EA or SEPA six months' prior notice of the abandonment of a mine or part of a mine. This should allow the EA or SEPA time to plan or advise on anticipated anti-pollution measures, especially pollution of controlled waters by accumulated mine water. This measure is important because mine water can be very toxic and cause serious damage to river life if it escapes.

Statutory nuisances

The Environmental Protection Act 1990 significantly improved the law of statutory nuisances.

Statutory nuisances (but only when they are prejudicial to health):

- Smoke.
- Fumes (including airborne solid matter smaller than dust) or gases.
- Premises in a state of disrepair.
- Dust, steam, smell or other effluvia arising on industrial, trade or business premises.
- Any accumulation or deposit.
- Noise (which includes vibration) emitted from premises.

Enforcement of the law is the duty of local authorities. They must take action if satisfied that a statutory nuisance exists or is likely to occur or recur. An Abatement Notice will be served on the person responsible, owner or occupier specifying what steps must be taken to deal with the nuisance. This may affect the management of construction sites.

The Clean Neighbourhoods and Environment Act 2005 made light pollution a statutory nuisance (except for defence, industry, trade or sport). Other measures included spot fines for abandoned vehicles, litter and graffiti.

Eco-management and audit

Eco-management and audit refers to a voluntary regulation to promote improvements in environmental performance at industrial sites through development of environmental management systems, regular auditing and the provision of information on environmental performance to the public.

This may be a source of work for landscape professionals, because it requires participating companies to identify all significant environmental issues relating to the industrial plant. However, if a landscape/environment practice undertakes an Environmental Audit their PII must reflect this aspect of work for liability claims.

Key Regulations – Control of Pollution

These are important regulations for landscape architects because it is the landscape architect's responsibility to check that the contractor is complying with all pesticide regulations.

Control of Pesticides Regulations 1986

Control of Pollution Act 1974, Pesticides Act 1998, Biocides Directive

- pesticide: a substance for destroying pests, especially insects (includes herbicides, fungicides, wood preservatives, plants and animal repellents and masonry biocides). Also rodenticides and avicides.
- Detailed requirements for aerial application.
- Users to take all reasonable precautions to protect health of human beings, creatures and plants.
- Commercial users must be competent.
- Employers must ensure employees have reached required standard of competence.
- Conditions applied to sale, supply and storage.
- Advertising is controlled.
- Certificate of competence for storing, selling, supplying of pesticides required.
- Users to comply with detailed directions for use.
- Listed adjutants (wetting agents) can be used.
- Only certain products can be tank mixed.

Control of Substances Hazardous to Health Regulations 1988 (COSHH)

Control of Pollution Act 1974.

The COSHH Regulations require employers, contractors, subcontractors and self-employed people to protect employees who may be exposed to health risks arising from hazardous substances they work with. The regulations require a written assessment of known risks or hazards and the action required to prevent or control them.

How COSSH affects landscape architects:

- Pesticides (check handling certificate and Certificate of Competence).
- Staining materials.
- Mulch from overseas (check bromide content).

Summary of COSSH requirements:

- Assess risks to health from hazardous substances arising in the workplace and determine action needed.
- Implement prevention or control programmes.
- Maintain and monitor those programmes.
- Provide health surveillance where appropriate.

- Inform, instruct and train employees in regard to work with hazardous substances.
- Keep records where required.

COSSH – safety and liability for pesticides

- COSHH assessment is comprehensive – check out all staff fully appraised.
- Check local water board.
- Prepare detailed specification and programme.
- Tender documents within requirements of HSE/HSC approved code of practice for safe use of pesticides for non-agricultural purposes.

Organization of Countryside and Conservation Authorities

The Environmental Protection Act 1990 split the Nature Conservancy Council (NCC) into three country agencies: English Nature, The Countryside Commission, and the Countryside Council for Wales, and also established the Joint Nature Conservation Committee. The Countryside Commission and the Rural Development Commission merged in 1999 to become the Countryside Agency. Scottish Natural Heritage was formed in 1991.

English Nature

English Nature is responsible for nature conservation in England.

The Countryside Agency

The Countryside Agency (formerly the Countryside Commission and the Rural Development Commission, which merged in 1999) is responsible for landscape conservation and countryside recreation in England.

The Countryside Agency's remit includes: conserving and enhancing the countryside; promoting social equity and economic opportunity for countryside residents; and promoting enjoyment for everyone of countryside recreation and tourism. Other areas included in the CA's remit are biodiversity, local distinctiveness, local character in food production, traffic management and access.

Statutory duties include designating national parks, AONBs and national trails, and mapping and opening up access to mountain, moor, heath and common land. The Countryside Agency also champions the provision of essential public services, housing needs, transport, businesses and towns in rural areas. (See 'Planning tomorrow's countryside' on the CA website at www.countryside.gov.uk)

Commission for Rural Communities

The Commission for Rural Communities (CRC) was established in 2005 as a division of the Countryside Agency. It is to be a rural advocate, expert advisor to the Government and independent watch-dog, concentrating on policy making rather than delivery. It is independent of Natural England.

Natural England

This is an independent agency, combining English Nature (the Landscape, Access and Recreation division of the Countryside Agency) and the environmental activities of DEFRA's Rural Development Service. It is a 'non-departmental public body' working on biodiversity, resource protection and landscape improvement, but its core aims do not include social and economic development. Socio-economic issues will be dealt with by local authorities and regional development agencies. The remit has been criticized for this apparent lack of integration. England's Forestry Commission could also be merged into the new organization.

Natural England was established in 2006 by the Natural Environment and Communities Act 2006. Natural England has responsibility for biodiversity, landscape and wildlife in rural, urban, coastal and marine areas.

The agencies and departments that will combine to form Natural England have been working together since April 2005 to:

- Promote nature conservation and protect biodiversity.
- Conserve and enhance the English landscape.
- Increase understanding and enjoyment of nature, promoting access to countryside and open spaces and encouraging open-air recreation.
- Contribute to social and economic well-being through management of the natural environment.
- Manage Environmental Stewardship, SSSIs, national parks and AONBs, NNRs and enforce relevant regulations.

The Countryside Council for Wales

CCW is responsible for landscape and nature conservation and countryside recreation in Wales.

The Joint Nature Conservation Committee

The JNCC acts as a co-ordinating body between the United Kingdom environmental agencies to provide a national, European and global dimension to nature conservation in the United Kingdom.

Scottish Natural Heritage

The Natural Heritage (Scotland) Act 1991 merged the Countryside Commission for Scotland and the Nature Conservation Council for Scotland to create Scottish Natural Heritage. SNH is responsible for landscape and nature conservation, promoting enjoyment and understanding of the environment, and encouraging sustainable use of natural resources.

The Farming and Rural Conservation Agency

From April 1997, this agency took over statutory work to do with rural land use planning, environmental protection, wildlife management, conservation, and the rural economy formerly handled by the Agricultural Development and Advisory Service.

Regional Development Agencies

RDAs were set up from April 1999. Their remit includes sustainable development.

Department for Environment, Food and Rural Affairs (DEFRA)

DEFRA was established in 2001 from a combination of the Ministry of Agriculture, Fisheries and Food and some functions from the Department of Environment, Transport and the Regions. Its main aim is sustainable development, defined as 'development which enables all people throughout the world to satisfy their basic needs and enjoy a better quality of life without compromising the quality of life of future generations'.

Sustainable development is to be achieved through five strategic priorities:
* Climate change and energy.
* Sustainable consumption and production.
* Protecting the countryside and natural resource protection.
* Sustainable rural communities.
* A sustainable farming and food sector including animal health and welfare.

Its task themes include:

* Integration of the environment with other government policies.
* Promotion of less wasteful uses of natural resources
* Prevention of animal disease outbreaks.
* Reform of the EU Common Fisheries Policy to preserve a healthy marine environment and sustainable fishing for the future.

These kinds of functions are performed in Scotland by the Scottish Executive Environment and Rural Affairs Department: SEERAD.

Cadw

Cadw is a Welsh word meaning "to keep". Cadw's remit is to protect, conserve and promote an appreciation of the built heritage of Wales. It was created in 1984. It is responsible for the preservation of and grant aiding of repairs to ancient monuments and historic buildings, and direct management of ancient monuments in Wales in direct state care. www.cadw.wales.gov.uk

English Heritage

This is an independent, government-sponsored body responsible for the historic environment of England. Its powers and responsibilities are set out in the National Heritage Act 1983. Its remit is to conserve and enhance the historic environment, broaden public access to the heritage and increase people's understanding of the past. www.english-heritage.org.uk

Historic Scotland

Historic Scotland is an agency within the Scottish Executive Education Department. It is responsible for safeguarding Scotland's historic environment and promoting its understanding and improvement. It was created in 1991. www.historic-scotland.gov.uk

5 Tendering

Work Stages

The Landscape Institute's *Landscape Consultant's Appointment* describes the preliminary and standard services that a landscape architect will provide from inception to completion for a normal design and implementation project. Work Stages F – H cover production information, Bills of Quantities (BQ) and tender action and follow on from the detailed proposals and approvals stage. The Landscape Consultants Appointment is due to be revised. Refer to The Landscape Institute or the website www. landscapeinstitute.org.uk).

Work Stage F: Production Information

Production information can be divided into three aspects:

> **• Illustrative •**
> Drawings (plans and details)

> **• Qualitative •**
> Specification

> **• Quantitative •**
> Bills of Quantities/Schedules/
> Schedules of Rates

The provision of one or all of these elements for a construction project is dependent on the procurement method adopted and the form of agreement used. (Refer to Chapter 6.)

Illustrative: Drawings

All construction contracts require some drawings, which may form part of the contract documents. Drawings illustrate the layout of the project and the detailing of the specified materials. They provide an accurate presentation of the work required in a consistent and clear format to communicate effectively with all members of the design and construction team. Ideally all drawings are issued at the date of the contract; however, dependent on the form of agreement being used they may vary in detail and timing of issue such as design and build contracts and management contracts.

Qualitative: Specification

The specification is a written document that describes the works generally and provides the detailed description of the quality required in terms of:

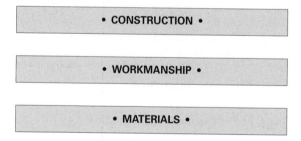

- CONSTRUCTION -

- WORKMANSHIP -

- MATERIALS -

The specification is divided into work sections that link with the Bills of Quantities and drawings. This system is known as the Common Arrangement of Works Section (CAWS), which was set up under the Government initiative 'Co-ordinated Project Information (CPI)', adopted in 1979 for drawings, specification and Bills aiming to produce a co-ordinated set of documents.

Where used, the specification forms part of the contract documents whether individual or contained within the BQ. In the JCLI form of agreement it is written into the contract if the specification is a separate contract document or if it forms part of the BQ. Specifications and Bills of Quantities are classified as design under the CDM regulations. In a JCT 'Without Quantities' form of agreement the specification is the over-riding description of the quality and quantity of the work required.

Employers Requirements/Contractors Proposals

In a design and build contract the specification acquires particular significance because it must set out the employer's requirements to which the contractors design, or detailed design must comply. The statement of 'employers requirements' can, at the employer's choice, be anything from a three-line performance specification to a completely developed scheme design with outline specification and drawings. In a JCT 'Contractor's Design 1998' form of agreement the concept of contractors' proposals is included. These are drafted by the prospective contractor in response to the employer's requirements and supplied together with the tender figure.

Methods of Specification

Where a traditional design and construction procurement route is adopted, the method of specification is linked to the form of agreement used, which will have standard systems relating to measurement and specification.

FORM OF AGREEMENT		SPECIFICATION SYSTEM	METHOD OF MEASUREMENT
1.	JCT	NBS (National Building Specification)	SMM7
2.	ICE	Specification for Road and Bridges Work	CESMM3
3.	GC WORKS	NBS	SMM7
4.	JCLI	NBS Landscape	SMM7

National standard systems are set up to ensure that consistency and accuracy is retained between all elements of the production information. Where a non-standard specification system is being used, a full descriptive specification can be prepared that is project specific and may have no references to trade products. Each item/product is specified in terms of its components, strength, colour, size, etc. Alternatively, many government departments and local authorities have in-house specifications which may be based on their standing orders or codes of practice.

Public Procurement: The Public Contracts Regulations 2006 (England, Wales and Northern Ireland)

EU Rules Governing Technical Specifications

A public contracting authority shall define technical specifications required for a contract either:

1. By reference to technical specifications in the following order of preference:
   - British Standards transposing European Standards (BS/EN/ISO); European technical approvals; common technical specifications; international standards, or other technical reference systems established by the European standardization bodies.
   - In the absence of these, by reference to British Standards or British Technical Approvals accompanied by the words *'or equivalent'*.
2. By reference to performance or functional requirements including environmental characteristics (eco-labels).
3. Unless justified by the subject of the contract, technical specifications must not mention products of a specific make, source or a particular process. The indication of trade marks, patents, types of a specific origin or production shall be prohibited unless the phrase 'or equivalent' is used where it is not possible to give a precise enough description of the subject for all parties concerned.

Quantitative: Schedules/Bills of Quantities/Schedules of Rates

Schedules are used to augment the drawings and assist in the preparation of Bills of Quantities. They are used to tabulate information for a range of similar items such as planting schedules, which list such items as species, type, size, location and unit rate.

Bills of Quantity and Schedules of Rates are described below more fully.

Work Stage G: Bills of Quantities

Bills of Quantities act as a link between the design and the implementation of the design. They consist of a list of items describing the works which when priced the total value equals the tender figure. They are prepared according to predetermined rules called 'Methods of Measurement' and they form part of the contract documents. The primary function of Bills of Quantity relates to their use with lump sum contracts. (Refer to Chapter 6)

Primary function
- Enable tenders to be submitted on the same basis.
- Enable interim valuations to be prepared.

In addition they can:

- Assist the contractor in assessing material, labour and plant requirements.
- Assist in the evaluation of tenders.
- Act as a basis for valuing alterations.
- Provide information for future estimates.

Layout and contents will vary but generally Bills of Quantities are set out under separate headings.

- PRELIMINARIES •

- MEASURED WORKS •

- PRIME COST, PROVISIONAL AND CONTINGENCY SUMS •

- GENERAL SUMMARY •

Preliminaries

The preliminaries cover the specific circumstances of the project under which the work will be carried out and which are not covered elsewhere in the tender documents. They comprise a list of items affecting the works as a whole, which are priced by the contractor, and these costs are carried forward to the general summary. The preliminaries form the backbone of the contractor's understanding of the working arrangements of the project and may influence the tender price.

Preliminaries

- Site description.
- Access and egress.
- Site security.
- Statutory approvals.
- Team accommodation/equipment requirements.
- Site meetings.
- Disturbance to third parties (noise, dust, cleaning of roads, access over land, temporary road closures).
- Warranties and bonds.
- Quality checks and samples.

- Health and Safety.
- Programme.
- Valuation and payment dates.
- Record drawings.
- Guarantees.
- Dayworks.

Payment of these items is due in the month/valuation period that they are expended. Normally they are paid as a proportion of the contract duration as it is unusual for the contractor to provide a break down of each item in the tender price.

Dayworks

Dayworks are set out in the preliminaries. They are works which cannot properly be measured and priced in accordance with the Bill of Quantities and therefore have to be dealt with on a labour, materials and plant basis, plus percentage for profit and overheads.
- Current agreed national rates for construction workers are used to value labour costs.
- Materials are valued as at actual cost to purchase
- There are set rates for plant costs published by the RICS and ICE. The method used should be stated in the dayworks section of the BQ.
- The tenderer states their percentage profit in the dayworks section of the BQ.

Measured works

This is the 'quantities' section of the Bill of Quantities and summarizes information from the drawings and specification. It is prepared in accordance with predetermined rules of measurement (rules of measurement relate to how items are quantified and how the Bill of Quantities is laid out) to produce a national general standard. The method of measurement is stated in the form of agreement used.

Four rules of measurement
- Civil Engineers Standard Method of Measurement (CESMM).
- Standard Method of Measurement of Building Works (SMM7).
- Method of Measurement for Road and Bridge Works.
- Code for the Measurement of Building Works in Small Dwellings.

SMM is based on the Co-ordinating Committee for Project Information (CCPI) common arrangement, adopted also for drawings and specifications (e.g. NBS), to produce a co-ordinated set of documents.

With SMM7, measurement is approached systematically through each work item or product, i.e. excavations, earthworks, topsoiling, cultivations, seeding and turfed areas, shrub and tree planting. Any departures from the standard measurement conventions must be specifically drawn to the attention of the tenderer.

With ICE contracts Bills of Quantities are shorter than standard building contracts and the method of measurement used is more concise. Complex and difficult operations may be described and measured as one item. For example, construction of a tunnel may measured as a singe item per linear metre.

Prime Cost, Provisional and Contingency Sums

Prime Cost Sum

This is a sum of money allowed in the Bill of Quantities for works, goods or services to be carried out or supplied by either the contractor, nominated subcontractor or nominated supplier for which the details are known at the time of tender.

Prime Cost sum

- An exact sum of money specified for an exact piece of work.
- When the contractor tenders they will allow in their rates the sum given in the Bill of Quantities plus their detailed profit and special attendance costs.

Provisional Sum

This is a sum allowed in the Bill of Quantities for works or goods, which cannot be accurately quantified or detailed entirely at the time the tender documents are issued. The contractor allows the sum plus percentage profit, except with a JCLI form of agreement where no percentage is allowed for profit. Provisional sums are identified under SMM7 as either defined work or undefined work.

Provisional sum

Defined work

Work not completely designed but includes information on:
- The nature and construction of the work.
- Approximate quantities that indicate the scope and extent of the work.

In this instance the contractor will be deemed to have made due allowance in the programming, planning and pricing of the preliminaries.

Undefined work

Work where no information is available. The contractor will not be deemed to have made any allowance in the programming, planning and pricing of preliminaries.

Contingency Sum

A sum allowed in the Bill of Quantities for works or costs required as a result of that which could not have been foreseen or accounted for. A contingency sum can only be expended in part or whole on the written authority of the landscape architect, e.g. soft spots at formation, reclamation, drainage. The sum can be expressed in two ways.

Contingency sum

- A specific sum entered in the Bill of Quantities.
- A sum calculated on a specific percentage of the contractor's tender; 2.5–5% is usual.

General Summary

This is the summary of costs from each section of the Bills of Quantities. The total of the general summary is the tender figure, which is carried to the 'form of tender'.

Schedules of Rates

Schedules of Rates are used where the actual quantities of work required are not known at the outset and are re-measured and valued only when the work has been completed.

A comprehensive Schedule of Rates including all that is likely to be required may often be little less than a Bill of Quantities without the quantities. In this situation approximate quantities can be included which are based on approximation of the area or volume envisaged. Although the work must be re-measured on completion the tender rates quoted are more likely to be accurate.

A Schedule of Rates can be used alongside a fixed quoted lump sum for the works (usually with very small projects using the JCT Minor Works Contract). The schedule will be used to value any additional works over that for which the lump sum has been quoted.

A Schedule of Rates can be used for serial tendering/measured-term contracts.

The Quantity Surveyor

The quantity surveyor is employed when the service he or she renders will be of value and economy in respect of the project. This should be for large contracts where proper cost control is essential. The quantity surveyor is either employed by the client or the landscape architect and is either paid directly by the client or the cost is included by the landscape architect in their fee.

The quantity surveyor is named in JCT forms of agreement, and in ICE contracts the duties of a quantity surveyor are placed on the engineer although in practice quantity surveyors are often appointed.

Role of the quantity surveyor (pre-contract)

Dependent on the level of appointment the QS will:
- Price the landscape architect's proposed scheme to enable the employer to compare all aspects of the designs.
- Prepare the Bill of Quantities by extracting the amounts of work from the landscape architect's drawings and descriptions in the specification.
- Prepare pre-tender probable costs.
- Check the priced Bills of Quantities submitted by the lowest tenderer.
- Report to the client via the landscape architect on the tenders recommended for acceptance or not.
- Amend or negotiate with the lowest tenderer.

The training of quantity surveyors includes contract administration and legal studies and consequently they can become involved in claims and disputes.

Work Stage H: Tender Action

The procurement route of the works must be agreed prior to the selection of the contractor and may take the form of a traditional, design and build, or management contract, etc. (Refer to Chapter 6). The method of selecting the contractor is normally by tendering either competitively or by negotiation.

Types of Tender

A tender is the price for which the tenderer (contractor) offers to carry out and complete, in accordance with the conditions of the contract and statutory requirements, the works shown on the drawings and described in the Bills of Quantities and/or specification.

There are two main types of tendering – non-competitive and competitive – although some types of tendering combine aspects of both. Within each of these types there are different methods of obtaining tenders.

• COMPETITIVE •
Selective (single or two stage)
Open
Serial

> • **NON-COMPETITIVE** •
> **Nominated**
> **Negotiated (single or two stage)**

Competitive Tendering

Selective Tendering (Single and Two Stage) JCT Practice Note 6 – Main Contract Tendering

The Code of Procedure for Single Stage or Two Stage Selective Tendering by the National Joint Consultative Committee for Building (NJCC) 1996 is no longer published. Practice Note 6 (2002) published by the Joint Contracts Tribunal Ltd (JCT) is intended to be a successor and includes single-stage, two-stage and design and build tendering. It sets out the rules that govern selective tendering that should be adhered to in order to obtain fair and competitive tenders. They do not however have to be followed unless it is stated in the tender documents that they are to be used.

Single-Stage Selective Tendering

A shortlist of tenderers is drawn up and they are issued with a full set of tender documents for pricing. The object of selection is to make a list of firms, any one of which could be entrusted with the job. If this is achieved, then the final choice of contractor will be simple – the firm offering the lowest tender. Only the most exceptional cases justify departure from this general recommendation. (Refer to page 245 for this process in more detail.)

Two-Stage Selective Tendering

This form of tendering is particularly suited to large or complex schemes where close collaboration with the contractor during the design stage will assist the search for the best solution for the employer in terms of cost, programme and design.

The professional team is able to make use of the contractor's expertise when finalizing the design; the contractor has an opportunity to become involved in the planning and key decision-making process for the project and build working relationships.

First stage

• The first stage is similar to single-stage competitive tendering, except in the level of information provided to the shortlist of tenderers, who have usually been included on the basis of their track record.

- Preliminaries, overheads, outline programme and pricing documents and partial design information are provided to a number of tenderers. It is not intended that a contract is entered into after the first stage process only that a tenderer is selected for the second stage where the pricing information is used in negotiation.

Second stage

- Negotiation based on the information provided at tender stage. It involves collaboration between the design team and the selected contractor in finalizing the design and development of production drawings, the health and safety plan and the Bills of Quantities for the works, and will result in a final agreed sum for the works. It will also include methods of working, value engineering, advice by the contractor on 'buildability', negotiation and allocation of risk, management of the site, detailed programming and the procurement of subcontractors and suppliers.
- Once an agreement on the contract sum has been agreed, a contract can be completed between the contractor and client.

All JCT Practice Note Model Forms can be adapted to suit two-stage selective tendering.

Open Tendering

Anyone is invited to apply to tender for the contract. Advertisements can be put in the press and tender documents are issued to those applying, normally on receipt of a deposit that is refunded when a tender is returned.

The Public Contracts Regulations 2006 and the Utilities Contracts Regulations (England, Wales and Northern Ireland). (Scotland will be implementing the Directive under separate regulations) covers the requirements of tendering public works or supply contracts Europe-wide to achieve fair competition. Supply contracts refer to Housing Associations, government agencies, local authorities or anybody subsidized by Government funds. The Regulations include new provisions on e-procurement systems, framework agreements, and competitive dialogue that helps the award of complex projects. It requires tenders expected to be over a certain value to be advertised in a Europe-wide tender journal (*OJEU*) inviting offers. The threshold value is stated in ECU's excluding VAT and is subject to regular amendment. The general principles are to ensure an equal and transparent treatment to all, which will still prevail regardless of the financial threshold.

The final selection of tenderers can however be by selection, negotiation or open tendering depending on the individual client and their own governing regulations.

Serial Tendering

Serial tendering is a combination of competitive and non-competitive tendering often used where there will be a number of similar repeat contracts. The contractor tenders for a project knowing that, if their performance is satisfactory, they will be awarded subsequent contracts.

The contract sum for the subsequent contracts will be negotiated from the original tender updated for any fluctuations in labour rates, materials, fuel, tax, etc. since the date of the tender. It is suitable where a number of similar projects will follow on from each other such as streetscape enhancement within a town centre where similar materials and details are used. The similarity of the works produces a learning curve for the contractor providing the client with savings in time and cost.

Non-competitive Tendering

Nominated Tendering

One contractor is nominated for the job. This typically occurs where the client has a preference for a particular contractor due to work previously carried out, or if the project requires a particular specialism that the contractor can offer. As competition is eliminated the price will normally be higher than that obtained through competition.

If recommending this form of tendering the landscape architect must be sure the benefits outweigh the potential additional cost to the client as it is very rare to have a totally nominated tender (most will be by negotiation).

Negotiated Tendering (single stage and two stage)

The contract price is negotiated between the client (or quantity surveyor if appointed) and the contractor.

> **Use of negotiated tendering**
> - The contractor has an established working relationship with a client.
> - Time for construction is limited.
> - There are specialized building techniques involved and the contractor's expertise could be valuable.
> - A project involves additional work.

Single-Stage Negotiation

To speed up the procedure of negotiation the contractor will normally price the tender documents and forward them to the QS for checking. The QS will check the rates and prices within the tender documents noting any contentious items. These will be the items discussed during the negotiation stage, all other items being accepted as priced. When agreement on all the items is reached a contract will be entered into based on the revised, negotiated tender sum.

Two-Stage Negotiation

Two-stage negotiation attempts to introduce some of the advantages of competitive tendering by obtaining tenders from a number of selected contractors. The tenders will consist of an ad hoc selection of rates for the major items of work, e.g. bulk excavations, topsoil, together with a priced preliminaries section, an outline programme and samples of all in labour rates, plant rates and materials prices expected to be used on the contract. On the basis of these rates, and in most cases an interview, a preferred bidder will be selected and negotiation similar to single stage will take place based on the rates already provided.

Two-stage negotiation is often used to select a management contractor under the JCT Management Contract form of agreement (refer to Chapter 6) or where it is important to have a contractor on board before all the design work is completed.

Advantages and Disadvantages of Alternative Types of Tendering

Single-Stage Selective Tendering

Advantages

- This process reduces abortive aggregated costs of estimating.
- Tenderers should be capable of the works and in a favourable financial situation.
- Tenderers have confidence that they are in a group facing similar conditions.

Disadvantages

- Cost level of tenders tends to be slightly higher due to better quality of tenderers and reduced competition.
- More upfront work required by the employer in putting the tender package together.
- Inflexible and no negotiation allowed for.
- Possibility of malpractice due to price fixing (there are still a few sectors of the industry and geographical locations where 'cartels' exist and price fixing, cover bidding, bid suppression and bid rotation is practiced). The Office of Fair Trading is currently clamping down on anti-competitive activities.

Two-Stage Selective Tendering

Advantages

- The design does not require to be finalized at tender stage and therefore the process is more flexible.
- The design can be developed with the contractor.
- Better project management by the contractor means that costs of changes are minimized.

Disadvantages

- No obligation on the employer to award contract.
- The price is likely to increase during the second stage as the approved stage 1 contractor has heavy bargaining power and the scope of work is not finally determined until stage 2.

Open Tendering

Advantages

- Competitive prices are usually obtained.
- Provides opportunities for firms wishing to diversify.
- Eliminates potential malpractice and price-fixing rings.
- Eliminates the potential charge of favouritism on a client.

Disadvantages

- Lowest tender may be submitted by a contractor inexperienced in tendering and may therefore have made a number of errors.
- Lowest tenderer may be unsuitable for the type of project or be financially unsound. Obtaining references may offset this slightly.
- Total cost of tendering is increased as all tenderers have to recoup costs eventually in other successful tenders.

Negotiated Tendering

Advantages

- Useful when time is limited and an early appointment of contractor is desired.
- Allows potential cost or time savings by using the contractor's expertise and skills during the design development and planning stage.
- Useful when contractor's expertise is known and required for design development.
- Useful when client/design team and contractor have an established relationship.

Disadvantages

- May lead to higher pricing.

Procedure for Single-Stage Selective Tendering

Practice Note 6: Main Contract Tendering published by the Joint Contracts Tribunal (JCT) 2002

This document is for use with all JCT Standard Forms of Building Contracts except JCT Form of Management Contract or Trades Contracts under the JCT Construction Management document. The Institute of Civil Engineers does have a separate tendering procedure for use with ICE-type contracts entitled 'Tendering for Civil Engineering Contracts' published in 2000.

Shortlist

A shortlist of tenderers is drawn up but no guidance is given on numbers in the practice note. Generally, a maximum of six tenderers for each project are chosen. (If there is likely to be extensive quantification, specification, specialization and calculation then this should be a maximum of four.)

Shortlist criteria

- Location of the firm.
- Financial standing and record.
- The firm's general experience, skill and reputation in the area in question.
- Adequacy of the firm's technical and management structure for the type of contract envisaged.
- The firm's competence and resources in respect of statutory Health and Safety requirements.
- The firms approach to quality assurance systems.
- Whether the firm will have adequate capacity at time of tender.

The object of shortlisting is to make a list of firms, any one of which will be capable of carrying out the contract.

This information could be obtained:

- By requesting references from previous employers and landscape architects.
- From your own, your colleague's or your client's knowledge/experience of the contractor.
- From BALI listings.
- From the client's approved list of contractors.

Preliminary Enquiry

A model 'form of preliminary enquiry' is contained within Appendix A of the practice note. It is in the form of a letter and includes the project information schedule and questionnaire.

Project information schedule

Model form contained within the practice note that allows for adjustments to design and build contracts using the JCT Building Contracts (with contractor's design), two-stage tendering process or partnering.

The form includes:
- Project information (title, description, location).
- Approximate cost range.
- Extent of design, if any, to be carried out by the contractor.
- Timing of the works (start and duration).
- Access to the site.
- Employer's requirements affecting order and methods of working.
- Anticipated date of tender issue and tender period.
- Proposed numbers of tenderers.
- Contact details of employer, consultants and planning supervisors.
- Form of contract and method of execution (simple or as deed).
- Details of listed, named or nominated subcontractors.
- Details of collateral warranty requirements.
- Details of guarantees or bonds required.
- Details of alternative tenders (e.g. price and other criteria).
- The criteria for assessing tenders, either price and/or other criteria (e.g. time, approach, resources, subcontractors and supply chain, technical ability, environmental proposals, management, customer care, design and build criteria).
- An indication of weighting or other means of assessment to be used should be provided.
- Correction of priced bills – alternative 1 or 2 to be used. (NB alternative 1 cannot be used with two-stage selective tendering or partnering).

Questionnaire

A model form is contained within Practice Note 6 and requests the following information:
- The company's experience in dealing with the type of project being tendered, to standards and timescale required.
- The company's technical skills for the project (including design capabilities where relevant).
- Management and personnel: management structure; management team for the project; company policies on staff development; and Health & Safety arrangements for liaising with the employer, the consultants, the subcontractors and the public).
- Current capability including current and expected workload.
- Company's financial standing and record.

The aim of the preliminary enquiry should be to make assessment of the eventual tenderers as straightforward as possible and, where relevant, a matter that can be judged on price alone. The preliminary enquiry should be sent out 4–6 weeks before the date set for the issue of tender documents. Responses should be received within 10 days unless the project/ questionnaire is more detailed.

Invitation to Tender

A shortlist of tenders is drawn up on the basis of responses to the preliminary enquiry. Documents to be issued include a 'Form of Invitation to Tender' in letter format (see Appendix B of the JCT Practice Note 6) and also:

- Project title and location.
- Employer details.
- Two copies of drawings listed on attached schedule.
- Two copies of specification, schedules of work or BQ or approximate quantities.
- Employer's requirements.
- JCT Form and other conditions.
- Any information changed from the preliminary enquiry information.
- Two copies of the pre-tender H&S plan.
- Other documents (e.g. collateral warranties, guarantee requirements, etc.).
- Form of Tender (see Practice Note 6 Appendix C for pro-forma).
- Tender return envelope, including tenderer's name.
- Instruction to tenderers (tendering procedure, date and time of return of tenders, inspection of the site and drawings or other documents).
- Signed and dated.

Separate Forms of Tender should be issued for each alternative offered.

In England and Wales it is common practice that the priced documents are not supplied with the tender unless errors are found on examination; the priced document of the successful tenderer will be supplied and examined. However, the employer may properly call for priced documents to accompany the tender, as in Scotland.

The Form of Tender is expressed to remain open for acceptance for a 28-day period from submission date. Tenderers should not withdraw their offer prior to this date, unless alternative 1 is used. An offer can lapse if not accepted within the specified period.

Tender Return

The tenderer should complete the Form of Tender enclosed with the invitation and return within the time specified. A minimum period should be allowed for the return of tenders and is stated in the Invitation to Tender (depending on the size and complexity of the job). This can be extended during the tender period if required by the employer, if an error in the tender documents is notified by a tenderer, or if a change is made by the employer.

Tender return procedure

- Tenders are opened at a specific time stated in the Invitation to Tender (usually 12 noon).
- In Scotland Bills of Quantities are submitted as a whole within the tender return. In England just the price of the tender is submitted, but following this the lowest tenderer is given four days to submit the bill for checking.
- A list of openings is prepared and witnessed (one in England and two in Scotland).
- In local authorities tenders go to the chief executive. The chairman of the committee that authorizes funding of the project signs the tenders and accepts them subject to checking. (The professional then does all the checking of tenders).
- Tenders received after time should not be admitted to the competition.

Checking of Tenders and Notification

In England the lowest tender is submitted and checked only. (Only if there are computational errors are the second and third lowest bills requested). In Scotland the three lowest tenders are arithmetically checked before rates are checked for any anomalies. Any obvious errors are recorded.

As soon as the tenders have been opened, all tenderers (except for the three lowest or best value) are informed immediately that their tenders have been unsuccessful. The second and third lowest (or best value) tenderers should be informed that their tenders were not the most favourable but that they may be approached again (this allows for withdrawals or errors in the lowest tender). Design information prepared by unsuccessful tenderers should be returned to them.

Qualification of Tender

Tenderers should not attempt to vary the identical basis of the tender by qualifying their tender. A tenderer who submits a qualified tender should be given the opportunity to withdraw the qualification without amendment to the tender; if they fail to do so their tender is rejected. Negotiation of a non-compliant tender is contrary to the principle of equal treatment.

Examination of Priced Documents and Errors in Tender Prices

The object of examining priced documents is to detect errors of computation before a contractor's offer is accepted. Tenderers sometimes make mistakes in their tender prices. The quantity surveyor (or landscape architect where no QS has been appointed) will check each item (rate and price) of the tenders. Good tendering procedure demands that a contractor's price should not be altered without justification.

The JCT Practice Note 6 recommends two simple alternative procedures for dealing with errors, which are specified in the formal Invitation to Tender and the Form of Tender.

Alternative 1: confirm or withdraw

(Correction of the overall tender price is not permitted – the tender price remains the same.)

The tenderer is informed of the errors and given the opportunity to confirm or withdraw their offer. This does not allow for the tender figure reported to the client to be corrected and the tender price remains the same.

- If the tenderer withdraws, then the second lowest tender is checked.
- If the tenderer confirms the tender as it stands, then an endorsement is added to the priced Bill of Quantities. This indicates that all rates or prices (excluding preliminary items, contingencies, prime cost and provisional sums) are considered reduced or increased in the same proportion as the corrected total of priced items exceeds or falls short of such items. For example, if there is a 10 per cent error, each valuation is reduced or increased by 10 per cent.
- Both the client and tenderer sign the endorsement.

Government bodies or local authorities often prefer this alternative, as the tender figure is the one that is reported and there is no chance of any negotiation occurring with the tenderer. However, it may be inconsistent with a partnering approach and is not appropriate for two-stage tendering procedures.

Alternative 2: confirm or amend

(Correction of the overall tender price is permitted – tender price can vary.)

The tenderer is given the opportunity to confirm their offer or amend it to correct genuine errors. This allows for the tender figure to be amended.

- If the tenderer confirms, Alternative 1 procedure is followed. (This is likely for only minor errors).

- If the tenderer chooses to amend their offer (this is likely if the error is commercially unviable), the new price is checked to ensure that it does not exceed the next lowest tender. If it does, the new lowest tender is checked.
- If the amended price is still the lowest tender, the tenderer has to be allowed access to their original Bill of Quantities to correct the details and initial them, or they will be required to confirm all the alterations in a letter. If the tenderer is subsequently successful in their tender, this letter should be joined with the acceptance and the amended tender figure and the rates in it substituted for those in the original tender.

It is important to ensure that it is genuine error and not negotiation, otherwise Alternative 2 becomes open to abuse if not properly supervised.

Tender Report and Recommendation

Tender report contents

- A statement of what the project comprises and the form of tendering used.
- The list of the tenderers and an explanation of any tenders not made or withdrawn.
- The range of tender prices.
- A note of obvious errors and the modifications made as a result.
- Amendments made to the tender documents during the tender period.
- In Scotland a detailed comparison of prices for the three lowest tenders (i.e. comparison of daywork rates, preambles, preliminaries and prime cost sums).
- A comment on rates in the context of the present state of the market.
- Confirmation that tenders were fairly, accurately and consistently priced.
- Recommendation.

Usually the lowest tender is recommended for acceptance. Only in exceptional circumstances should the landscape architect recommend other than the lowest tender because all are supposed to be suitable.

If tenders are over budget the tender report can incorporate a statement of any savings that could be made to bring the lowest tender within budget. A Bill of Reductions can be produced after negotiation with the lowest tenderer.

Acceptance of Tender

The tender report is sent to the client with a request for approval of the recommendation. If the client accepts, then either the client, or the landscape architect on the client's behalf, writes to the tenderer accepting their offer. This acceptance of an offer initiates a contract.

Post-tender Period

Notification of Tenders

Once the contract has been let, the JCT Model Form of Invitation to Tender provides a post-award notification to tenderers of a list of those tendering (alphabetical order) and a separate list of tender prices (in ascending order). These prices should not be attributable to individual bidders.

In terms of best value assessments contractors need to know how they have performed against the various criteria; each should, on request, be supplied with their own individual scores and the range of scores relating to each of the criteria.

Contract Preparation

Upon receipt of the letter of acceptance from the client or landscape architect, all documents become contract documents and the tenderer becomes the contractor. All the contract documents are signed and witnessed (two witnesses in Scotland).

If the project is notifiable, the CDM regulations state that the contractor cannot commence work until the Health and Safety Executive has been notified (Form F10) and the Contractors Construction Stage Health and Safety plan approved by the planning supervisor.

6 Contract and contract administration

Types of Contract

When a client decides they would like to carry out a project, whether it be an engineering or a building contract, there are a number of decisions that have to be made:-

- Who will design the works?
- Will the works be designed before the start of the contract?
- How firm a price is required?
- Is speed and early completion of the project important?
- Who takes the risk?

There are particular types of contract to suit the client's requirements:

Management contracts

If the client is looking for speedy completion of the project, which has the added advantage of possible savings, then a management contract is the best option.

The contractor works alongside the design team and cost consultants providing a construction management service on a number of professional bases. The management contractor does not undertake either the design or construction work directly. The design is not detailed when the contractor is engaged, therefore the design evolves as work proceeds.

The design requirements are met by letting each element of the construction to specialist subcontractors/consultants in parallel.

Fixed price or lump sum contract

Landscape architects, when working on simple landscape contracts, will in most cases use lump sum contracts. These are usually procured through the traditional method of tendering. Lump sum contracts are used when the client requires total control of the costs and a firm price at the outset.

Design and build or 'all in' contract

Where the contractor is designing the works (or this is done on his behalf) and building the works, a design and build contract is used. The burden of risk is with the contractor.

Standard Forms of Contract

There is a form of contract/agreement for every type of contract. Standard forms are produced for the following reasons:

CERTAINTY

The required performance of each party involved in the contract is known and clearly stated.

STANDARDIZATION

Wide use of standard forms enables contractors and professionals to be familiar with the rules laid down. This saves time, helps avoid confusion and provides a tried and tested framework for the successful completion of a contract.

SUITED FOR PURPOSE

There are several standard forms of agreement. Each has been designed for particular kinds of projects. Part of the professional's job is to choose the appropriate form of agreement for the job in hand.

Forms of Contract

Listed below are some of the main forms of agreement with which landscape architects may be involved:

- ICE -
- NEC -
- GC WORKS -

> - **JCT STANDARD FORM OF BUILDING CONTRACT**
> - **JCT STANDARD FORM OF MANAGEMENT CONTRACT**
> - **JCT INTERMEDIATE**
> - **JCT MINOR BUILDING WORKS**
> - **JCT INTERMEDIATE LANDSCAPE SUPPLEMENT**
> - **JCLI**

ICE Form (Institute of Civil Engineers)

Designed for large civil engineering contracts (i.e. bridges, motorways, slagheaps, sewage works, etc.). A very simple form for a few trades with wide powers, i.e. an engineer can dictate sequence of execution and simple quantities. All work is re-measured as it proceeds and therefore the final price is uncertain. The contractor is entitled to extensions of time and extra payment if they encounter physical conditions or artificial obstructions not reasonably foreseen by an experienced contractor.

New Engineering and Construction Contract

The Institute of Civil Engineers also produced the NEC (New Engineering Contract). NEC represents a very different approach to contracts and non-confrontational approaches to working within a contract.

GC Works – Government Contracts

There are three versions of GC/Works/1 for major building and civil engineering work: with quantities; without quantities; single-stage design and build.

> - GC/Works/2 for minor building and civil engineering work.
> - GC/Works/3 for mechanical and electrical engineering.
> - GC/Works/4 for small building, civil, mechanical and electrical work.
> - GC/Works/5 procurement of professional services.

JCT Standard Form of Building Contract (Joint Contracts Tribunal)

This is incorrectly also known as the RIBA form. Now a very complex document in a variety of forms, i.e. with/without quantities, private/local authority, approximate quantities, phased completion variants. Used for building contracts. Various forms for nominated subcontractors (NSC) are used with JCT and are discussed later in this chapter.

JCT Standard Form of Management Contract

This contract is used for large construction contracts where speed is of importance. There are incentives in place for the contractor to complete as quickly as possible. The contractor is accountable for all 'works' contractors.

JCT Intermediate

This also known as IFC (Intermediate Form of Contract) and is slightly simpler than JCT. There is no nomination of subcontractors, just 'naming'. Suitable for contracts of less than 12 months.

JCT Minor Building Works

Designed for use on relatively low value private or local authority, new and amended fixed price contracts. Very useful for a wide variety of projects including landscape, except it lacks the clauses for variations, objections to a nomination, penultimate certificate, fluctuations, and malicious damage or theft, which are included in the JCLI form.

This form is much simpler and easier to understand than JCT. Involving less administration, it is also cheaper to use than JCT. However, some clauses are omitted and therefore certain matters are undefined, e.g. there are no provisions for extensions of time and the valuation of variations is uncertain. There is no provision for nominated subcontractors and therefore it is not appropriate where specialist subcontractors are required.

JCT Intermediate Landscape Supplement

A supplement to the JCT Intermediate Form with provision for increased costs, vandalism, dead plants and partial possession by the employer.

In July 2005, JCT began its sequential publication of the new suite of contract documents. The new documentation is intended to simplify and shorten the contracts, ensuring that they match subcontracts and their fitness for purpose.

Changes that have occurred since 1998 which affect the JCT suite of contracts are:

Amendment 1 – construction Industry Scheme (CIS) (June 1999).
Amendment 2 – Sundry amendments (January 2000).
Amendment 3 – Terrorism cover/joint fire cost/CIS (January 2001).
Amendment 4 – Extension of time/loss and expense/advance payment (January 2001).
Amendment 5 – Construction skills Certification scheme (July 2003).

JCLI (Joint Council for Landscape Industries)

In 1998 the JCLI (Joint Council of Landscape Industries) form of agreement was updated and split into two contracts:

JCLI Agreement for Landscape Works '98

There are some fundamental differences to the previous version of the contract:

> - There is no provision for maintenance after completion; a separate JCLI agreement for landscape maintenance works is available for this purpose.
> - Provision has been included in the document to allow the release of retentions as various defects periods expire.

This contract is in the process of being updated.

The JCLI Form of Contract is a very simple contract originally based mainly on the JCT Minor Works contract. It does allow for nominated subcontractors, the penultimate certificate, malicious damage or theft and fluctuations, but more importantly it allows for options regarding differing lengths of soft defects liability and post practical completion by the employer or contractor. (Refer to Chapter 7 for more information.)

JCLI Landscape Maintenance Agreement '98

The JCLI Agreement for Maintenance Works '98 is appropriate for use in two different circumstances:

> - With the construction contract to cover maintenance during the planting defects period.
> - For the landscape maintenance works not associated with a construction contract.

This contract is in the process of being updated.

The contract allows for periodic payments and annual accounts. A bonus scheme can be applied for completion of work as programmed. Liquidated damages can be applied to items not carried out by the contractor on time or in accordance with specification.

If a landscape architect wishes to provide a contract for both landscape and maintenance works the two documents must be used and should be tendered together and signed at the same time.

Subcontracts

There are usually two types of subcontract:

NOMINATED SUBCONTRACTS
or
DOMESTIC SUBCONTRACTS

Nominated subcontracts

The landscape architect nominates the subcontractor when specialist techniques are required, early ordering is necessary and work of a particular quality is essential. With nominated subcontracts either a single firm is nominated within the document or a list of subcontractors is given.

In both cases, either before letting the main contract or during its early stages, the landscape architect invites tenders from a number of firms he or she thinks capable of performing the nominated subcontractor works. Then the landscape architect instructs the main contractor to accept a firm as a nominated subcontractor.

The conditions of contract for the subcontractor must be no more or less onerous than those binding the main contractor and the client. This applies to insurances too.

Several forms known by the letters NSC (nominated subcontractor) are used in association with JCT:

- **NSC/T**   Part 1 – Invitation to Tender.
            Part 2 – Standard form of nominated subcontractor tender.
            Three parts: Invitation.
                         Tender.
                         Conditions.
            Part 3 – Particular conditions (between main and subcontractor).
- **NSC/A**   Agreement between nominated subcontractor and contractor.
- **NSC/N**   A nomination instruction.
- **NSC/C**   Standard conditions of nominated subcontract.
- **NSC/W**   Employer and nominated subcontractor warranty.

If a nominated subcontractor delays completion of the works, the main contractor is entitled to an extension of time. Equally, the client suffers a loss of right to apply liquidated and ascertained damage if a delay is due to a nominated subcontractor.

Payment of Nominated Subcontractors
It is usually stipulated that subcontractors must be paid within 14 days of certified completion of their works.

If the nominated subcontractor is not paid, the landscape architect is entitled to raise this issue with the main contractor because the subcontractor is bound by the same contractual conditions as the main contractor and the valuation has been certified and therefore the subcontractor must be paid. If there is no action by the main contractor then the landscape architect advises the client to pay the subcontractor directly and issue certificates directly to the subcontractor.

Domestic Subcontracts

With domestic subcontracts the contractor chooses the subcontract and is responsible in all ways. The contractor lists the subcontractor in the tender and the landscape architect may have the right to disapprove him.

The landscape architect will have nothing to do with a domestic subcontractor and is not responsible for payments to the subcontractor. The contractor and subcontractor usually have a good working relationship.

Named Subcontractors

This is specific to IFC. The firm you require to do the work is named in the specification. The contractor enters a subcontract with the named firm. The contractor has the right to object to the named firm. The subcontractor becomes a domestic subcontractor.

Roles of People Engaged in Landscape Contracts

The parties to a landscape contract will be the client and the contractor. In traditional design, tender and construct situations there are the following teams (these are different for design and build contracts):

THE DESIGN TEAM
Client
Landscape architect or contract administrator
Project manager
Quantity surveyor
Other consultants
Clerk of works
Planning supervisor

THE CONTRACTOR
Contracts manager
Site agent/foreman
H&S representative
Subcontractors

The client, the landscape architect, the quantity surveyor, the contractor, the nominated subcontractor are all mentioned in most standard contracts. Other consultants are not and their position will depend largely on what form of agreement they have with the client or the landscape architect.

The Client

A private client may be unaware of the sequence of the design and construction process or of the functions and responsibilities of those engaged in a landscape contract. He or she also has additional responsibilities under CDM regulations. The landscape architect, as the client's agent, should advise him or her of their role.

The client as the employer will be responsible for the following:

- Either deciding the functions which the scheme is to fulfil or instructing the landscape architect to investigate these functions and thereafter agree them with him or her.
- Deciding the approximate budget.
- Appointing a landscape architect; also a quantity surveyor and a clerk of works or other professionals if required.
- Signing the legal agreement or contract that contains the clauses governing the conduct of the parties to the contract, namely the employer and the contractor.
- Appointing a competent planning supervisor and principal contractor under the CDM regulations and ensuring that sufficient resources will be allocated to enable the work to be carried out safely.
- During the course of and at the end of the contract paying any money due for services directly to the contractor, the amount being shown on certificates issued by the landscape architect and in the time specified in the contract.

What should the client be aware of?
- Their responsibilities and obligations, including adherence to these in a timely manner.
- Terms of engaging a professional person and the methods of working.
- Delegation of responsibility to the professional person as their agent.

The Landscape Architect/Contract Administrator

The landscape architect is the agent of the employer and is either appointed by the employer directly or as a consultant to an architect or engineer who is an appointee of the employer. The landscape architect is required, in accordance with the *Landscape Consultant's Appointment* or their agreement with the client, to:

- Advise the client on the appointment of the contractor and the responsibilities of the client, the contractor and the landscape consultant under the terms of the contract documents.

- Prepare the contract documents and arrange for them to be signed by the client and the contractor and provide production information as required by the contract.
- Administer the contract during operations on site including control of the clerk of works where appointed.
- Visit the site at intervals appropriate to the contractor's programmed activities to inspect the progress and quality of the works.
- Check and certify the authenticity of accounts.
- Make periodic financial reports to the client and identify any variation in the cost of the works or in the expected duration of the contract.
- Ensure the client understands their responsibility regarding CDM regulations including notifiable work and the appointment of a planning supervisor.
- Carry out all design and specification work in accordance with CDM regulations and prepare a risk assessment. Provide information to the planning supervisor.

The Project Manager

For larger, more complex projects a project manager is employed by the client. Project management is defined as 'the overall planning, co-ordination and control of the project from inception to completion'. The key role is to motivate, manage, co-ordinate and maintain the morale of the whole project team. The project manager is responsible for:

- Acting on behalf of and representing the client.
- Providing a cost-effective and independent service.
- Managing different disciplines and expertise.
- Satisfying the objectives and provisions of the project brief from inception to completion.

The Quantity Surveyor – Contract Period

(The responsibilities of a QS in the pre-contract period are covered in Chapter 5.)

The quantity surveyor will be responsible for:

- Measuring work carried out on site and valuing any materials held on site, at intervals.
- Agreeing, with the contractor's representative, the value of the interim measurement.

- Preparing and submitting these valuations to the landscape architect, who will use the figures to prepare interim certificates.
- Giving estimates of the cost of additional work involved and also of any consequential savings of work omitted because of variation orders.
- Agreeing the value of such work with the contractor.
- If requested, preparing variation Bill of Quantities to cover such work.
- Measuring and calculating the value of work carried out, and agreeing this value with the contractor on completion of the work.
- Submitting the valuation to the landscape architect.
- Generally advising the landscape architect of financial aspects and implications of the labour and material costs, insurance charges, etc. involved in any design or change of design in construction.

The Clerk of Works

The clerk of works is engaged by either the client or the landscape architect. They will work under the supervision of the landscape architect and their duties will include the following:

- Maintaining a register of drawings and all contract documentation.
- Notifying the landscape architect of any errors or discrepancies in the contract documents.
- Notifying the landscape architect immediately of any significant problems on site, or if any decisions or variations are required.
- Inspecting materials and goods for compliance with the stated standards and to make sure that they are properly stored and protected. Inspecting delivery notes and obtaining necessary certificates.
- Inspecting work for execution in accordance with the contract documents and with instruction or variation orders; witness and record any tests.
- Issuing verbal instructions. These must be confirmed in writing by the landscape architect within two days.
- Maintaining a daily diary recording such things as weather, instructions issued, details of attendance at dayworks, labour on site, delays, records of any tests.
- Submitting weekly reports on the state and progress of the works completed with the master programme.
- Attending site progress meetings and confirming accuracy of the contractor's progress report.
- Observing health and safety requirements with particular reference to CDM regulations.
- Measuring/inspecting work which may be buried if required.

A BUILDING CLERK OF WORKS

If you are working with a clerk of works who knows about building but not about landscape work:

- Go through the drawings, bills and specification with them to make sure they understand what is involved and what is important.
- Show them what a sample of good quality topsoil looks like.
- Have all plants delivered to the site labelled by species or at least have a labelled sample of each species to hand for comparison or ensure that you have checked them or tagged them at the nursery.

The Planning Supervisor

The planning supervisor has overall responsibility for:

- Co-ordinating the health and safety aspects of the design and planning phase and for the early stages of the health and safety plan and the health and safety file.
- Ensuring the principal contractor registers with the HSE for construction work which is notifiable.

Other Consultants

Consultants act purely as advisors to the landscape architect on specialist aspects of design or construction. They act under the landscape architect and cannot issue instructions directly. Evidence of consultants' PII should be sent to the landscape architect's insurers for verification.

The Contractor

The contractor enters into a legal agreement with the client and signs the contract document. He or she will be responsible for:

- Carrying out and completing the work in accordance with the contract documents and to the satisfaction of the landscape architect.
- Providing materials, goods and workmanship in accordance with the contract documents.
- Complying with statutory requirements and local by-laws.
- Ensuring that all the requirements of necessary legislation and regulations such as HASAW, CDM and Building regulations are complied with, such as registering with HSE for notifiable work, providing training for employees in Health & Safety and ensuring that adequate funds are made available for Health and Safety.
- Appointing an H&S officer and preparing the Health and Safety plan in accordance with CDM regulations. Ensuring that other subcontractors carry out a risk assessment of operations on site. Providing information for the Health and Safety file.

- Complying with the landscape architect's instructions or variations.
- Provide appropriate insurances and certificates.
- Organizing the sequence of the works and preparing the detailed programme.
- Co-ordinating the works of all subcontractors and suppliers.
- Keeping a competent person in charge of the works.
- Give notice of expected delays and the reasons for them.
- Make good any defects.
- Payment of wages/deduction of income tax for all employees.

Site Agent/Foreman

The site agent is the contractor's representative and will be responsible for all items listed under the main contractor that are applicable to the working of the site, and also for the following:

- Taking charge of the drawings, specification, Bill of Quantities, etc.
- Layout of site including any plant and huts.
- Organizing the labour teams, and day-to-day running of the site.
- Supervision of the work.
- Phasing the delivery of materials.
- Receiving instruction from the landscape architect.
- Presentation of the firm's policy to the workers.
- Feeding back information to the firm.
- Feeding back any complaints he or she cannot deal with.
- Probably the most important – showing a profit on each site

H&S Representative

- Responsible for all requirements relating to CDM & Health Safety including risk assessments method statements
- H&S file.
- Subcontractors (Ref. to p. 286/257).

HOW TO OBTAIN GOOD QUALITY IN A LANDSCAPE JOB

- Contract running is an important part of design work.
- Be meticulous, careful and accurate in running a job.
- Keep a diary, correspondence, minutes.
- You must provide time for contract administration.
- You must create the right atmosphere to get the best possible job.
- Remember quality starts on the drawing board.
- Relations with the contractor are important.
- Use a clerk of works.
- Use samples of workmanship or materials to guard against you and the contractor having different understandings about the specification.

The Pre-Start/Pre-Contract Meeting

When the contractor has been appointed by the client and the contract placed, an initial project meeting with the contractor and all others concerned should be arranged prior to works commencing on site. The meeting is held to establish contract procedure and administration and is usually chaired by the landscape architect (contract administrator). An agenda should be issued prior to the meeting that will include the following items for discussion:

**INITIAL PROJECT MEETING/PRE-START MEETING
SPECIMEN AGENDA**

1. Introduction
2. Project
3. Contract
4. Statutory obligations
5. Health and Safety matters
6. Contractual matters
7. Clerks of work's matters
8. Consultant's matters
9. Quantity surveyor's matters
10. Communications and procedures
11. Meetings

Introductions

This is the introduction of the representatives and parties to the contract. Individual roles should be clarified and an indication of any specialist appointed by the client for the contract should be given.

Project works

This is a brief description of the project, and its principals and objectives, and a description of the details of the site and any special restrictions such as access.

Contract

This is when the confirmation of the contract takes place, i.e. the exchange of letters between the contractor and client is required and the status with regard to preparation and signature of documents. It is usual to hand over all production information necessary for carrying out the works and review the situation regarding issuing other information. Insurance documents must be viewed and confirmed as valid.

It is the landscape architect/contract administrator's responsibility to ensure that the client receives all necessary evidence to their satisfaction and that the contractor is properly insured throughout the course of the contract until the issue of practical completion. The landscape architect/contract administrator should also remind the contractor to check the subcontractor's insurance. The contractor's tax exemption certificate should be checked and the requirement of a bond confirmed or otherwise. At this stage it should be checked that the client has registered with the Health and Safety Executive if required to do so.

Confirmation of the timing for the contract is also necessary and the date of possession, date of commencement, date of completion and maintenance period times or dates are confirmed.

Statutory obligations

Compliance with statutory requirements regarding noise, safety, building regulations, local by-laws and restrictions, Health and Safety Executive, etc. is discussed at this stage.

Health and Safety issues

In relation to CDM regulations, the Health and Safety Plan will be discussed and the planning supervisor will highlight the roles of the individual parties.

Contractor's matters

Note should be made that the work programme supplied by the contractor must be in the form required, e.g. bar chart. It must contain adequate separate work elements to measure their progress and integration with service installation, allocate specific dates for nominated subcontract work and relate to landscape architect's instructions and be kept up to date.

Agreement should be reached on site organization, such as location of site compound and facilities, services and access to the site.

Quality control should be discussed to cover the definition of the contractor's duties to supervise, the landscape architect's or contract administrator's duty to inspect, and the clerk of works or supervisory staff's duties in connection with the works.

Specialist works require a review of outstanding requirements for information to or from the contractor in connection with specialist works, and clarification that the contractor is responsible for co-ordinating specialist works and for their workmanship and materials.

Other issues such as testing and statutory undertakers should also be discussed at this stage.

Clerk of work's matters

The contractor must provide the clerk of works with adequate facilities as well as all relevant information on site staff, equipment and operations for the clerk of work's weekly reports to the landscape architect. Procedures for quality checks through certificates, vouchers and samples of material, samples of workmanship, test procedures set out in the Bill of Quantities, adequate protection and storage and visits to suppliers/manufacturer's works are discussed.

Consultants' matters

This requires a description of what the consultants are employed to do and confirmation that all instructions are to be issued by the landscape architect/contract administrator. Also, a timetable for specialist drawings should be established.

Quantity surveyor's matters/payments

Procedures are to be agreed for valuations in accordance with the client's instructions regarding timing. The percentage retention is to be clarified along with clarification of percentage value of goods and materials to be taken into account.

It is worth confirming that Dayworks will only be accepted on written instructions and that day sheets are required within seven days for signature by the landscape architect.

Tax requirements both for the client and contract concerning VAT should be agreed.

Communications and procedures

- It should be established that:
- Requests for information should be in writing.
- The landscape architect will respond to queries quickly.
- Technical queries are raised with the clerk of works initially.
- Policy queries and discrepancies are referred to the landscape architect for resolution.
- All information issued by the contract administrator will be via standard forms (certificates). Distribution and numbers of copies of drawings and instructions required by recipients is to be agreed.

Clarification is required that only written instructions from the landscape architect are valid and that all oral instructions will be confirmed in writing within 48 hours. The contractor must notify the landscape architect of any written confirmations outstanding. Claims are to be strictly in accordance with the terms of the contract. Any events should be raised immediately the relevant conditions occur.

Meetings

Types of meetings necessary require to be established, e.g. progress, site or design team meetings and their frequency.

Progress Meetings

Progress meetings are held to establish the progress of the contractor in relation to the programme. They are also a mechanism for keeping all parties informed of the situation with the contract and any issues arising from the contract. They should be held at regular intervals over the contract period suitable to the length of the contract.

Typical agenda for a progress meeting

1 Present
2 Minutes of last meeting
3 Matters arising from last meeting
4 Contractor's progress
 - General report
 - Subcontractor's report
 - Progress and comparison with programme
 - Percentage of main items complete
 - Causes for delay
 - Claims arising
 - Information received since last meeting
 - Information and drawings required, instructions required
5 Clerk of works report
 - Site matters – weather and general quality control
 - Lost time
6 Consultant's report
7 Qs Report
 - Valuation and measurement
 - Updated cost reports
8 Health and Safety matters
9 Communication and procedures
 - Drawings issued
 - Meetings held
 - Instructions issued
10 Contract completion date
11 Technical matters
12 Any other business
13 Date, time and place of next meeting

Definitions

The next few pages describe some of the issues relating to definitions within contract documentation or situations arising from contracts and explain how the various parties deal with them. In most cases the JCLI Agreement for Landscape Works is referred to unless otherwise stipulated.

Certificates

The Conditions of Contract state that the contract administrator is to issue certificates. Pro formers for all certificates can be downloaded from the Landscape Institute website. There are two types of certificate:

> **CERTIFICATES OF PAYMENT**
> **CERTIFICATES OF PROGRESS**

Certificates of Payment

> *The Progress Payment Certificate*

The JCLI Agreement for Landscape Works contract conditions require the contract administrator to certify progress payments at intervals of not less than four weeks (or at certain specified stages of the work) in respect of the value of the works properly exercised (as agreed by the landscape architect), materials on site and deduction of retention money.

The amount due to the contractor is written on a standard form and a copy is sent to the contractor, quantity surveyor and client. The client must pay within the time specified in the contract.

> *The Penultimate Certificate*

Within 14 days of issuing the certificate of practical completion the contract administration must issue a penultimate certificate of payment. It is priced on the basis of 97.5 per cent of the contract sum adjusted for the cost of variations, prime cost, provisional sums and any fluctuations to which the contractor is entitled, and the release of half the retention money. The valuation of this certificate must be accurate since the contract does not provide for the issue of any other before the final certificate.

> *The Final Certificate*

Having received from the contractor all the necessary documentation within the specified period from practical completion, the contract administrator must issue a final certificate. This must be issued within 28 days and will cover the balance due to the contractor. The payment should be honoured by the client within the period specified in the contract. In most circumstances the amount specified will include all outstanding monies and the final half of the retention money. However there are options in the JCLI Agreement for Landscape Works to issue the final certificate with retentions associated with unexpired defects liability periods. It will be issued on a standard form and copied as before.

JCLI Maintenance Certificate of Payment

The JCLI Maintenance Agreement allows for periodic payments to the landscape contractor at intervals of one month. There is no retention but there is a system whereby the client can deduct monies for individual items of work not being carried out or not in accordance with the specification or on time. There is also a bonus that can be added to the contractor's annual certificate if the contractor is performing well.

Certificates of Progress

The Practical Completion Certificate

The contract administrator must certify the date when in their opinion the works have reached practical completion, i.e. whether work is sufficiently complete to be safely used for the purpose for which it was designed. There is a standard form for most contracts but with ICE conditions, a letter is issued.

Implications of practical completion

- All parties know that works are finished.
- The contractor is no longer required to carry insurance for the works.
- The contractor can apply for release of bond.
- The contractor can apply for half retention money.
- The period of final measurement may start.
- The defects liability period begins.

There is also a certificate of non-completion required to start the liquidated and ascertained damages process.

The Certificate of Non-Completion

Implications of non-completion

- All parties know that the works are not complete on the due date.
- The contractor must continue to complete the works.
- Liquidated and ascertained damages can be sought from the contractor.

It is the contract administrator's responsibility to ensure that the planning supervisor has all the information required for the Health and Safety before this certificate is issued.

The Certificate of Making Good Defects

The contractor has to make good any defects both in the hard works and soft works (pre-practical completion) within a specified period after practical completion. The contract administrator has a duty to certify when the contractor has made them good with a Certificate of Making Good Defects. If the contractor is responsible for the maintenance of the soft works (post practical completion) he or she will be required to make good any defects within a specified time after practical completion. The contract administrator has a duty to certify when the contractor has made them good.

Instructions

A written instruction to proceed with, omit or change any aspect of the works provided it is a minor change with small monetary value. It can also be used to omit prime cost and provisional sums. Instructions are issued by the contract administrator on a standard form and must follow a verbal instruction within two days.

Variations

The contract administrator can issue instructions for the following reasons:

A variation

- In the expenditure of a prime cost.
- In the expenditure of a provisional sum.
- Any major addition.
- Any major omission or change in the works.
- A major change to the order or period in which the works are to be carried out, which is necessary.

If this involves time or money, it is called a 'variation'. Variations are issued on the same forms as instructions.

It is the contract administrator or quantity surveyor's responsibility to value the variations, but usually it is agreed between the landscape architect or QS and the contractor.

> **Valuing of variations**
> - The same work under similar conditions at the contract rate and prices.
> - Similar work under different conditions based on contract rates.
> - Different work for which no rates exist, at fair and reasonable rates.
> - Works that cannot be measured at dayworks' rates.

Dayworks

Dayworks are used where a specific set of works are to be undertaken which are not included within the original contract documents. A contingency sum is allowed in the documents and can only be expended on written authority of the landscape architect.

Dayworks must always be authorized beforehand and it is important to check that the rates, prices, quantity of labour and materials are correct.

The valuation of work on a daywork basis consists of the actual (prime) cost to the contractor of labour, materials and plant to which are added the incidental costs, overheads and profit and expressed as a percentage addition.

The contractor must keep records of amount of labour, time worked and the plant used. The clerk of works keeps a close eye of the works and checks daywork sheets. Daywork sheets are required to be submitted on a Monday following the work. The landscape architect must approve the daywork sheets.

Penalties

The following are penalties against the contractor for not completing the works at all or on time:

> **Bond**
> A bond is an assurance against the contractor not completing the works. It is taken out by the contractor in the name of the client and the contractor and placed in a bank account. If the contractor does not perform, the client has the money. It is written into the contract documents as a sum or percentage.
>
> **Retention money**
> A deduction from each interim certificate of payment is made, which is usually 5 per cent of the contract. Half will be given back to the contractor at practical completion, half at end of defects liability period.
>
> **Liquidated damages**
> This is an assessed sum of money that is to be paid by the contractor if they fail to complete the works in the period of time required. It is based

on an assessment made by the client of loss due to non-use or non-trading on the site, and is written into the contract documents.
- Liquidated: failure to operate, i.e. bank loan amount or failure/loss of revenue.
- Ascertained: specific failure, i.e. 10 car parking spaces × amount per car. It is an exact amount.

Liquidated and ascertained damages can only be applied with a certificate of non-completion. If the contract administrator fails to take off L&A damages, the client is entitled to do so.

Extensions of Time

Contracts provide for the contractor to notify the contract administrator if it becomes apparent the works will not be completed by the contract completion date 'for reasons beyond the control of the contractor'.

In most large building contracts there are 13 relevant events:

Reasons for an extension of time – JCT

- 'Force majeure'.
- Exceptionally adverse weather conditions.
- Civil commotion.
- Compliance with instructions.
- Opening up work that was proved to be satisfactory.
- Late instructions.
- Nominated subcontractor's delay.
- Delay by other contractors or suppliers organized by the employer.
- Statutory powers or reasons beyond the contractor's control affecting the use of labour or securing of goods essential to the works.
- Statutory undertaker's work.
- Prevention of ingress or egress by the employer.
- Postponement of the works by the employer or architect.
- A release schedule by the architect.

In JCLI it is quoted 'for reasons beyond the control of the contractor including compliance of any instruction of the contract administrator whose issue is not due to a default of the contractor'.

The contract administrator must make in writing an extension of the time for completion that is reasonable. (An event that causes delay does not automatically result in an extension; it must cause delay to the critical path of the contract). In addition, the landscape architect must ascertain the amount of loss and expense involved to the contractor if notified by the contractor and include it in any progress payments.

Determination

By the client/employer

The client can determine the contractor's employment if the contractor fails to proceed diligently with the works or wholly suspends carrying out the works or if the contractor becomes bankrupt, makes a composite arrangement with his or her creditors or has a provisional liquidator appointed or a winding up order made.

In the first situation the employer must give seven days notice in which they require the default to be ended. In the case of bankruptcy determination is by notice and is actioned on the date of notice.

Determination is by notice (registered post or recorded delivery) and is actioned on the date of the notice. The date it is received the contractor must cease activities and immediately give up possession of the works. Upon receipt of the notice, determination is immediate. The client may require the contractor to remove their equipment and assign all delivery agreements to any new contractor the client employs.

By the contractor

The contractor can determine their own employment if:
- The client fails to make progress payment under the provision of the contract or makes a default with regard to VAT.
- The client obstructs the issue of any certificate due.
- If the client or their representative interferes or obstructs the works or fails to make the site available for the works.
- The client suspends the works for a continuous period of one month.
- If the client goes bankrupt, makes a composite arrangement with their creditors or has a provisional liquidation appointed or a winding up order made.

In first three situations determination must be by notice (registered post and recorded delivery). This notice specifies the default and requires it to be ended. After receipt of the notice the client has seven days to cease any of the activities described, otherwise the contractor will service further notice to determine the contract. Determination shall take effect on the date of receipt of that notice.

If the client goes bankrupt determination is by notice and it takes effect upon the date of the notice by the client/employer.

WHEN DISASTER STRIKES!
- You must keep the client informed; you must act on their agreement.
- Assess any financial implications of any decision made.

- Set out, especially in a dispute, to act with balanced judgement and act reasonably.
- Imagine your opinion being put to an arbiter at a later date.
- Act quickly (discuss the matter with colleagues).
- Do not hesitate to bring in outside advice or expertise.
- Keep the fullest possible documentation of your contract.
- Ensure the clarity and precision of the documentation before going to tender – it is important.

Action Following Determination

Determination by Employer

The contractor ceases to occupy the site and the employer may recover additional cost to him or her for completing the works and any expenses incurred as a direct result of the determination, i.e. consultants fees, retendering or approaching second lowest contractor.

Determination by Contractor

The contractor prepares an account setting out the total value of the work executed and materials on site, costs of removing site equipment and direct loss/damage caused by the determination. The employer must then pay the contractor the amount due within 28 days of its submission by the contractor.

Dispute Resolution

If a dispute arises within the contract, the parties to the contract should try resolving it themselves. If this is not possible there are a number of options as follows:

Litigation

This is the process of dispute resolution before a court. It takes place in the Technology and Construction court, which is a specialist division of the High Court, or in the County Court. Lawyers act on each party's behalf.

Arbitration

The process whereby parties of a contract agree to refer a dispute to the determination of one or more independent persons, in a judicial manner. The decision of the arbiter is expressed in an award which will be binding on the parties and enforceable in law. Arbitration must be agreed by both parties. (Arbitration Act 1996.)

Adjudication

This is the process by which disputes between parties to a contract are decided by a third party adjudicator. It is used to obtain a quick, neutral decision on disputes arising from a contract.

Mediation

The process of structured negotiation aided by a third party mediator. The mediator does not decide the dispute; the matter is for the parties' own agreement. The process is voluntary and consensual. If an agreement is reached, the parties can decide whether to set out the agreement in a written signed document with the intention of it becoming a binding agreement.

7 The JCLI Agreements

There are two JCLI Forms of Agreement used by practising landscape architects. The JCLI Agreement for Landscape Works and the JCLI Agreement for Landscape Maintenance works. Both are lump sum contracts. The original documents were produced in 1998 and the most recent edition is 2002, but in the process of being updated.

If the client wishes to carry out both landscape works and maintenance under the same contract, then the JCLI Agreement for Landscape Works and the JCLI Agreement for Maintenance Works must be used and should be tendered together and signed at the same time.

The JCLI Agreement for Landscape Works

Outlined below are explanatory notes to be read in conjunction with the contract document. The Landscape Institute publishes Practice Note 5 to aid in the use of this form. The JCLI Agreements differ from other standard contracts by containing clauses which allow for partial possession, differing lengths of defects liability periods and allowances for payment in final certificates for release of retention as each defects period expires. (All actions by the landscape architect are to be carried out pre-tender. All actions by the contract administrator take place whilst the works are ongoing.)

> **JCLI Agreement for Landscape Works. 1st, 2nd and 3rd Recitals.**

It is the landscape architect's duty to decide on the relevant production information and fill the form in correctly. It is essential that the right information is given to allow the tenderer to price on the right basis.

It should be noted that the contract administrator is named in person.

4th Recital

It should be noted that the quantity surveyor is named in person. If there is no quantity surveyor working on the project this section should be deleted.

5th Recital

This clause refers to CDM regulations and should be considered and deleted according to the relevant alternatives by the landscape architect, pre-tender.

Article 1 and Article 2

The 'consideration': this is filled in by the contract administrator once the contract sum has been agreed.

Articles 3 to 7C

The articles basically state in principle what each party to the contract will do. It is the contract administrator's duty to fill in the consideration and the relevant names.

Articles 4 and 5 only require to be completed if CDM regulations apply.

Article 7 gives the parties to the contract the choice of method of dispute resolution.

1.0   Intentions of the Parties
1.1   Contractor's obligations

'The contractor shall, in a good and workmanlike manner, carry out and complete the works in accordance with the contract documents using materials and workmanship specified to the reasonable satisfaction of the contract Administrator'.

1.2 Contract Administrator's duties

The contract administrator's duties are to:

- Issue further information.
- Issue all certificates.
- Confirm all instructions in writing.

1.3 Reappointment of Planning Supervisor or Principal Contractor – notification to Contractor

The above is only relevant if CDM regulations apply. It is the contract administrator's duty to notify the contractor in writing.

1.4 Alternative B2 in the 5th recital – notification by Contractor – regulation 8(5) of the CDM Regulations

The landscape architect is to retain or omit this clause depending on the CDM requirement.

1.5 Giving or service of notices or other documents

It is the landscape architect's responsibility to decide what should be the relevant means of giving notice and should retain or omit this clause.

1.6 Reckoning periods of days

It is the landscape architect's responsibility to decide if this should be the case and retain or amend this clause.

1.7 Applicable Law

In Scotland the Law of Scotland shall apply.

1.8 Bills of Quantities and SMM

It is the landscape architect's responsibility to check that this is the case.

1.9 Contracts (Rights of Third Parties) Act 1999 – contracting out

2.0 Commencement and completion

2.1 Commencement and completion

The commencement and completion dates are to be inserted by the landscape architect.

2.2 Extension of contract period

The contractor shall be given an extension of time for reasons beyond his control. This is quite vague and the contract administrator will have to make a fair and reasonable judgement as to the reasons for an extension of time. The contractor may seek guidance from other Forms of Contract such as JCT (refer to Chapter 6). The contract administrator's response must be in writing. Refer also to Clause 7.3.1, 2 and 3.

2.3 Damages for non-completion

It is the landscape architect's responsibility to work out the amount of damages. It is not possible to estimate accurately the loss of interest an employer will suffer when a contract is delayed, but a reasonable estimate can be made by carrying out the following calculation:

For example,

Estimated Contract Value	£75,000.
Bank Base Rate + 2%	9%

$$\text{Interest} = \frac{£75\,\text{K} \times 9\%}{52\ (\text{weekly rate})} = £129.80 \text{ per week}$$

The contract administrator must issue a certificate of non-completion.

2.4 Practical Completion

The contract administrator issues this certificate when he believes the works are complete. Where the contract administrator is unable to certify due to, say, seasonal planting requirements, he can certify upon receiving the contractor's written undertaking to complete the planting within an agreed time. The relevance of practical completion is outlined in Chapter 6.

2.5 Defects Liability

This relates particularly to hard landscape works. If a 12-month defect period is required in the contract, the landscape architect must make the necessary amendments to this clause. A Certificate of Making Good Defects is issued by the contract administrator at the end of the Defects Liability Period when all works have been 'made good'.

2.6 Partial possession by Employer

It is important to ensure that insurance is sorted out by both parties for partial possession.

2.7 Failures of plants (pre practical completion)

This clause is relevant only to plant failures and sub-standard plant material pre practical completion.

2.8A 1 & 2 Plants defects liability and post practical completion care by Contractor

Either section 1 or 2 or the next clause is relevant and has an implication on whether or not the JCLI Form of Agreement for Maintenance Works is included in the contract documentation. If this section 1 is relevant, the landscape architect must ensure before tender that both Forms of Contract are included in the contract documentation, tendered and signed at the same time. It is the landscape architect's responsibility to fill in the relevant sections. Maintenance works will commence at Practical completion. If Partial Possession, it is better for the maintenance to be concluded on one date and not be staggered. Practice note 5 recommends defects liability periods for grass, shrubs, trees and semi-mature trees; it is the landscape architect's responsibility to ensure the most appropriate period for each is considered and inserted.

> **2.8B**   *Plants defects liability and post practical completion care by Employer*

This clause is only relevant should the employer be responsible for maintenance of the site following practical completion. This is generally not good practice and is not recommended due to lack of guarantee and assessment of plant failure at practical completion.

> **2.9A & B**   *Malicious damage or theft (before practical completion)*

The landscape architect must choose the most relevant clause for the site and location of the works.

> **3.0   Control of the Works**

> **3.1   *Assignment***

> **3.2 1 & 2**

Section 1 implies that it is the contract administrator's duty to ensure written consent has been given to any subcontractor.

Section 2 implies that the subcontract should provide for payment by the contractor to the subcontractor in the proper manner.

> **3.3   *Contractor's representative***

> **3.4   *Exclusion from the Works***

> **3.5   *Contract Administrator's instructions***

It is of upmost importance that the 48 hours are adhered to by the contract administrator; likewise with the seven days by the contractor (although there are few situations where this is possible depending on the type of works being carried out).

3.6   Variations

The contract administrator is required to decide on the best option and act accordingly.

3.7   PC and Provisional Sums

Refer to practice note 5 in which it is noted that no cash discount is allowable by subcontractors or suppliers arising out of instructions in respect of prime cost sums.

4.0   Payment

4.1   Correction of inconsistencies

No one part of the contract documentation takes precedence; it is entirely the decision of the contract administrator who has to weigh up the various options and ensure that the desired option can be afforded by the client.

4.2.1   Progress payments and retention

It is the contract administrator's duty to prepare progress certificates of payment and include the reduction of retention until practical completion. If the figure requires to be more or less than 5% retention then the landscape architect shall insert the appropriate amount before tender.

In most situations, the employer is unlikely to be able to pay the contractor within the stipulated 14 days. It is essential that the landscape architect establishes the appropriate period of payment for the client; otherwise clause 4.2.1 shall apply.

4.3   Penultimate certificate

The contract administrator issues the certificate after awarding practical completion. This certificate releases half the retention monies. Again, note the 14-day limit may require to be altered.

4.4   Notices of amounts to be paid and deductions

4.5 0.1, 0.2, 0.3, 0.4 & 0.5   Final Certificate

This will or will not release the retention monies depending on the period after practical completion written into the clause, the relationship of this time period with the defects liability period and whether the client or the contractor is caring for plants after practical completion. It is a complicated process dependant on how many expiries of defects liability periods there are in the contract. It would prudent of the contract administrator to ensure all defects liability period expiry dates are recorded and information is easily accessible to allow the contractor to be paid on time in accordance with the contract. Again, the 14-day period for payment may require to be altered to suit the client's payment periods.

4.6   Contribution, levy and tax changes [s]

This clause should be deleted if the contract is for a short period.

4.7   Fixed price

4.8   Right of suspension by Contractor

5.0   Statutory obligations

5.1   Statutory obligations, notices, fees and charges

This clause implicates the landscape architect to ensure that all relevant information is in the contract documentation. It is useful to put a note on the drawings regarding the accuracy of public utilities information and the onus on the contractor to accurately locate all services.

5.2   Value added tax

It is recommended that the contract administrator writes a letter with the payment certificate expressing the amount of VAT to be paid to the contractor and reminding the client of their obligations to pay VAT.

5.3   Construction Industry Scheme (CIS)

The tax exemption certificate allows the contractor to be exempt from income tax under the Corporation and Taxes Act 1998. It is essential that the contract administrator checks the validity of the CIS 4 registration card or certificates 5 or 6.

6.0   Injury, damage and insurance

All insurance requirements should be completed by the landscape architect in agreement with the client at the outset.

6.4   Evidence of Insurance

It is essential that the landscape architect sees evidence of the contractor's insurances and makes a note of expiry dates.

7.0   Determination

Refer to Chapter 6.

The contract administrator must ensure the client is fully informed at all times.

8.0   Settlement of disputes

It is the landscape architect's responsibility to choose the appropriate form of dispute settlement. (Refer to Chapter 6 for more information on the types of dispute settlement.)

The JCLI Agreement for Landscape Maintenance Works

This contract is intended for landscape maintenance contracts with a value of up to about £150 000.00 per year.

This agreement makes no provision for implementing landscape construction works.

It can be used as a maintenance contract and incorporates considerable flexibility to accommodate different circumstances. It can also be used with the JCLI Agreement for Landscape Works for the maintenance of landscape works. If a defects period is required for plants, a separate agreement between the contractor and employer is required for the after-care of plants during this period.

Where this is the case:

- The maintenance contract should last for at least the longest soft land-scape defects period in the construction contract.
- Partial possession under the construction contract will cause phased commencement of the maintenance contract, but the end of the maintenance should be the same for all parts. Phased commencement will constitute an instruction.

The following relate specifically to the maintenance contract:

- There is no reference to CDM regulations, as maintenance is not a construction issue.
- There are no references to Bills of Quantities and SMM.
- Sections 2 and 4 are adapted to suit the circumstances relating to maintenance.
- It omits the Statutory Deduction Scheme provisions because this scheme does not apply to maintenance works.
- There are no provisions for PC sums and nominated subcontractors.
- There is no insurance of the works.
- There are slight revisions to the determination clauses to suit maintenance works.

Index

Access, 208–218
  Access Agreements and
    Orders, 216–217
  Countryside and Rights
    of Way Act 2000,
    213–215
  Disability
    Discrimination
    Act, 218
  long distance paths, 218
  new access rights,
    213–215
    access land, 214
    excepted land, 214
    restrictions, 214–215
  Public Path and Orders
    Agreements,
    217–218
  public rights of way,
    209–215
    in England and
      Wales, 209–213
    in Scotland, 215
Adjudication, 275
Agency, law of, 58–59
Agenda, pre-start
  meeting, 264–267
Agricultural Development
  and Advisory
  Service, 229
Amenity and landscape,
  designations, 174–183
Arbitration, 274
Areas of Great Landscape
  Value, 176–177
Areas of Outstanding
  Natural Beauty,
  180–182
Ascertained
  damages, 272

Badgers, 188–189
Bats, 189–190
Bills of Quantity, 234,
  234–238, 247
  general summary, 238
  layout, 235
  measured works,
    236–237
  preliminaries, 235–236

primary function,
  234–235
prime cost, provisional
  and contingency
  sums, 237–238
purposes of, 234–235
Biodiversity, 191–192
Birds, 184–185, 203
Bond, 272–273
Breach:
  Code of Conduct, 3
  contract, 33, 51, 67–68
  management agree-
    ments, 206–207
Business development, 26

CDM Regulations, 45, 72,
  74–81
  application of, 74–75
  breach and prosecu-
    tion, 79–80
  commencement of
    work, 251
  design, 232
  duties of parties, 75–77,
    258–259
  Health and Safety File,
    78–79, 262
  Health and Safety
    Plans, 78, 262
  planning supervisor, 262
  revisions, 80–81
  risk assessment, 77
  tender questionnaire,
    246
Circulars:
  Circular 11/95, 126, 134
  Circular 13/1991 Nature
    Conservation, 184,
    192, 196
  Circular 42/55, 175
Clerk of Works, 261–262,
  266, 267
Client:
  contract with landscape
    architect, 33
  determination of
    contract, 273–274
  duties under CDM
    regulations, 76

integrity and
  standing, 31
landscape architect's
  liability towards,
  66, 68–69
landscape architect's
  responsibility to,
  7–9
public sector, 9–10
quantity surveyor, and,
  238
role, 258–259
why employ a
  landscape
  architect, 1
Code of Conduct, 3–7
  Architects Registration
    Board, 3
  breach, 3
  clients, 33
  guidance, for
    employees, 7
  sections, 3–4
  standards, 4–7
Code of Procedure for
  Single Stage Selective
  Tendering, 240,
  243, 245
Collateral warranties, 45,
  58, 68
Collateral warranty, 45,
  57–58, 68
Commencement and
  completion, JCLI
  agreements, 279
  contract period
    extension, 279
  defects liability, 280
  employer, partial
    possession, 280
  malicious damage/
    theft, 281
  non-completion,
    damages for, 279
  plants defects liability
    and post practical
    completion care:
    by contractor, 280
    by employer, 281
  plants failures, 280

Commencement and
  completion, JCLI
  agreements (*Contd*)
practical completion,
  279–280
Commission for Rural
  Communities (CRC),
  228
Cadw, 230
Countryside Council for
  Wales (CCW), 228
DEFRA, 229
English heritage, 230
Farming and rural
  conservation
  agency, 229
Historic Scotland, 230
Joint Nature
  Conservation
  Committee
  (JNCC), 228
Natural England, 228
Regional development
  agencies (RDA),
  229
Scottish Natural
  Heritage (SNH),
  229
Common Agricultural
  Policy (CAP), 155–157
Common Arrangement
  of Works Section
  (CAWS), 232
Communication in
  contract, 266–267
Companies, 16–20
accounts and finance, 17
bankruptcy, 16
Certificate of
  Incorporation, 16
directors, 16
dissolution, 18
formation, 16
liabilities, 18
limited liability, 16–17
management, 16
and partnerships, key
  differences, 19–20
public limited
  company, 17
registered number, 16
retirement and
  death, 16
shareholders, 16–17
size, 17
unlimited liability, 16–17
Conservancies,
  responsibilities of,
  228–230

Consortia, 22
Consultants:
appointment of a
  landscape
  consultant
  methods, 26–31
other professionals,
  25–26, 262
planning supervisor,
  76, 262
quantity surveyor,
  238–239
Contaminated land,
  223–224
Planning Policy
  Statement, 224
remediation, 224
Contingency sum, 238
Contract:
agency, 58
agreement, 52–53
all in contract, 253
ascertained damages,
  272
bond, 271
breach, 51, 67–68
certificates:
  making good
    defects, 270
  non-completion,
    269–270
  payment and
    progress,
    268–270
claims, 266–267
consideration, 52
dayworks, 236, 271
defects liability period,
  269
definitions, 51
discharge of, 53–54
dispute resolution,
  274–275
essential of a valid,
  52–53
forms, 253–256
GC Works, 254
ICE, see main entry
instructions, 270
instructions by
  landscape
  architect, 266
JCLI, see main entry
JCT, see main entry
JCT Minor works, 238,
  255
landscape architect and
  client, 33, 34
legality, 53

liquidated damages,
  271–272
lump sum, 253
  schedules of rates, 238
making good defects,
  270, 286
management
  agreements,
  206–207
measured term schedule
  of rates, 238
non completion, 269–270
offer and acceptance, 52
offer and revocation, 52
penalties, 271–272
practical completion,
  269
pre-start meeting, 264
privity, 57
  collateral warranties,
    58
  Contracts Act 1999, 57
retention money, 271
standard forms, 253–254
  purpose, 253
  types, 253–254
subcontracts, 257–258
terms, 54–55
value added tax, 266,
  273
variations, 270–271
in writing, 55
Contractor:
actions at pre-start
  meeting, 265
CDM Regulations, 77,
  262–263
Control of Pesticides
  Regulations, 226
COSHH, 226–227
determination by, 273,
  274
duties of main
  contractor, 262–263
foreman, 263
nomination for work,
  246
preliminaries, 235–236
progress report, 261, 267
site agent, 263
special skills and
  tendering, 241
Contracts Act 1999, 57
Control of Substances
  Hazardous to Health
  Regulations 1988
  (COSSH), 226–227
Convention on
  International Trade in

Endangered Species of Wild Flora and Fauna (CITES), 184, 187
Co-operatives, 21
Copyright:
duration, 47–48
effect, 48
ownership, 48
protected works, 47
Cost control, 238
Country parks, 177
Countryside Agency, 179–180, 213, 230
Countryside Commission, 179, 227
Countryside Council for Wales, 173, 213, 228
Countryside Stewardship, 161–162, 183

Dayworks, 236, 261, 266, 271
Department for Environment, Food and Rural Affairs (DEFRA), 87, 128, 171, 219, 229
Design competitions, 28
Determination, JCLI agreements, *see* Determination of contract
Determination of contract, 273–274
Development plan documents (DPDs), 93
Disbursement, 40–41
Disputes, settlement: in JCLI agreements, 284
Diversion orders (DO), 210
Duty of care, *see* Collateral warranties

Eco-management and audit, 225
Electronic documents, 56
England:
community forests, 170
Environmental Protection Agency, 219–220
National Forests, 170
planning guidance, 88
return of tenders, 247–248
English Nature, 227, 228

Entrust, 222–223
Environmental Impact Assessment, 104, 129–130, 141–146
environmental statement, 143–144
extent of, 152–153, 154–155
landscape assessment, 146–148
Natura 2000, 201–205
planning legislation, 141–146
decision process, 146
implementing and monitoring, 146
key legislation, 141–142
need, 142
screening, 143
significance, 142–143
submission procedure, 145
scope, 145
Environmental legislation, 152
access to the countryside, 208–218
amenity, landscape quality and natural habitat, protection, 174–187
amenity and landscape, designations, 175–183
species and special habitats, designations, 183–187
commission for rural communities, 228–230
Convention on International Trade in Endangered Species (CITES), 187–206
development, 152–153
development plans, 154
organization of countryside and conservation authorities, 227
planning law, 153–155

pollution control, 219–227
scarce resources, management, 155–174
specific sites and species, 206–208
Environmental stewardship, 163–164
Environmental trusts, 222–223
Environmentally Sensitive Areas (ESA), 160–161
European law:
'assessment of the effects of certain public and private projects on the environment', the, 141
Bern Convention of European Wildlife and natural Habitats 1979, 201
Biocides Directive, 226
Birds Directive 1979, 201
conservation of natural habitats and wild flora and fauna 1992, 201
Construction Directive 1992, 73
Specifications Directive 2006, 234
Treaty of Amsterdam 1997, 153
Water Framework Directive 2000 (WFD), 173
Work Directive 2000, 72
European Spatial Development Perspective (ESPD), 91
Extensions of time, 272

Farming and Rural Conservation Agency, 229
Farming areas, residential property, 154
Fees, *see* Landscape Architect, fees
Finance:
capacity of landscape practice, 31
companies, 17
debts in partnership, 12–13

Finance (*Contd*)
  fees, *see* Landscape
    Architect
  income tax, 12
  payment certificates,
    268–269
  systems, 24
Foreman, 263
Forest Design Plans
  (FDP), 167
Forest plans, 167
Forestry, *see* Trees
Forms of agreement:
  Appointment of
    Landscape
    Architect, and,
    31–33
  See also Contract, ICE,
    JCLI and JCT
Forms of organization,
  9–22
  private sector:
    companies, 16–20
    consortia, 22
    co-operatives, 21
    group practice, 22
    limited liability
      partnerships
      (LLPs), 14–15
    partnerships, 11–15
    sole principal, 20–21
    trusts, 21–22
  public sector, 9–10

General summary in Bill
  of Quantity, 238
Grants, 165–166
Greenbelt, 175–176
Group practices, 22

Habitat creation, 223
Hazardous substances,
  226–227
Health and Safety:
  Act 1974, 72–73
  CDM construction
    phase, 78
  CDM file, 78–79
  CDM pre-tender plan,
    77–78
  CDM Regulation, 74–81
  pre-start meeting, 265
Hedgerows, 182–183
Human rights, European
  convention on, 50–51

ICE form of agreement:
  form of contract, 254
  tendering, 246

IFC Contract, 255
Injury and damage, JCLI
  agreements, 284
Insurance:
  collateral warranties, 58
  contract, 85
  employer's liability, 85
  other consultants'
    professional
    indemnity, 262
  professional indemnity,
    24, 83–85
  public liability, 85
Insurance, JCLI
  agreements.
  evidence, 284
Integrated Coastal Zone
  Management, 201
Integrated pollution
  prevention and
  control (IPPC) 96/91,
  220–221

JCLI form of agreement:
  certificates of payment
    and progress,
    268–269
  extensions of time,
    272
  form of contract,
    254–255
  for landscape
    maintenance
    works, 284–285
  for landscape works:
    commencement
      and completion,
      279
    determination,
      284
    disputes, settlements,
      284
    injury, damage and
      insurance, 284
    intentions of parties,
      277–279
    payment, 282–283
    statutory obligations,
      283–284
    works, control,
      281–282
  maintenance certificate
    of payment, 269
  specification, 233–234
JCT form of agreement:
  contractors proposals,
    233
  employers requirements,
    233

forms of contract,
  254–255
  specification, 232
JCT Intermediate, 255
  Landscape
    Supplement, 255
JCT Landscape
  maintenance
  agreement, 256
JCT landscape
  supplement, 255
Joint Nature Conservation
  Committee, 227–230

Landfill, 222
Landscape architect:
  appointment of a, 26, 35
  capacity to undertake
    work, 31
  certificates of payment
    and progress,
    268–269
  Code of Conduct, 3–7
  conditions of
    appointment, 35
  confirming
    appointment, 31–36
  duties in contract,
    259–260, 264–272
  duties under CDM
    Regulations, 75, 260
  fees, 36
    calculating, 36–37, 43
    calculation methods,
      apportionment,
      41
    ceiling figure, 40
    charging, 36–37
    expenses, 40
    incentive, 40
    Landscape
      Consultant's
      Appointment,
      The, 35
    lump sum, 39
    non payment, 41–42
    payment, 40
    percentage, 37
    programmed
      instalment, 41
    retainer/term
      commissions,
      40
    schedule of fees, 36
    submissions, 42
    tendering, 28, 42
    time, 38
    unit price, 40
  instructions, 266, 270

Memorandum of
    Agreement, 32, 34
obligations, 7–9
planning legislation, 139
professional compe-
    tence, 5, 8, 31
professional title, 2
public inquiries,
    137–138
quasi-arbitrator/
    arbiter, 9
relationship with client,
    7–9, 32–33
responsibilities, 7
responsible agent, 8–9
role in contract,
    259–260, 264–272
services, 35–36
Landscape assessment,
    146–148
Landscape character, 128
Landscape character
    assessment, 155
Landscape Institute:
    Charter of
        Incorporation, 2–3
    Code of Professional
        Conduct and
        Practice, 3–7
    Guide to Procedure for
        Competitive
        Tendering, 42
    landscape assessment
        guidelines, 146–147
    Landscape Consultant's
        Appointment,
        The, 33–35, 231
    members, 3
    objects of, 2
    Professional
        Performance
        and Conduct
        Committee, 3
    Royal Charter, 2
    Standard Memorandum
        of Agreement, 32
    standards, 4–7
Latent damage, 82
Law:
    Acts of Parliament, *see*
        Legislation
    agency, 58–59
    blame, 82
    civil, 51
    common, 50
    contract, 51–59
    criminal, 51
    defamation/libel, 65
    delict, 65

duty of care, 60
English, 50
European, 50
latent damage, 82
legislation, *see main entry*
liability, *see main entry*
negligence, 60
nuisance, 62
planning, 86
Rylands v. Fletcher, 61
Scots, 49
strict liability, 61
torts, 59–65
trespass, 65
written, 50
Legal entity:
    companies and, 16
    partnerships and, 11
Legal systems, of UK,
    49–51
Legislation:
    Agricultural Land
        (Removal of
        Surface Soil) Act
        1953, 158
    Agriculture Act 1947,
        158
    Agriculture Act 1986,
        160
    Alkali Act 1960, 219
    Ancient Monuments
        and Archaeological
        Areas Act 1979,
        118
    Asylum and
        Immigration Act
        1997, 72
    Badger Act 1973, 188
    Brine Pumping
        (Compensation
        for Subsidence)
        Act 1981, 174
    Civil Liberties
        Contribution Act
        1982, 82
    Clean Air Acts
        1956–1993, 219
    Coal Mining Subsidence
        Act 1957, 174
    Companies Act 1985,
        16, 18
    Companies Act 1989,
        16, 23
    Conservation of Wild
        Creatures and
        Wild Plants Act
        1975, 183–184
    Control of Pollution
        Act 1974, 219, 226

Countryside Act 1968,
    177, 206, 209,
    216–217
Countryside (Scotland)
    Act 1981, 177, 192,
    206, 218
Countryside and Rights
    of Way Act 2000,
    183, 184, 205, 209
Defective Premises
    Act 1972, 72
Disability
    Discrimination
    Act 1995, 72, 218
Employer's Liability
    (Compulsory
    Insurance)
    Act 1969, 72
Employment Act 1980,
    72
Employment Protection
    (Consolidation)
    Act 1978, 72
Employment Relations
    Act 1999, 23, 72
Employment Rights Act
    1996, 23–24, 71, 72
Environment Act 1995,
    130–131, 179, 182,
    219, 223
Environmental
    Protection Act 1990,
    97, 219–223, 227
Equal pay Act 1970, 72
European Communities
    Act 1972, 50, 201
Finance Act 1996, 222
Forestry Acts 1919,
    1967, 1979, 1986,
    1991, 164
Greenbelt (London and
    the Home counties)
    Act 1938, 175
Health and Safety at
    Work Act 1974, 24,
    72–73
Highways Act 1980, 136,
    209, 217
Housing Grants and
    Regeneration Act
    1996, 33
Industrial and Provident
    Societies Acts
    1965–1975, 21
Land Reform (Scotland)
    Act 2003, 215–216
Limitations Act 1980, 82
Local Government Act,
    10

Legislation (*Contd*)
  Local Government
    Act 1985, 96
  Mineral Working Act
    1951 and 1971, 174
  National Minimum
    Wage Act 1998, 72
  National Parks
    (Scotland) Act
    2000, 179
  National Parks and
    Access to the
    Countryside Act
    1949, 179–180, 192,
    199, 206, 209, 216,
    218
  National Heritage
    (Scotland) Act
    1992, 182
  Nature Conservation
    (Scotland) Act
    2004, 185
  Noise and Statutory
    Nuisance Act
    1993, 219
  Occupier's Liability
    Act 1954, 71, 73
  Offices, Shops and
    Railway Premises
    Act 1963, 24, 72–73
  Partnerships Act 1890,
    11–12, 23
  Pesticides Act 1998, 226
  Planning (Listed
    Buildings and
    Conservation
    Areas) Act 1990,
    87, 116–117
  Planning (Listed
    Buildings and
    Conservation
    Areas) (Scotland)
    Act 1997, 89, 116,
    117
  Planning and
    Compensation
    Act 1991, 91,
    96–97, 101, 111, 131
  Planning and
    Compensation
    Act 2004, 91–92,
    94–95
  Pollution Prevention
    and Control Act
    1999, 219
  primary, examples of, 87
  Protection of Animals
    (Scotland) Act
    1912, 186
  Protection of Badgers
    Act 1992, 188
  Protection of Birds Acts
    1954–1967, 183
  Protection of Wild
    Mammals
    (Scotland) Act
    2002, 186
  Public Health (Scotland)
    Act 1987, 219
  Race Relations Act
    1976, 72
  Restrictive Trade
    Practices Act 1976,
    33
  Rights of Way Act 1990,
    209
  Rivers (Prevention of
    Pollution) Acts
    1951 and 1965, 219
  Scotland Act 1998, 89
  Sex Discrimination Act
    1975, 72
  Supply of Goods and
    Services Act 1982,
    72
  Town and Country
    Amenities Act
    1974, 116
  Town and Country
    Planning Act 1947,
    86, 104, 176
  Town and Country
    Planning Act 1971,
    132, 137
  Town and Country
    Planning
    (Minerals) Act
    1981, 130, 174
  Town and Country
    Planning Act 1990,
    87, 101, 116, 117,
    132
  Town and Country
    Planning (Scotland)
    Act 1997, 89, 101,
    110, 130, 133
  Transport and Works
    Act 1992, 136
  Water Act 1973, 172
  Weed Act 1959, 158
  Wild Animals
    Protection Act
    1996, 185–186
  Wild Mammals
    (Protection) Act
    1996, 184
  Wildlife and
    Countryside Act
    1981, 188, 190,
    192–193, 206, 208
  Wildlife and
    Countryside
    (Amendment) Act
    1985, 188, 192
Letters of intent, 56
Liability:
  in companies, 18
  contract, 67
  negligence, 66
  of partnerships, 11
  practice, 68–69
  professional, 67
  statutory, 71
  tort, 66
  vicarious, 71
Limestone pavements, 190
Limited liability
    partnerships (LLPs),
    14–15, 69
  accounts, 15
  dissolution, 15
  finance, 15
  formation, 14
  legal status, 14–15
  liabilities, 15
  management, 14–15
  power, 15
  size, 15
Liquidated damages,
    271–272
Litigation, 274
Local authorities:
  Areas of Outstanding
    Natural Beauty,
    180–182
  best value, 10
  compulsory competitive
    tendering, 10
  country parks, 177
  Environmentally
    Sensitive Areas, 160
  litter, 221–222
  management
    agreements,
    206–207
  national parks, 177
  National Scenic Areas,
    182
  nature reserves,
    199–200
  public paths, 217
  rights of way, 209–215
  standing orders, 10
  statutory nuisances,
    225
Local planning
    designations, 155

Marine nature
    reserves, 200
    designation, 201
    Integrated Coastal
        Zone Management
        (ICZM), 201
    purpose, 201
Mediation, 275
Meetings:
    precontract, 264
    prestart, 264
    progress, 267
Minerals:
    abandoned mines,
        224–225
    Act 1981, 130
    generally, 102, 130–132
    guidance, 87–88
    plans, 96–97
Mulch, 226

National Assembly for
    Wales (NAW), 88
National Parks, 179
National Parks
    Commission, 179
National Scenic
    Areas, 182
Natura 2000, 201–205
Nature Conservancy
    Council, 227
Nature Conservation
    Order, 207–208
    characteristics, 207–208
    special, 208
Nature Reserves, 199–200
Negotiation:
    for landscape work,
        27–28
    in tendering, 242–243,
        244
Northern Ireland, 90
    Environmental Service,
        220
    heritage, 110
    planning guidance,
        100

Obligations:
    liabilities, 65–66
    partnerships, 11–12

Parties intentions, JCLI
    agreements:
    Alternative B2 in 5th
        recital, 278
    applicable law, 278
    bills of quantities and
        SMM, 278–279

contract administrator's
    duties, 278
contractor's
    obligations, 277
Contracts Act 1999,
    279
giving or service of
    notices or other
    documents, 278
planning supervisor's
    reappointment, 278
principal contractor's
    reappointment, 278
reckoning period of
    days, 278
Partnerships, 11–15
    accounts, 12
    agreements, 12
    and companies, key
        differences, 19–20
    contract debts and
        torts, 12–13
    criminal actions, 13
    dissolution, 13–14
    finance, 12
    income tax, 12
    junior partners, 12
    liabilities, 11–15
    management, 12
    no audit required, 20
    obligations of partners,
        12
    personal assets, 11
    profit and loss, 12
    property of, 11
    recognition, 11
    retirement or death of
        partner, 13
    rights, 12
    salary, 12
    in Scotland, 11
    senior partners, 12
    size of, 12
    types, 12
    unlimited, 11–14
Payment, JCLI
    agreements:
    contribution, 283
    deductions, 282
    final certificate, 283
    fixed price, 283
    inconsistencies,
        correction, 282
    levy, 283
    notices, 282
    penultimate certificate,
        282
    progress payments and
        retention, 282

suspension right, by
    contractor, 283
tax changes, 283
Personal issues, 26
Pesticides, 225–227
Planning guidance:
    circulars, 88–90
    in the countryside,
        153–154
    in England, 87–88
    mineral guidance in
        Wales, 89
    Mineral Policy
        Guidance
        (MPG), 88
    Mineral Planning
        Guidance Note 13,
        131–132
    Northern Ireland, 90
    Planning Advice Notes
        (PAN), 90
    planning guidance,
        Wales, 88
    Planning Policy
        Guidance Notes
        (PPG), 88
    PPG1 (General policy
        and principles), 113
    PPG7, 106
    Regional Policy
        Guidance Notes
        (RPG), 88
    in Scotland, 89–90
    Technical Advice Notes
        (TAN), 89
    in Wales, 88–89
Planning legislation and
    law:
    activities not
        considered to be
        development, 105
    advice, *see* Planning
        guidance
    aftercare conditions, 130
    agriculture, 106
    ancient monuments, 118
    appeals, 136
    archaeological
        areas, 119
    Areas of Outstanding
        Natural Beauty,
        106, 182
    Article 4 Direction,
        106
    authority decision
        options, 133–134
    bad neighbour
        development,
        104, 107

Planning legislation and law (*Contd*)
building acts and regulations, 124, 149
England and Wales, 149–150
Northern Ireland, 151
Scotland, 150–151
building preservation notice, 118
business improvement districts (BIDS), 110
change of use, 102–103
community strategies, 97
conditions, 134
conservation areas, 106, 116–117
designated development, 104, 107
development, 87
development always requiring consent, 106–107
development control, 87, 101–107
development plans, 87, 154
in England, 91–92, 98
local development frameworks (LDFs), 93–94
Northern Ireland, responsibility, 100
regional spatial strategies (RSS), 92
responsibility, 98–100
role, 91
Scotland, responsibility, 99–100
Scotland and Northern Ireland, reform, 94
transition period, 95
in Wales, 91–92, 99
Welsh reform, 94
District Wide Local Plans, 96
duration of permission, 134–135
enforcement, 139–141
enterprise zones, 105, 108
environmental impact assessment, *see main entry*

gardens and designed landscapes, 119–120
heritage, 110–120
landscape assessment, 146–148
methodology, 147–148
landscape design, 125–126, 135–139
listed buildings, 117–118
Local Development Frameworks (LDFs), 93
minerals, *see main entry*
national parks, 106, 179–180
National Scenic Areas, 182
necessity for planning permission, 104–105
non-compliance, penalties, 112–120
operations notice, 119
overhanging trees, 116
permitted development, 104–106
planning inquiries, 137–139
planning obligations, 132–133
planning permission process, 120–151
application process, 120–133
calling in, 127
character maps, 128–129
consultation, 127–128
decision, 125
E-planning, 124
fees, 124
landscape design, 125–126
local authority, 124–125
reserved matters, 121
site visit, 127
tranquil zones, 128–129
types, 120–121
planning policy, 87
public inquiries, 137–141
refusal of permission, 135
Regional Development Agencies, 108
Regional Spatial Strategies (RSS), 92

Section 52 Agreements, 132–133
Section 75 Agreements, 133
Section 106 Agreements, 132–133
Simplified Planning Zones, 105, 108
Special Development Areas, 107–110
SSSI, 106
strategic environmental impact assessment (SEA), 148–149
structure plans, 96
transport plans, 97
tree preservation orders (TPO), 111–114
trees and woodlands, 112
trees dangerous, 114
UDP, 96
urban development areas and corporations, 108
Use Class Orders, 103–104
unitary development plans, 96
waste plans, 97
Planning Policy Statement (PPS23), 224
Pollution, 219–227
abandoned mines, 224–225
contaminated land, 223
Control of Pesticides Regulations 1986, 226
Control of Substances Hazardous to Health Regulations 1988, 226–227
eco-management and audit, 225
Entrust, 222–223
Environment Agency, 201, 219
Environmental Service in Northern Ireland, 220
European Environment Agency, 220
integrated pollution control, 220
landfill tax, 222
litter, 221–222
pollution linkages, 223

Scottish Environmental
Protection Agency,
201, 219–220
statutory nuisances, 225
waste:
authorities, 221
management
licenses, 221
Potentially damaging
operations, 193, 194,
207
Preliminaries, 235–236
Prime cost sums, 235,
237, 270
Private practice:
accepting work in, 31
establishing a, 22–26
finance, 24–25
insurance, 24
management, 23–24
Production information,
231–234
Project manager, 260
Protected species,
183–187
Provisional sums, 235,
237, 270
Public rights of way:
England and Wales,
209–215
bulls, 212
categories, 209
changes to routes, 210
cycle tracks, 213
definitive maps,
209–210
diversion of routes,
210–211
extinguishment of
routes, 212
improvement plans,
213
new routes, 212
ploughing, 212
sign-posting, 212–213
wardens, 212
Scotland, 215

Quality, 45–47, 232–263
Quality-based
selection, 28
Quantity surveyor,
238–239, 260–261,
266, 270
Quid pro quo, 52

Ramsar sites, 205
Recoverable expenses,
40–41

Regulations:
Conservation (Natural
Habitats etc.)
Regulations 1994,
201, 208
Construction (Design
and Management)
Regulations 1994,
72, 74–81
Control of Pesticides
Regulations 1986,
226
Control of Substances
Hazardous to
Health Regulations
COSHH, 226–227
Environmental
Assessment
Regulations, 105
Environmental Impact
Assessment
(Scotland)
Regulations
1999, 142
Environmental
Information
Regulations
2004, 224
European Wildlife Trade
Regulations 1997,
184, 187
Habitats Regulations
1994, 192, 202
Health and Safety, 73–81
Hedgerow Regulations
1997, 182–183
Highways (Assessment
of Environmental
Effects) Regulations
1988, 136
Landfill Tax Regulations
1996, 222
Partnerships (unre-
stricted size) No 14
Regulations
1970, 12
Planning
(Environmental
Impact
Assessment)
(Northern Ireland)
Regulations 1999,
The, 142
Set-aside regulations,
158
six pack, 73
Town and Country
Planning
(Assessment of

Environmental
Effects) Regulations
1988 (England and
Wales), 141, 143
Town and Country
Planning (Control
of Advertisements)
Regulations
1992, 107
Town and Country
Planning (Listed
Buildings and
Conservation
Areas) (Scotland)
Regulations
1997, 89
Town and Country
Planning
(Environmental
Impact
Assessment)
(England and
Wales) Regulations
1999, 141, 144
Town and Country
Planning (Tree
Preservation
Order) Regulations
1999, 111
Transport and Works
(Assessment of
Environmental
Effects) Regulations
1995, 136
Work Regulations 1999,
Management of
Health and
Safety, 81
Retention money, 271
Rights of Third Parties Act
1999, *see* Contracts
Act 1999
Risk assessment, 77
Royal Charter, 2
Rural stewardship scheme
(RSS), 162–163

Sanctuary Order, 185, 207
Scarce resources,
management, 155
agricultural land, 158
agri-environment
schemes,
158–160
European policy,
155–157
national strategic
resources, 157–158
Schedules of rates, 231, 238

Scotland:
  bad neighbour
      development, 104
  consideration in
      contract, 52
  delict, 65
  indicative forestry
      strategies, 170
  interdict, 64–65
  law, 50, 51
  nuisance, 64
  partnerships in, 11
  planning guidance,
      89–90
  public rights of way,
      215–216
  return of tenders,
      247–248
Scotland Act 1998, 89
Scottish Environmental
    Protection Agency,
    172, 219
Scottish Executive, 89
tender report, 250
Town and Country
    Planning (Scotland)
    Act 1997, 89, 101,
    103, 106, 110,
    130, 133
Scottish and National
    Planning Policy
    Guidelines
    (SPPGs), 89
Scottish Forestry Strategy,
    169–170
Scottish Natural
    Heritage, 182
Set-Aside Regulations, 160
Site agent, 263
Sites of Special Scientific
    Interest (SSSI),
    192–199, 203, 207
  amendment, 199
  by-laws, 197
  change of owner, 197
  compulsory
      purchase, 197
  condition, 198
  consequences,
      194–195
  critique, 199
  designation procedure,
      193–194
  emergency operations,
      195
  funding, 198
  management, 196
  penalties, 197–198
  planning, 195

  public right of access,
      195
Six pack 1992, 73
SMM7, 233, 236
Sole principal, 20–21
Special Areas of
    Conservation (SAC),
    201–202
Special Nature
    Conservation
    Order, 208
Special Protection Areas
    (SPA), 203
Species and special
    habitats, designations,
    183–187, 206–208
  management agree-
      ments, 206–207
  Nature Conservation
      Order (NCO),
      207–208
  sanctuary order, 207
Specification:
  British Standards, 234
  European Standards,
      234
  JCT, 233
  National Building
      Specification, 233
  SMM7, 233
Standard term contrasts
    (STCs), 56
Standing Orders, in local
    authorities, 10
Statutory Instruments
    and Orders:
  Ancient Monuments
      (Class Consents)
      Order, 118
  interim development
      order, 131
  Planning (Northern
      Ireland) Order
      1991, 90, 101, 110
  Pollution Control and
      Local Government
      (Northern Ireland)
      Order 1978, 222
  special development
      orders (new
      towns), 105
  Town and Country
      Planning (General
      Development)
      (Scotland) Order
      1997, 103
  Town and Country
      Planning (Mineral)
      Act 1981, 130–132

  Town and Country
      Planning (Use
      Classes) Order
      1987, 103
  Town and Country
      Planning Act
      (General permitted
      Development)
      Order 1995,
      101, 152
Statutory obligations,
    JCLI agreements:
  Construction Industry
      Scheme (CIS), 284
  notices, fees and
      charges, 283
  value added tax, 283
Sub-consultants,
    appointments:
  CDM, regulations
      and dispute
      resolution, 45
  collateral warranties, 45
  fees and expenses, 45
  liabilities, insurances
      and management,
      44
  obligations, of parties, 44
  selection, 44
Sustainability:
  European objective, 153
  waste management, 221

Technical proposal, 28
Tendering, 231
  acceptance, 250–251
  bills of quantity, 234
  checking, 248
  competitive, 239
  competitive fee
      tendering, 28–29
  dayworks, 236
  definition, 239
  errors in prices, 249
  information issued to
      tenderers, 247
  invitation to tender, 247
  for landscape work, 31
  measured works, 236
  negotiated, 242–244
  nominated, 242
  non-competitive, 242
  notification, 248
  open, 241, 244
  post-tender period, 251
  preliminaries, 235–236
  priced documents,
      examination,
      249–250

prime cost, provisional and contingency sums, 237–238
production information, 231–233
qualification, 248
recommendation, 250–251
report, 250
return of tenders, 247–248
selective, 240
serial, 242
single stage selective, 240, 245
specification, 232
two envelope system, 28
two stage selective, 240, 243–244
types of tender, 239–243
work stages, 231, 234, 239
Treaty of Amsterdam 1997, 153
Treaty of Union 1707, 49
Trees:
ancient and veteran, 169
dangerous, 114
felling, 168
Forestry Commission, 164–171
forestry standard, 164–165

grants for planting, 165–166
overhanging, 116
preservation, 111
Trusts, 21–22

UKBAP, 191–192
Urban parks and green spaces, 177–178
Valuations, 125, 266
Variations, 270–271
Visual impact assessment, 147

Wales, planning guidance, 88
Water:
COSHH, 226–227
marine nature reserves, 200–201
pollution, 172
Ramsar sites, 205
recreation, 177
resources, 171–173
strategic planning guidance, 173–174
Water Framework Directive (WFD), 173
Weather, adverse, 272
When disaster strikes!, 273–274

Wildlife:
habitat creation, 223
legislation in Scotland, 187–188
protection, 183–187
Woodland and tree organizations:
Arboricultural Association, 171
Countryside Around Town (CAT), 171
International Tree Foundation (ITF), 171
Tree Council, 170–171
Woodland Trust, 171
Woodland assurance scheme, 168–169
Woodland grant scheme (WGS), 165–167
Works control, JCLI agreements:
assignment, 281
contract administrator's instructions, 281
contractor's representative, 281
exclusion from work, 281
sub-contract, 281
variations, 282
World Heritage Sites, 206